I0493596

The Anatomy of a Growing Company
A Handbook for Hands-On Managers

Second Edition

With a New Section for Start-Ups

By Dick Dadamo

The Anatomy of a Growing Company—Second Edition
Copyright © 2014 by Dick Dadamo

All rights reserved. No part of this book may be used or reproduced by any means, graphic, electronic, or mechanical, including photocopying, recording, taping, or by any information storage retrieval system without the written permission of the publisher except in the case of brief quotations embodied in critical articles and reviews.

Information provided in this publication is derived from various sources, standards, and analyses. Any errors or omissions shall not imply any liability for direct or indirect consequences arising from the use of this information. The publisher, authors, and reviewers make no warranty for the correctness or for the use of this information, and they assume no liability for direct or indirect damages of any kind arising from technical interpretations or technical explanations in this book, for typographical or printing errors, or for any subsequent changes.

ISBN: 978-1497441521

Printed in the United States of America

Acknowledgements

2013
I want to thank all those would be entrepreneurs whose numerous presentations I endured through the years and inspired me to add Section 3 to the book.

2009
This is my seventh book, and it seems like any acknowledgment I can think of except one are the same as books number 1-6.

Let me start with the exception, my friend of many years, Phil Harding. My plan was to select good stuff from the previous books, but that meant I would have to read all of them again. As a result, the idea had been sitting on my cluttered desk for years. Phil and I have done several management things together, and most recently I was director of a company where Phil was the CEO. He managed to drive the company from a few hundred thousand in annual revenue to well over $500 million in annual revenue. He took a profitable company public in 2004. Although he moved far beyond small company environments, many of our discussions bordered on the same problems and challenges of small companies.

I asked Phil if he could find time to review some of the stuff I was writing. He obliged, and everything I sent was returned shortly. This kept me on my toes and forced me to keep feeding him.

Thanks to my daughter Susan for wrestling with the bits and pieces of paper I called notes.

Thanks also to all the people, too many to mention by name, who listened to my observations along the way and encouraged me to put them into book form.

Table of Contents

Preface

This is my eighth book related to management. I believe I have more to add and hope I live long enough to accomplish..

"I would like to dedicate this book to all the people who have asked me for advice through the years, especially those people who have actually paid for it. Strangely, my wife and children have never asked me to advise them, even though I would never charge them for my services. But I feel it is appropriate to include them in this dedication because they have inspired me by laughing every time I mentioned a (new) project. They may yet have the last laugh, if I get no further than this."

You can see my family has had a lot of laughs, as this will be my eighth book. This book will also be like a handbook and actually will include selected material from some of my other books on planning, inventory, marketing, engineering and accounting, especially from The Laws of Management Physics.

I believe one of the criteria for a rapidly growing company is for the management staff to understand the role of all the staff functions. This will minimize the level of frustration, as growth often requires compromise. At the same time, the staff must wear several hats in rapid growth.

On this basis, I try to write the books to give insight to all the staff members. For instance, the marketing book is not based on making a marketing manager even better (but at times it might). It is more to have the technical manager or accounting person understand marketing.

The original book—*The Laws of Management Physics: A Handbook for Hands-On Managers*—was meant to lay the foundation for the need for culture change in growth. It has been effective through the years, and the 100 Laws are replicated in this book. Up to now, I have not tried to personally make money from the books. I have turned over any sales dollars annually to a selected charity. My reward was more for my ego, particularly when someone would quote a law or material from one of the books.

As an example, I could quote Law 1, "*The Goesinnas have to exceed the Goesouttas* (referring to cash) or Law 3, "*A staff that stays together cannot grow together…at the same rate.*" Then there is an excerpt from the chapter Management Lies: "The hiring manager says to the candidate for a key position, 'Don't worry. Join our company now, and within 30 days we will work out a bonus plan.'" Promises, promises. I am still waiting for several of those plans that never did develop along the way.

The objective of this book is to recognize there are many ways to do some things, and yours may not be the only way. I also believe good managers have to be a little cynical to be their best, something that may be difficult for an inexperienced manager who doesn't know what lies ahead in a growth situation. I hope with this book and the others in my Busting $10 Million series that the reader can find help. Anatomy of a Growing Company is not meant to be a "How-To" book for executives and managers in a growing company. I hope the reader sees it as an expression of wisdom that I have tried to convey to all the people who worked for me and clients that I consulted for in my career. If successful, it will give the reader the proper mind-set to tackle and solve almost any new and difficult situations along the way to successful growth.

I do not believe I am an expert, but I do have fifty years in management in most all of the junior and senior roles in a company. That's fifty years of observing and learning.

The Dadamo Creed.

"I do not profess to be an expert, but I do profess to be an observer. So listen to my observations, which are built on years of experience, and accept that there is more than one way to do things! In fact, listen to how I have done things wrong as well as right so you can avoid the same mistakes. Then, if I have challenged your mind-set and encouraged you to consider alternatives, I have accomplished my task." Enjoy the book.

Introduction

After spending the first half of my career in big public companies, I started a consulting firm, RJD Associates, Inc. My goal was to help companies grow, including small companies that wanted to change, investment start-ups and student incubator start-ups. I have played roles as advisor, served on Boards of Directors, and member of advisory boards.

The book has 3 sections. Section 1 is material from the first edition of The Anatomy of a Growing Company and is important to all growing companies. Section 3 is dedicated to start-ups but can help small businesses planning robust growth. Section 2 should be covered by the reader with interaction with either section 1 or 3. Forgive me if their seems to be redundancy throughout the book as I want to be sure the reader would cover section 2 as well as 1 or 3 as chosen.

Since my books have been the best kept secret from the public, many of you may not have heard of Dick Dadamo before you picked up this book. You can find the list of previous books in Appendix B.

I had my first taste of management over fifty years ago, when I was put in charge of an engineering project and found out how lonely management can be. My first unpopular management decision was to change the weekly work schedule from four ten-hour days plus an eight-hour Friday to six eight-hour days Monday through Saturday. The result was that all of the sudden, the team didn't have to do the overtime on Saturday to keep up with the schedule. Actually, the two hours for overtime each day Monday through Thursday were just bull sessions anyway, and as expected, no one wanted to give up their Saturday. But since the team also lost the overtime pay for those extra hours, they didn't have a warm feeling for me. Also being the youngest guy in the group didn't help my popularity.

By the way, the project was for a high-speed printer. I mention it to show the improvement in quality and performance over time—whereas the "high-speed printer" shipped with a complete set of spare parts, my HP printer, which is several years old, keeps chugging along and has never died in need of a part.

I started my professional career as a design engineer, but early on lost interest in engineering. Most engineering designs were deemed successful if a light went on and off when the circuit was activated.

It did not take long to be surrounded by boredom. In looking back, I remember one task was to design a circuit known as a "flip flop," complete with a light to indicate what state it was in—one or zero. The challenge was to fit this one in a 19" rack. I haven't looked lately, but I know the technology today allows semiconductor manufacturers to get over a billion flip flops on a chip.

After twenty-five years in all phases of corporate management, I had my fill of big company culture, and I left to be a consultant.

During my corporate experience, I helped a company to grow to over $100,000,000 in revenue and left as the President. After building a regional sales office and starting a company in Hong Kong, I worked for Japanese and French companies and operated an International group of companies based in Italy. During the last couple years in corporate management, I did turnarounds and divestures. This gave me the idea to do consulting.

After leaving the big company world, my main source of income for paying my mortgage came from mentoring company presidents. During my consulting career, I have, from time to time, been dragged back into the problematic corporate world, being a CEO on two occasions and, a director of a $700 million public company. My real love is working with smaller companies, because it is a teaching task that I totally enjoy.

Much of my success in mentoring comes from understanding the difference between advice and counseling. Advice can be good, but many times it falls short in solving a problem. Counseling is advice that can be accomplished within the system and with the resources available.

There is another great advantage to working with small companies. "They" are sitting there in every meeting. There is no need to get corporate approval from some place called Cleveland or New York. The management can make decisions on the spot and reverse them instantaneously, if necessary.

I am still very active, working as a director and advisor for several recent start-ups. I find the material from all my books still useful and timely in helping the presentations of these companies.

I call myself an observer rather than an expert. Most of the consulting I provide can only be gained from experience, and I have tons of it. I have tried to get my experience into *The Anatomy of a Growing* Company, as well as the books before it, to help executives become aware of what they *do not know* lies ahead. Please let me know if I have succeeded.

"Growth company: A company that grows at a greater rate than the economy as a whole and that usually directs a relatively high proportion of its income back into the business"

Webster's New Collegiate Dictionary, 1977.

Section 1

Chapter 1: You Don't Know What You Don't Know!

I can't think of a more appropriate cliché that defines what a management team in a growing company faces than: "You don't know what you don't know." You don't know when you will have to:

- make changes in your management style.
- borrow money for the business for the first time.
- start to trust subordinates.
- delegate sacred decisions you previously protected.
- pay lawyers in spite of your perceived idea of exorbitant rates.
- do a forecast that extends beyond a week.
- become an expert in cash management.
- engage in formal planning.
- establish priorities, continue to review them, and reorder as needed.
- recruit superstars who will grow in capability to help you bust through the revenue barriers of $10 million, $50 million, and $500 million.
- enter new markets and conceive of new products.

The thing you really don't know is when and how you will need to change the present culture so you can go forward with rapid growth rates. And along with that, you don't know growth comes with the pressure that will grow proportionally from your stakeholders, including investors, customers, employees, suppliers, and your family.

Most likely the most important factor with growth is the need to compromise to develop a different, more effective management style. High growth rates are synonymous with compromise.

No longer can you take the time you would like to think things out before making a decision.

You can't have forever to solve a customer problem.

You have to make decisions at a much faster pace than you have been used to. In other words, you must make decisions with the information and resources available and in the time allowed.

You have to be fast on your feet to be in position for change should your original decision be wrong. Hang in there reading this book, and you will get the answers you need to succeed.

Accountability—The First Drink Is the One that Kills You

It is common for companies from start-up to a certain level of revenue to operate with the "I" culture, wherein Number One makes all the decisions. Revenue commitments are only made if there is money in the company to cover them. As a result, inventories are not built up, and special skills people are not put in place until a customer's order is received. This inability to respond to needs in a timely manner limits growth, because the customer must wait for the business to catch up to his or her needs.

If the product and output continue with just more of the same the company can grow up to about $3 million in revenue depending on the product and service mix and the lead time to deliver a customer's order.

For robust growth, management needs to assume some financial risk and put additional assets and skills in place without customer commitments. Bank borrowing becomes available but is limited by the assets available for the bank to "own" if the company defaults on the loan.

If new ideas, a disruptive technology, and an emerging market are available, equity investment may be possible for the funding the company's growth.

The bigger and more robust the growth desired, the higher the risk becomes by putting capital in jeopardy. Planning and priorities become more a part of the culture, and the proper perspective and perception on the company team are necessary. As the company requires investments in facilities and products to be put in place for future growth needs, all staff needs to work together to help all programs perform satisfactorily.

Engineering Accountability

The following is an example how a company can get off track by a perceived small glitch in the program.

What appears to be a modest slip in commitments at the beginning of a program can have a devastating effect on its long-term outcome. Windows of opportunity are often fragile, so a manager must be sensitive to their importance, catch them when they're open, and address them with the high priority and commitment level they require. How often have I heard, "We'll only be a month late with the product!"

Unfortunately, that one month often has a tremendous impact on the big picture.

Case Study: Company X could finally reach a point in their market that could make them a proactive company rather than a reactive company, always chasing the competition. They believed they had a new technology that would scoop the market and could double annual sales in the first year of shipments. If they came anywhere near their more realistic projections for sales, profit, and cash generated, the company could be in position for an IPO or selling to a strategic investor. If this happened all the employees and investors in the company would end up with a great financial reward.

All of the staff needed to participate in the program called "Success" to make the program work. It took days of planning; starting with schedules and output. Engineering needs to release the product on time. Manufacturing must put the resources in place to produce at the projected costs. Marketing and sales team up to provide all the advertising and collateral needed to reach the sales goals. Finally, the finance division must ensure that the cash will be available to cover all the costs to get to a cash-breakeven point.

The first year plan was to manufacture and sell 166 units for a revenue of $4.1 million. After overcoming the early cash output requirement, the cash coming in from the sales at a later month would turn the net cash positive for the year

Shortly before the engineering release in a progress meeting, the head of engineering casually announces there will be a slight delay in the schedule for the product release. After much uproar, the head of finance quickly runs off all the new numbers on a basis of maybe "only one month" as the engineering says, but plans on two months as well. The results are disastrous for the first twelve months of the product. The revenue sales drop over half, and most important, the cash net will be a negative $1.07 million. In the original plan the worst cumulative cash needed got to $140,000, which Finance could borrow to cover. The company is unable to come up with the cash combining the need for at least $1.07 million program initiation and the cash needed for all the "Success" costs already in place. Because of the unplanned extra two months the company has to kill the program. The following graphs show the difference a couple of months can make.

The Review

The message was loud and clear

- Revenue Down: This kills any growth plans they had for the year.

- Gross Margin Down: This falls so low that it will force a staff reduction.

- Profit Down: Kiss your bonus goodbye, and feel for Paul, the CEO when he has to tell the board.

- Increased Manufacturing and Engineering Expenses: Expenses will exceed budget and require actions that may end up hurting the program even more.

- Development: New program development will be delayed, hurting future company performance and pushing out the IPO they had hoped to do in eighteen months.

- Negative Cash: Cash will fall far short of the plan, and that may force a private equity offering at giveaway prices, diluting the value of the stock for the present stockholders.

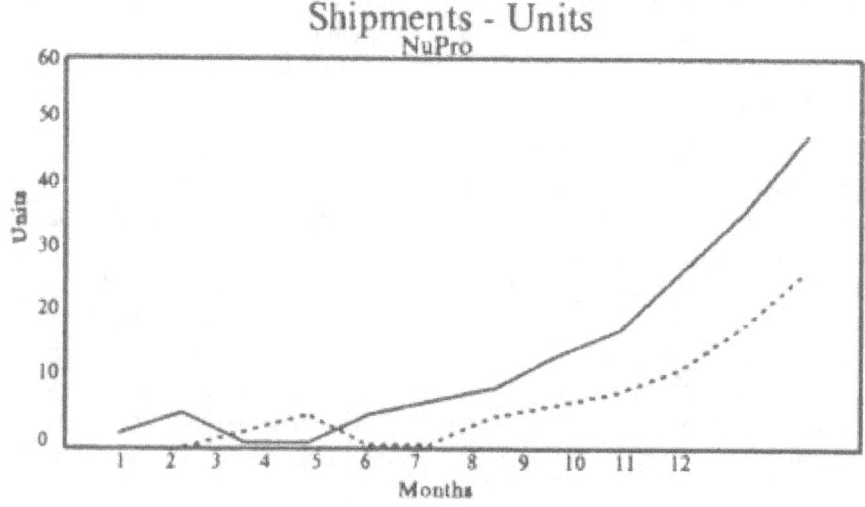

Graph 1. Shipments in Units

Solid line = original plan, dotted line = two-month slip

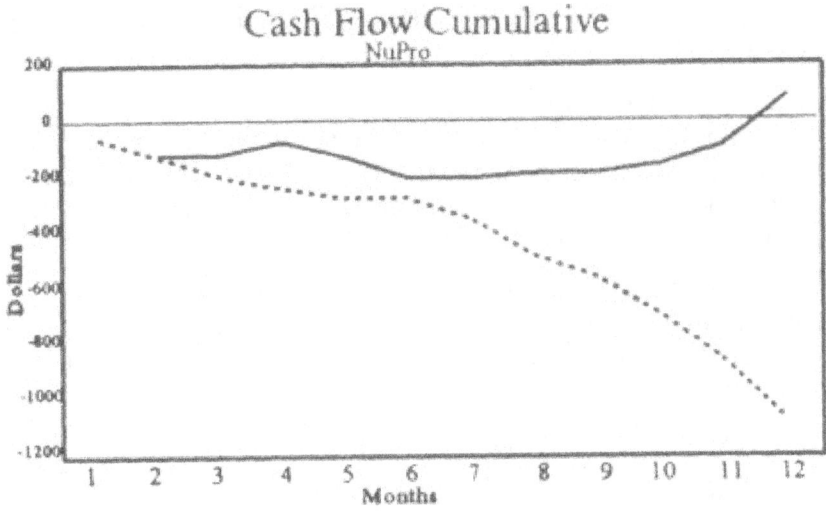

Graph 2. Cumulative Cash Flow

Solid line = original plan, dotted line = two-month slip

Growth requires intensity and commitment to meeting goals, impossible though they may seem. Certainly management cannot permit casual schedule changes. In the above case, Engineering broke down the entire program by the slippage, and what is even worse, they had no recovery plan to get back to the original schedule.

Supplier Accountability—"Tell Me Why I Shouldn't Worry"

Here is a case study to illustrate the need for a customer to feel comfortable believing the supplier will be able to meet the customer needs.

Once when I was a division manager, we had a purchase order from a Fortune 100 company. We wouldn't even have been considered for the order if we hadn't been one division of a multibillion-dollar corporation. The customer wanted their deadlines met, and the supplier wanted their reputation preserved, so both were watching the situation very closely. My staff was in complete disarray because of the pressure we were all feeling and their inexperience in dealing with a company of this magnitude.

In this situation, I received a visit from the customer's representatives. They wanted to make sure that we had the right attitude and were giving a high priority to their purchase order and needs. After everyone was seated, the first thing the customer wanted to know was, "Tell me why I shouldn't worry about you meeting the schedules for the first article and subsequent production buildup."

Surprising even myself, I was able to remain very calm as I gave him my well thought out answer. (I later realized that I was able to remain so calm because I was underpaid, and therefore had very little to lose.) I had anticipated the question, and I was prepared. I began, "I will give you several reasons why we will not slip schedules."

"First off, if we miss the dates, every day we are late will cause cost overruns, hurting our bottom line and cash availability. Also, if we miss dates, we tie up personnel resources that we need for other planned projects, hurting our chances for future successes. Third, if we fail, all hell will break loose at corporate headquarters, so you can bet they'll be watching with great interest. Finally, if we miss our revenue and profit forecasts, it will affect our bonuses, and maybe even my job. So, I assure you that I will be watching the program personally, and as soon as I see a problem that could cause us to miss a major milestone, I will force my staff to find alternatives to make very sure our final schedule commitments are met."

The man glared at me for what seemed like a lifetime, and I was certain that he had interpreted my remarks in the worst possible way. However, when he finally replied, it was to tell me that he was very impressed with all the reasons, but that the last one had really hit home. He went on to make it clear that they were part of the team, and if I could see any way in which they could be a part of any alternatives, I should call them. What happened? We got the order, and we performed to everyone's satisfaction.

Attitude Problems

I have worked with this idea in mind over the years, and I try to get it across to everyone I work with: Missed schedules create extra costs and delayed revenue streams, and as a result they delay profit and, most importantly, risk losing the customer and the product's market window. Because keeping schedule commitments is so important, staff must always have alternatives prepared that will enable them to stay on schedule and be ready to implement these on short notice. It is important to prevent one bad program from knocking down all the others like dominos.

Management Accountability

The way many companies can tolerate missed commitments has always frustrated me. That's one reason I've consistently had trouble relating to big company environments—they are often more tolerant of such slippage than smaller companies can afford to be. Misguided accountability can often hurt more than the original party or group causing the problem.

For example, I was working in a $400 million dollar group that had centralized sales at the group level for all divisions. The sales organization would give sales forecasts to the divisions in September to start off the budgeting process for the coming year. Division budgets were due in October, but the divisions were being squeezed between the sales forecast on one side and the corporate revenue and Return on Investment targets on the other, making it difficult for the divisions to make ends meet.

Then, usually by the end of October, sales would issue a revised forecast that was down by as much as 17 percent. Then management at the group level would hammer the divisions to reduce their budgeted expenses across the board, with some arbitrary percentage for profit required to meet the corporate consolidated profit goal. As could be expected, this created severe morale problems because sales was let off the hook by putting pressure on the operating divisions who had less control over the process.

In reality, the new forecast for the group had dropped over $60 million in sales and $5 million in profit. Would you think that management at the group level would tell sales to find alternatives that would enable them to stick to their original commitment? Even if it required investments above the original budget, the overall results might still be improved, and with far less pain and risk.

The point is this: from the very beginning, the focus must be on setting goals and making commitments that will stick, and then being accountable for sticking to them.

Accounting—The Evolution of a Management Report

Early on in many companies, cash is king and the only consideration for operating. Nothing is spent unless there is cash to provide for it. Unfortunately this can only take a company so far. Eventually, risk commitments need to be made to continue growth and entering larger markets.

In the manufacturing companies, inventory has to be built up and paid for before receiving funds from the customer. In service companies, employees need to be hired and paid before they cover their costs. As the company grows the president and the management team roles expand; getting detailed knowledge of the cash flow becomes more difficult.

Formal forecasting of cash flow with the ins and outs becomes a necessity. At the same time, even with increased cash data, it is not necessarily the only financial data needed to plan and run the company. Accounting becomes important to organize the data in an accurate and timely fashion to turn it into information. Organizing the data requires growth in accounting skills and financial management of the company

The following is a history of how the accounting function needs grow from bookkeeper to head of finance to be more useful to management in providing financial information and recommendations in the growth of the company.

Management reports are a necessary evil of running a company. Unfortunately, they are also the weakest and most inefficient tool that I have encountered in my consulting activities. Often, the initial phase of my work at a company is severely hampered by the lack of factual and sufficiently detailed reports. In struggling companies, proper reports that supply the information needed to run the company are scarce, and those that do exist are generally weak and untimely.

What Makes a Good Management Report?

Companies create data from all directions within the company, but at the same time, provide very little in the way of useful reports until they learn how to convert that data into meaningful information. Even in companies with sophisticated MIS systems, reports may be plentiful but useless. Many operating managers have complained to me that they are embarrassed because the reports are piling up unread. There simply isn't enough time to read them all, but they are afraid to complain for fear that it will be perceived as a negative reflection on their management abilities. However, the more serious problem is the fact that most of those reports are useless, because they do not provide the timely information needed to run the operating departments.

Inadequate reporting results from the fact that the accounting and MIS managers are deciding what reports they think others will need, so that's what they produce. This thinking is completely backward. Accounting and MIS need to produce an accurate and timely product that serves their customers, the department heads. In order to do this, they should begin by asking each department head what reports they need to support their work and run their department.

It is astounding how many MIS managers will talk for hours about the vast quantity of reports their department turns out but have no idea how (or even if) they are used. They don't know whether the information is useful; they haven't learned that a few reports containing meaningful information are far more valuable than many reports full of useless data.

Reports are generally more useful when presented graphically and when the data is plotted against other relevant information such as the budget or last year's performance. In the manufacturing company environment, I have found that several graphs, a balance sheet, a profit and loss statement, and a cash flow statement provide sufficient information to run a profit unit, be it a division or an entire company. These graphs should include revenue, profit, inventory, accounts receivable, accounts payable, bookings, and backlog.

A more subtle aspect of the art of reporting is that when you demand a report from your organization, you can be sure that those who prepare it have to review the situation in the process. In addition, reports are also the tools that support management controls, and a report that combines information with recommended actions provides the president/general manager with a basis for making decisions without the inefficient effort of having to dig and probe for information.

The following demonstrates how basic accounting data can be expanded and transformed into useful information that can help management make tough decisions. This is not to imply that all the accounting additions are made by different individuals, but rather by the different disciplines of accounting. In a small company, these additions may all be made by one person.

The Evolution of the Management Report

As data flows from accounting to management, it gets molded, expanded, and adapted until what results is a report combining meaningful information presented in a meaningful way with recommendations for action. These financial reports start in the accounting department and have different slants depending on who prepares them and for what purpose. That report may pass through bookkeeping, the controller, the financial analyst, and the head of finance before it becomes a useful management tool.

Initially, financial accounting was a product of the need to report tax liabilities. The accounting department still performs these tasks, but far more is required to manage a growing company. What used to be a basic procedure has developed into an art, with multiple depreciation methods, reserves for many expense accounts, accruals such as payroll, and several ways to report inventory, leading to absorbed and unabsorbed overhead.

With financial reporting such a subtle and complex process, how is a general manager to make sure that the cash "goesinnas" continue to exceed the cash "goesouttas"?

To make it even more difficult, accountants have created a report referring to the sources and uses of funds. I have yet to attend an operations review or board of directors meeting where the group didn't get bogged down trying to review the source and use of funds report. Adding insult to injury, accountants inevitably use brackets instead of good old pluses and minuses, always requiring further explanation. I am sure this report helps accountants increase their job security, but it drives me crazy, especially when I'm left in a room to figure it out for myself.

What is really needed is a "real cash" report. First, it should lay out all cash that comes into the company from customers, investors, banks, or the sale of assets. Then, it should lay out all cash going out of the company by major categories, including payroll, materials, rent, purchase of assets, dividends, interest, and principal repayment. Finally, get the calculator out and subtract the "goesouttas" from the "goesinnas."

If you subtract the "goesouttas" from the "goesinnas" and consistently get a negative number, you'd better get into the system and figure out what action is needed to make it positive. It doesn't matter if the profit and loss statement shows a positive profit, the law still holds: "The goesinnas *must* be greater than the goesouttas."

To overcome the accounting mumbo jumbo, the general manager or president must think cash and cash flow. In small companies driven by cash, all departments and functions should be summarized in a convenient and easy-to-understand format. In more complex situations with departments and divisions, each unit's cash should also be summarized to aid the management staff in their responsibilities.

In the following example, for simplicity, several small accounts have been combined and all department accounts have been summarized so they have one set of numbers.

Step 1/Table 1 (in thousands of dollars)

Table 1	(1)
RJD, Inc.	x1000$
Operating Report	Aug.
Net Sales	$232.0
Material	100
Direct Labor	32
Indirect Salaries	36
Other Employee Costs	27.5
Bonus	1
Outside Services	2.5
Commissions	0
Supplies	8.25
Equipment	0.5
Auto Expense	0
Building	5
Utilities	4
Telephone, Fax	2
Travel/ Entertainment	0.1
Advertising	0
Catalog/Manuals	0
Freight In	2.3
Freight Out	0.6
Bad Debt Reserve	1
Total Operating Expenses	$???.75
Operating Profit	9.25
Depreciation	0.09
Amortization	3
Interest Expenses	7
Other	2.5
Total Costs	236.15
Net Profit	-4.15

This report is prepared by the bookkeeper, and lists the sales and expenses for a given month. It has one column listing the sales and costs for the month.

Although this report is very accurate, there is no way for a department head to tell from this data if business is good, bad, according to plan, up to expectations, or heading for disaster! There is nothing to which the department head can relate the data, and about the only meaningful thing this report indicates is that the company lost money.

Step 2/Table 2 (in thousands of dollars)

Table 2	(1)	(2)
RJD, Inc.		
Operating Report	Aug.	% Sales
Net Sales	$232.0	100%
Material	100	43%
Direct Labor	32	14%
Indirect Salaries	36	16%
Other Employee Costs	27.5	12%
Bonus	1	0%
Outside Services	2.5	1%
Commissions	0	0%
Supplies	8.25	4%
Equipment	0.5	0%
Auto Expense	0	0%
Building	5	2%
Utilities	4	2%
Telephone, Fax	2	1%
Travel / Entertainment	0.1	0%
Advertising	0	0%
Catalog/Manuals	0	0%
Freight In	2.3	1%
Freight Out	0.6	0%
Bad Debt Reserve	1	0%
Total Operating Expenses	$222.75	96%
Operating Profit	9.25	4%
Depreciation	0.09	0%
Amortization	3	1%
Interest Expense	7	3%
Other	2.5	1%
Total Costs	$236.15	102%
Net Profit	-4.15	-2%

The accountant has calculated each item as a percentage of the sales revenue for the month. It helps to know the percentages of sales income that go to pay for material or go to profit, but it is difficult to tell if the data is good or bad relative to other companies, current trends, or even *the previous* month. The loss has been quantified to be 2% of sales, but again, compared to what? At this point the data produce far more questions than answers.

Step 3/Table 3 (in thousands of dollars)

Table 3	(1)	(2)	(3)	(4)	(5)
RJD, Inc.			Bud.		Dif
Operating Report	Aug.	% Sales	Aug.	% Sales	Act – Bud
Net Sales	$232.0	100	$240	100	–$8
Material	100	43%	96	40%	4
Direct Labor	32	14%	29	12%	3
Indirect Salaries	36	16%	34	14%	2
Other Employee Costs	27.5	12%	26	11%	1.5
Bonus	1	0%	1	0%	0
Outside Services	2.5	1%	1	0%	1.5
Commissions	0	0%	0	0%	0
Supplies	8.25	4%	7	3%	1.25
Equipment	0.5	0%	0.5	0%	0
Auto Expense	0	0%	0	0%	0
Building	5	2%	5	2%	0
Utilities	4	2%	3.5	1%	0.5
Telephone, Fax	2	1%	2	1%	0
Travel / Entertainment	0.1	0%	0.1	0%	0
Advertising	0	0%	2	1%	–2
Catalog/Manuals	0	0%	0	0%	0
Freight In	2.3	1%	2.4	1%	–0.1
Freight Out	0.6	0%	0.1	0%	0.5
Bad Debt Reserve	1	0%	1	0%	0
Total Operating Expenses	$222.75	96%	$210.6	88%	$12.15
Operating Profit	9.25	4%	29.4	12%	–20.15
Depreciation	0.09	0%	0.09	0%	0
Amortization	3	1%	3	1%	0
Interest Expense	7	3%	5	2%	2
Other	2.5	1%	2	1%	0.5
Total Costs	$236.15	102%	$221.5	92%	$14.65
Net Profit	–$4.15	–2%	$18.5	8%	–$22.65

The controller has added the budget for each account and calculated each item as a percentage of budget. There is also a column to compare the actual dollars to the budgeted dollars. The report is now starting to emerge as an indicator of performance. It is the controller's role to track actual expenses to the budget, and this report can now be his guide as he discusses the variances with the responsible managers. For starters, he can see the costs of material, labor, salaries, consultants, and supplies are above budget. He can now go back into the system and look at the same report on a departmental basis.

Step 4/Table 4 (in thousands of dollars)

Table 4	(1)	(2)	(3)	(4)	(5)	(6)	(7)	(8)
RJD, Inc.			Bud.		Dif			
Operating Report	Aug.	%	Aug.	%	Act –	Y/D	%	Y/D by
Net Sales	$232.0	100%	$240	100%	–$8	$1948	100%	$244
Material	100	43%	96	40%	4	784	40%	98
Direct Labor	32	14%	29	12%	3	253	13%	32
Indirect Salaries	36	16%	34	14%	2	302	16%	38
Other Emp. Costs	27.5	12%	26	11%	1.5	222	11%	28
Bonus	1	0%	1	0%	0	8	0%	1
Outside Services	2.5	1%	1	0%	1.5	19.8	1%	2
Commissions	0	0%	0	0%	0	5	0%	1
Supplies	8.25	4%	7	3%	1.25	70	4%	9
Equipment	0.5	0%	0.5	0%	0	4	0%	1
Auto Expense		0%		0%	0	1	0%	0
Building	5	2%	5	2%	0	65	3%	8
Utilities	4	2%	3.5	1%	0.5	47	2%	6
Telephone, Fax	2	1%	2	1%	0	17	1%	2
Travel/Ent.	0.1	0%	0.1	0%	0	1.2	0%	0
Advertising		0%	2	1%	–2	13	1%	2
Catalog/Manuals		0%	0	0%	0	2	0%	0
Freight In	2.3	1%	2.4	1%	–0.1	13	1%	2
Freight Out	0.6	0%	0.1	0%	0.5	2	0%	0
Bad Debt Reserve	1	0%	1	0%	0	8	0%	1
Total Operating	$222.75	96%	$210.6	88%	$12.15	$18.37	94%	$230
Operating Profit	9.25	4%	29.4	12%	–20.15	111	6%	14
Depreciation	0.09	0%	0.09	0%	0	7.2	0%	1
Amortization	3	1%	3	1%	0	12	1%	2
Interest Expense	7	3%	5	2%	2	50	3%	6
Other	2.5	1%	2	1%	0.5	18	1%	2
Total Costs	$236.15	102%	$221.5	92%	$14.65	$1924.2	99%	$241
Net Profit	–$4.15	–0.02	$18.5	8%	–$22.65	$23.8	1%	$3

In Table 4, the financial analyst has added information comparing the present figures with the year-to-date figures (Y/D). This step can identify large discontinuities, such as a one-shot advertising bill. This part of the report can help avoid panic by showing that the year-to-date is still on track. A quick preventive for this kind of panic is to divide the year-to-date totals by the number of months in the year to date and then comparing this average month to each of the actual months. The analyst may also graph information from a series of months looking for trends.

Here, the analyst immediately goes after indirect and direct labor and material. He can see that August was higher on a cost of sales basis, when compared to both the budget and the year-to-date average. As he gets into the system, he finds out that with a softer backlog, material is being expedited (with higher costs of freight in), and there is unbudgeted overtime being expended to get the maximum shipments out.

Exploring why the shipments are getting tougher to make, he concludes that the product mix is changing more rapidly than originally planned. The larger customers are phasing out as the product mix changes, and with the reduced commitments, the backlog isn't as high, and manufacturing has to scramble more to meet the planned shipping levels. In fact, the entire organization is working harder, and the sales department has more people than budgeted for in order to try to recover lost bookings.

All of these conclusions are added to Table 4 as the information is prepared for the head of finance, who will make his recommendations to the president.

Step 5/Table 5 (in thousands of dollars)

Table 45	(1)	(2)	(3)	(4)	(5)	(6)	(7)	(8)	(9)
RJD, Inc.			Bud.		Dif				Last
Operating Report	Aug.	%	Aug.	%	Act–Bud	Y/D	%	Y/D mo.	%
Net Sales	$232.0	100%	$240	100%	–$8	$1948	100%	$244	100%
Material	100	43%	96	40%	4	784	40%	98	38
Direct Labor	32	14%	29	12%	3	253	13%	32	11
Indirect Salaries	36	16%	34	14%	2	302	16%	38	
Other Emp. Costs	27.5	12%	26	11%	1.5	222	11%	28	
Bonus	1	0%	1	0%	0	8	0%	1	
Outside Services	2.5	1%	1	0%	1.5	19.8	1%	2	
Commissions	0	0%	0	0%	0	5	0%	1	
Supplies	8.25	4%	7	3%	1.25	70	4%	9	
Equipment	0.5	0%	0.5	0%	0	4	0%	1	
Auto Expense	0	0%	0	0%	0	1	0%	0	
Building	5	2%	5	2%	0	65	3%	8	
Utilities	4	2%	3.5	1%	0.5	47	2%	6	
Telephone, Fax	2	1%	2	1%	0	17	1%	2	
Travel/Ent.	0.1	0%	0.1	0%	0	1.2	0%	0	
Advertising	0	0%	2	1%	–2	13	1%	2	
Catalog/Manuals	0	0%	0	0%	0	2	0%	0	
Freight In	2.3	1%	2.4	1%	–0.1	13	1%	2	
Freight Out	0.6	0%	0.1	0%	0.5	2	0%	0	
Bad Debt Reserve	1	0%	1	0%	0	8	0%	1	
Total Operating	$222.75	96%	$210.6	88%	$12.15	$18.37	94%	$230	
Operating Profit	9.25	4%	29.4	12%	–20.15	111	6%	14	
Depreciation	0.09	0%	0.09	0%	0	7.2	0%	1	
Amortization	3	1%	3	1%	0	12	1%	2	
Interest Expense	7	3%	5	2%	2	50	3%	6	
Other	$2.5	1%	$2	1%	$0.5	$18	1%	$2	
Total Costs	236.15	102%	221.5	92%	14.65	1924.2	99%	241	
Net Profit	–4.15	–0.02	18.5	8%	–22.65	23.8	1%	3	

18

After the financial analyst report is given to the finance head, he or she will probably ask the analyst to add one more column to show last year's percent of sales for labor and materials. This will yield more background on the changing product and customer mix.

Step 6

In this step, the head of the finance department adds his recommendations. It is part of his responsibility as staff to provide his assessment of the results and his comments on what he believes should be done.

Finally, we have a full-fledged management report, ready for a review meeting. It not only provides the general manager/president with data on the month's performance, but it also provides both a good view of how the company is performing overall and recommendations for improvement.

Tasks, assignments, and priorities can now be made based on the data and recommendations. In his report, the finance head points out that although changes were anticipated with the changing product line and corresponding large OEM customers—and budgeted accordingly—the changes still seem to be accelerating. This is clearly illustrated by the difference between last year's cost-of-sales percentages for material, direct labor, and indirect labor compared to August and the budget. The backlog is lower as smaller customers are added, and replacing larger customers with smaller ones takes a lot more in energy and costs out of the sales department. His strongest recommendation is to raise prices, although he knows that sales will resist this.

Therefore, to fill out the report, he recommends that the sales manager do an updated forecast for the remainder of the year, including an analysis of why sales to larger customers are dropping faster than previously forecasted. He warns engineering that he will be raising the issue of their being late with the new product. He provides an exercise to show what payroll costs must be taken out to meet the profit objective. He also makes recommendations on other expense accounts, such as deferring the next advertising media release.

He also includes in his recommendations those hidden accounting expenses he has squirreled away, like the bonus accrual (that might not be needed) and the bad debt reserve (that he has treated very conservatively). Finally, to top it off, he suggests that the outside consultants be cut off for the near term.

The president now has sufficient background information to make the tough decisions that will affect both near- and long-term business. His responsibility is to decide which, if any, actions will be taken; realizing that price increases or elimination of key resources must be studied closely.

Keeping in mind that the general manager is one of their major customers, the finance department must rise to the occasion by taking almost useless data and transforming it into meaningful information that management can use to effectively run the company.

Accounts Payable—Danger Ahead?

All companies are aware of the accounts payable (A/P) even if they don't know them by name. If payments fall behind, they will know about A/P as the phone will start ringing off the hook.

Unfortunately, the money owed to suppliers and vendors has to be paid on time, or the vendors may cut you off. With customers who owe you money and are overdue on payments, it feels right to say we will cut them off, but because there is a risk of losing the customer, management must think carefully through such decisions. The vast majority usually are passed over, and the overdue payment even gets worse.

But here is the danger in slipping on overdue payments to vendors. You may lose their attitude as a partner. As a partner, they are there when you need dramatic up-or-down rates in the schedule, voluntary effort to reduce the cost of producing your product, and after a long good relationship, agreeable at tough times to let you stretch out payments.

Because What vendors owe you is really like a loan with no interest, and when cash is really getting squeezed, there is a tendency to put the vendors down the list to be paid.

When the level gets above the vendor's patience threshold, they will start to lose patience with you as a customer, and most likely your priority will slip down toward oblivion. Then when you really need their support with deliveries and cost, you won't get it. I have seen bad customers abusing suppliers, but when the tide turns, vendors tend to even kick their customer when they are down.

The best thing to do when it is clear payments will slip for a while is that Number One in the company should go and sit down with the vendors, explain the situation, and promise to keep any new payment commitment you make.

Accounts Receivable—Who Is Really the Culprit?

An important aspect of cash available is the quality of the Accounts Receivable A/R.

Banks say they will loan 80 percent of a company's A/R, but I have advised companies many times to only count on 50–60 percent, if a loan can be obtained at all.

Why is this discounted so badly? They may discard A/R over 90 days because of the high risk; international sales for which a company has no leverage to collect; government sales usually take too long to pay, and accounts in the A/R that are generally considered poor risks to pay (i.e., client's credit rating is low). Banks are not investors, and they need to minimize their risks to make money and cover their bad loan deals.

The obvious action is to improve the A/R quality. In my experience, the biggest improvement can come from better timely collections. Companies will blame poor collections on the customers. Many times this was more a perception than fact. The biggest reason for delay in payments is poor paperwork, wherein the invoice to the customer did not match the purchase order from the customer. I was able to help a company collect over $200,000 that was argued over for months by eliminating a $25 service charge added for units returned that had no problem. The total added was only $750, but the supplier had not informed the customer this was going to happen.

The second noncustomer problem was not receiving all the deliverables listed on the purchase order. The worst example I remember was not getting paid for an $110,000 software product for lack of a $1 floppy. Engineering played it down, but did finally admit that the customer would have to operate without the latest version of the software that they were promised on the purchase order but did not receive.

There is another noncustomer problem that is in total control of the supplier. This is getting the invoice out the door ASAP. I have seen systems where the process may take days to get a bill out. There are many companies today that allow the supplier to bill instantaneously online when the product is shipped.

There are methods to collect the A/R quicker than with the normal terms. If affordable many customers will pay sooner if given a discount like 2 percent for payments within ten days. And though companies do not like the idea, some finance companies will pay you for a discounted value of the receivable the day you ship. They will take more than 2 percent, and the lender may want the cash from the customers to go directly to them, but this turns many suppliers off because it reflects a bad image.

During my career, I got involved in turnarounds—companies bleeding cash and negative profit that were a step away from the spiral to oblivion. You can bet a company in deep trouble probably wasn't watching collections. The first priority for me was to understand the A/R to see how I could squeeze it for cash as soon as possible. I even got to know accounts payable clerks in big companies to understand why they were delinquent in their payments. These strategies helped, and they provided the life blood to keep the company moving forward.

Acquisitions and Mergers

Major reasons for acquisitions to fail:

1. Poor due diligence by both sides.
2. Poor planning for the post-organization.
3. Inexperience of teams assigned to make it work.
4. Personnel assigned to the task already have full-time jobs and have little time for an acquisition or merger
5. Differences in the company culture.

Following are several simple questions that can be applied in advance before moving forward and if ignored, can result in wasted time and use of resources (both personnel and cash-wise):

1. Are the strategic goals of the potential partners similar?
2. Are the staffs compatible? Who will be president? Will there be two CFOs available?
3. Are the cultures compatible?
4. Is the method to be used for valuation of each company agreed to in advance?

You can expect trouble if the answers are no to any of the above questions.

As an example I was involved in an acquisition that failed badly because:

- The acquiree management staff was an unknown.
- The foreign culture was different.
- The method of valuation defied logic.
- As a result after balking at the deal, the acquirer wanted to walk away before the papers were signed. What followed was legal suits developed, a foreign government agency getting involved and even a hedge-fund entered to sue the acquirer's directors.
- The purpose of the acquisition was political, but made no sense to the acquirer's independent directors, who represented a majority of the board of directors therefore they backed out. Ironically, the result was that the deal was ultimately rejected by the acquiree

shareholders. The acquiree company eventually won by losing but this cost them millions of dollars and over a year of fighting the deal.

Antigrowth—Killing the Golden Goose

I had clients that lived off the output of a golden goose for years and then got carried away with the false perception that to be a great manager, one has to grow in sales. They knew the market, had their arms around their business, and slept sound at night, but along came an opportunity "too good to be true" (it usually is), and they jumped on it. It came so fast, but little did they know what lay ahead, and the inexperience caused them take their eye off the true money maker.

The worst situation I remember for killing the golden goose involved a peripheral company called GG that had sales of $5 million in revenue a year and was making hundreds of thousands of dollars profit. A "great" opportunity came along from a Mr. Big offering a potential for all his company's new planned peripherals to be manufactured outside the company, and they had selected GG to be their source. This presented GG with an opportunity of potential sales above $20 million on an annual basis. GG put a program together with increased expenses in place, including three times the floor space and the addition of several senior staff.

The ramp started, but when the company got above $6 million in sales, Mr. Big's world for the new products collapsed. Mr. Big's company was having problems in the new computer market space they had entered, and since the program wasn't meeting milestones, they decided to shut the program down. It became apparent that Mr. Big had gone outside of the company for the peripheral product to minimize his company's risk in building up expenses. Mr. Big also did not have to let people go, usually a painful task for companies cutting down. By concentrating on Mr. Big, GG neglected the sales of their golden goose and weakened its activity in the market so it was impossible to build it up again in the time needed. As you can imagine this wreaked havoc with GG, a small company without significant reserves. By the time they reduced significant expenses their response was too late and not enough. As a result, within a year, they filed Chapter 7 bankruptcy and disappeared into *the spiral to oblivion.*

Cash Management—The Ultimate Skills for Success

One of the top reasons for start-up or small companies failing is from poor cash management—the inability to have enough cash available get through the difficult as well as the successful periods of a company.

The following will explain all the aspects of managing cash, but one of the first Laws of Management Physics explains it all: the goesinnas have to exceed the goesouttas. There must be more cash coming in than is needed to cover all the operating costs of in order to grow. Yes, this statement is basic, but if it were understood, there wouldn't be the thousands of bankruptcies in our country every year.

In simple terms, cash management is the managing of cash to be available to meet the objectives of the company. Cash in can be from investors, loans, profit, or the sale of assets. Cash out can be for investing needs, loan payments and interest on loans, employee compensation, operating expenses, and dividends. One of the pitfalls of poor cash management is mistaking profit for cash. Growth cannot depend on profit alone, and a good explanation of the difference between profit and cash is the second Law of Management Physics: profit is muscle, cash is blood. We can live without muscles, but cannot survive without blood. Profit will eventually be turned into cash, but the time delay from sales revenue to collections from a customer can kill a company.

The answer to good cash management is planning. Depending on the situation in a company, cash planning can ensure that the company meets the next payroll and covers all the costs that are going to be incurred to meet the revenue and profit forecasts. One of the subtle aspects of cash planning relates to the timing of cash in and cash out. Customer payments may be dragged out, but you can't drag out costs like payroll and rent. And vendors seldom have the same patience not to get paid on time as you may tolerate with your customers.

The cash flow projection should be planned on a regular schedule. A thirteen-week cash flow report done weekly on a rolling basis is a must. One would expect that operating cash elements would be paid during this period, and accounts receivable should be collected in this period. In many high-growth situations, the cash available might run dry if collections stop completely. It is good to mark that point on the forecast as to when that might to occur in the thirteen-week period in order to focus on it to make sure it doesn't happen.

Cash flow projections can be structured in many ways, but a straightforward way is as follows:

1. Cash available at the beginning of the week
2. Identify potential collections from vendors in during the week and when they might occur;
3. Add a line for any other potential cash in such as the sales of assets or equity investments;
4. Total cash in equals 2 plus 3;
5. The cash available during the week to cover committed (or planned) payments is 1 + 4;
6. Identify when bills related to the cost of sales (material) will be paid during the period;
7. Identify when expenses such as payroll, rent, and interest on loans will be paid during the each one-week period;
8. Total cash out during the week be the sum of 6 plus 7
9. Total cash ending each week and beginning the next will be 5 minus 8.
10. Determine the net cash per week for each of the next twelve weeks by repeating the steps above

It would add visibility going forward if a cumulative cash position is also calculated by summing step 9 for each week of the 13 week cash flow period.

Another good metric regarding measuring cash is called the burn rate—the cash needed monthly if there were no collections from revenue and there were no payments to be made for material to build the product or outside services. This can be calculated from the fixed cash related expenses in place excluding material, or from the cash flow projection eliminating the projections for collections and vendors supplying material.

There are small private companies who do not have a balance sheet as part of their financial report package. Their financial reports are geared more to tax related information. This might work for a steady business where the goesinnas continues to exceed the goesouttas. A balance sheet is a must for robust growing companies to understand working capital. Working capital is determined on a balance sheet and is defined by current assets minus current liabilities. The common assets consist of items like cash, debt payments, accounts receivables, and inventory. The current liabilities consist of items like short-term debt and accounts payable. This is a measure of the health of a company: they should expect that current assets are greater than current liabilities. It is expected that having working capital will allow a company to be in position to cover near-term liabilities. Any excess working capital above the current liabilities can be used to help grow the company and pay for additional personnel, extra inventory, and advertising. If a company has zero working capital, it only has sufficient assets to operate the company in the near–term, and there will be no cash left over to invest in the needs that will help the company grow.

Companies get in trouble for failure to understand working capital and the timing of it. I lost count of start-ups who believed profit would cover the robust growth, then fail because they learned this isn't often true. Unless the profit margin far exceeds the industry norm, the more successful the growth, the more cash is needed. This is why robust growth cannot normally be supported from the business, and therefore additional cash in is needed from loans or equity investors. Basically, growth requires putting resources in place before the present level of revenue can cover paying for them.

Since current assets comprise mostly items that will be covered in a sixty - to 90-day period, working capital gives about a quarter-year viewpoint of cash that will be available. For a shorter view, there is quick ratio that is a combination of cash available and accounts receivable divided by accounts payable. This is a much shorter period viewpoint on having cash to go forward. If the quick rate is less than 1.0, the company is in trouble. It says the cash available plus what is to be collected soon won't cover the payments to suppliers and vendors owed money. In addition, if short-term cash can only cover short-term supplier commitments and interest payments, there won't be enough for payroll and additional inventory needed for growth.

Management can get so caught up in sales and in the bottom line; it hardly gets around to the balance sheet. Many times I get a business plan to review that is void of a balance sheet. Yet, the balance sheet contains the vital signs of a company, including what the company owns, what customers owe the company, and what the company owes to employees, companies, vendors, and the government. What could be more basic? If what is owed (the liabilities) gets out of hand and exceeds the assets of a company, then bankruptcy is just ahead. If the current and quick ratios are not watched, trouble could develop. The availability of working capital is the foundation for a growing company, and it needs to be projected regularly to determine how robust the growth can be. If the working capital can't support growth, then money needs to be brought into the company through debt or equity investors.

Dick Dadamo—The Observer

I have been in Management for over 50 years. During that time I have seen an infinite number of unique challenges, management styles, and so-called management "experts." After all these years, I do not believe there are any "experts," and I do not believe there is only one way to successfully manage people and companies.

I have been fortunate to work in the corporate world for about half of my career and as a consultant for rapidly growing companies in the second half. This has given me balance and has provided the continual broadening of my experience. Even today, at this writing, I am a director of a $700 million dollar public company and director of three start-up companies. I have lost count of the numerous investment I have made in start-ups perhaps to forget those among the failures. But one of my real joys now is working with students at local colleges by coaching those who are would-be-entrepreneurs. In fact, I am learning more about the new culture as I am giving back about the real world management.

During many of my meetings I keep getting asked, "What is the greatest change in management and what is the tried and true staple that has never changed in good management?" For the first question, I would say the way management treats people. To use the clichés, we have come from the past as a mushroom factory, where workers were kept in the dark and led blindly, to the open kimono approach, wherein management has unveiled their mission and vision. In many cases, even the company's financial performance results are disclosed to all their employees.

An important aspect of good management that hasn't changed is the need for excellent communications. Several years ago almost all management books were written about communications. Today, the emphasis in new literature is all about new technologies and new processes. But good communication still prevails. I was challenged recently as to what I believed was the most significant innovation or technological advancement in the last 50 years. My answer surprised many in the group when I said the break-up of the Bell system. I believe this was the genesis of the Internet, which in turn improved communications around the world. The Internet has led to the increased efficiency and productivity across the board in all industries and markets. We would still be without the Internet if the Bell System had prevailed and if their slow operating pace continued. The Bell System, with its monopolistic control, would still be sitting on the creativity needed to invent the Internet.

So what is an observer all about? An observer can apply years of experience in a variety of management situations, not to provide what he believes is the best way to do it, but to show there are alternatives that can help companies open their minds to other possibilities. An observer can bring innovation to a group, innovation being the ability to bring what worked in another world to the present world of a company.

Equal Partnerships—Doomed for Failure

Several times in my career, in consulting for small businesses, I have seen companies with equal ownership by two or more persons hit a wall and stifle growth when the partners want to go in different directions

Disagreement prevents a company from reaching its full potential, and the company usually starts to come apart. Even the use of legal documents that define what can be done by each partner doesn't guarantee a clean separation when a serious disagreement arises. More than once I've seen companies break apart while legal experts are fighting over the carcass. This eventually kills the company for lack of leadership and direction while the battle goes on. The longer a resolution takes, the more bitter the relationship becomes. Eventually the last step on the way to oblivion is in when other people in the company start to take sides.

Some reasons for the ultimate problems are:

- One partner wants to expand while the other partner is happy with the way things are.

- One partner wants to start taking cash out and the other doesn't.

- The company requires additional capital to reach its goals, but the one partner doesn't want to invest or add debt.

- One partner believes the other is not putting equal time and effort into the company—and most of the time this is true.

- All though it has nothing to do with the business, bitterness develops between the owners' families.

- And most important, a serious disagreement occurs when there is no longer agreement about the strategy of the company going forward.

Disagreement and conflicting decisions create friction during tough times resulting in the development of negative attitudes even over trivial issues when the partners want to go in different directions.

It is just like a marriage that has gone sour. It would take just as long to get out of the bad situation that it took to get in. Most often, neither side wants to work at making that happen.

To prevent the friction, as soon as one partner sees the difficulty arising he should address the problem. The potential to resolve the problem is to have a mutually trusted third party help work out the differences. It is most important to avoid a crisis before it occurs. Having a legal backup before the friction can help, but once the problem goes to the lawyers, usually the company is doomed.

It helps to have legal involvement from the start of the relationship as a contingency if the breakup in a partnership becomes inevitable. However, there has to be a serious attempt initially to define the reasons that may cause a split so that the course of action can be defined should a breakup be necessary. Unfortunately many agreements only define what happens with success since the relationship is all positive at the beginning.

The document should also include a clear definition of the roles of each partner. A definition for each should state the authority each partner has and his or her individual decision-making levels, when each partner has to inform the other of what he or she is doing, and when a partner needs to consult the other for major decisions even within their individual responsibility and authority.

A lot of the problem can be prevented by a company if the partnership starts out with the same objective for growth. Part of the agreement should include a definition of when additional capital is needed and how ownership is adjusted depending upon how much capital each partner contributes. In this way, the partner that really wants to keep charging ahead and is willing to put whatever is necessary in the form of capital into the company can gain the advantage of majority ownership and control if the other partner doesn't match the investment. An experienced attorney can help with the arrangement by suggesting how to handle the various unpredictable situations that may occur that could affect a partnership's success.

If over half of all married partners can't sustain a partnership, why should we expect two partners in a business would be able to sustain a relationship forever?

Ethics—Not In-House (NIH)

Although I have offended managers (particularly engineers), I believe a "not-in-house (NIH) attitude" to be a serious ethics' problem. If managers and engineers block good ideas because they are not developed in-house—even though doing this could hurt their company—I consider this to be ethics because passing on outside ideas and opportunities may very well restrict the success of the company.

Ethics—Crossing the Line

Our government's/politicians' definition of ethics includes: hypocrisy, lying and, quite frankly, lots of BS. In my private life the meaning of ethics depends on how a child is brought up and what they see going on around their own home and within their family. Of course, a child has a better chance if there are two parents to help them while they're growing up.

However, business ethics are difficult to define because depending upon the situation there's a very fine line that defines the situation at hand at any given point in time; therefore, as far as business is concerned, bad ethics is when you cross that very fine line.

In my experience, I can honestly attest to the act that almost all robberies in my clients' companies were perpetrated and/or caused by employees within those companies. I can also say that the majority were in companies where the top executive(s) possessed the bad ethics that were involved.

For example:

Company A: In a board of directors meeting, we were given a presentation on how the company embraced the quality (the presentation even included a copper-etched plaque with signatures of the management staff!). In this instance, before month's end and the end of the fiscal year, I received a call from an employee advising that at the direction of management to meet the year's forecasted revenue numbers, they were shipping product to a major customer, even though the system had failed the final acceptance test.

Company B: Like many manufacturing companies, it seemed that the vast majority of monthly revenue forecasts were shipped on the last day of the month—which, to management, seemed to be on Saturday or Sunday, despite the fact that the accounting month ended on Friday. The company was having numerous problems, which somehow seemed to be part of the culture that existed at that time. Since it was impossible for me to stop it immediately, I ultimately managed to solve the problem over the necessary period of time required to "smooth out" shipments on a monthly basis.

Company C: At this writing, the worst experience I can immediately recall occurred with a group of executives in a multimillion dollar company. The "boss" at the time had left the company prior to the arrival of his replacement, who became my boss when I joined the company. I was given an assignment that involved six of the 28 divisions not meeting the group's requirements (i.e., expectations). I found several things taking place that literally "blew my mind."

For example, one of the company's divisions had management forming their own travel agency, thus reaping income from all inside deals/ arrangements. Another division included individuals who were actually shipping product to their homes in order to meet monthly forecasts, only to return the product the next month. It was apparent the group executive put tremendous pressure on each division's general manager in order to meet the required "numbers."

To be expected this group executive went on to other companies, eventually becoming chairman of a well-respected Silicon Valley company. Predictably, however, his style caught up with him. Also as the Chairman of a computer peripheral company, it, too, encountered difficulties/troubles because it was [literally] learned that it was shipping bricks in boxes to represent disk drives—again to meet the "numbers." Management got caught, and the chairman went to jail (which obviously ended his career in the industry!).

Recap so far…

Company A – Bad Ethics

Company B – Questionable

Company C – Really Bad Ethics—way over the line

The negativity from bad ethics (with or without pressure from the top) occurs from the example set by management. If management crosses over the [obvious] lines(s), employees may see nothing wrong in their own actions by doing the same in their area.

And then…there's Company D, a small engineering design company with which I became involved. To establish a basic foundation, we redefined the vision, mission, and ethics by having company meetings on a regular basis.

When it appeared that the president was ready to finalize the ethics' section, the young man who headed the IT department posed the following question: "You talk about your ethics' plan, but how come we have lots of software for which we are not paying licensing fees?" This question turned out to be the moment of truth for the president because he could have responded: "This is the norm for our market, so lets move forward with it." If he said that he would have wasted all past efforts that had been undertaken to establish "wrong position." But, instead, he said: "Work on a number, and let's go over it as soon as we can." Although it cost several thousands of dollars for this small company, I believe it helped the culture—and equally as important, the eventual growth of the company.

In reality it is difficult to define ethics based on bad management and what is illegal; but, when all is said and done, management's ethics depend on where *they* draw the line.

Ethics Overdone

When the Sarbanes-Oxley Law was passed defining new governance rules—some of which elements were driven by ethical requirements—I was on board of a public company, so it became necessary to live by those new laws.

In the board meetings that followed, it became apparent that we seemed to be putting too much emphasis on governance issues. For example, a meeting starting at nine in the morning continued with governance topics until mid-afternoon—leaving only a small amount of time to delve into other business and strategy issues.

At the time, in this particular company in subsequent meetings our chairman finally put out agendas where the company business came up first; therefore; the disproportionate concern about doing something wrong minimized the necessary discussion time on other, very important topics. In other words, frankly speaking, too many directors prioritized the need to cover their tails to ensure there would be no problems in the future. *(See the chapter on Advisory Boards as a way to overcome this type of problem)*

Image—"Dress for Success"

Although dress codes have changed over the years from a suit and tie to beards and pony tails along with casual wear, there is still a code that has not changed to creating the proper image to a customer.

- Make the customer see that you have a positive attitude.
- Make the customer see that you are a winner.
- Make the customer want to deal with you.
- Make the customer see that you are a partner.
- Make the customer believe that you are the best.
- Make the customer see that you are the first person to approach to solve his need.
- Make the customer see you as a leader in your market and his.
- Make the customer believe he is your number one priority.

Create a mystic for the company to differentiate you from the competition.

A very large company descended on a $10 million division I was running in a very big company. We had been chosen to build one step in a process that they were not yet ready to do for themselves. The visiting team had more people than my entire staff. The question was how they could be sure we would be able to meet our commitment. We had done some research on their product and were able to stress how we saw the importance of their need. We showed them the plan that corporate people helped us put together, and I pledged a daily report over the ten week period of the program. We showed them product that had been successfully built without a process. But there were a couple of major points that helped create the comfort that initiated their visit. First, I made it clear that if we failed, I would probably be fired because of our two companies' existing great relationship. Second, my request and offer to let them help us to make it happen was a high point—a true indication of a partnership and not a vendor with an arms-length relationship.

Incremental pricing

Often an opportunity comes along in a growing company where revenue can increase significantly. A new Mr. Big customer might provide a chance to double the revenue, but there will be one big problem with Mr. Big: He will put pressure on you to lower your prices, and this will affect your product margin and bottom line profit percentage.

Often the rationale is, "We don't have to increase all the supporting costs proportionally to the revenue, so this can be a great deal." But here is a simple example to illustrate the result and what can happen.

Company Z, before Mr. Big came along, was making pretax profit of $50,000 on $2 million in sales. The product margin was 25%. These sales were going on year after year and providing the owner a nice life style. Mr. Big offered the chance to do an additional $2 million in revenue in the next year, but at a 10% margin. The rationale for accepting the lower margin for the company was that the new revenue would provide a pick up in the additional $2 million that would yield at 10%, $200,000, in incremental margin. It was also believed that the additional product would add no nonmanufacturing costs to the company. Wrong.

Mr. Big brought a mix of many more parts, straining the manufacturing organization and additional costs to support Mr. Big as a customer. This was an additional increase of $50,000 across the board in operating expenses.

The first year looked good, and the results were $4 million in sales revenue and a resulting total pretax profit of $175,000. This was fine, but as Mr. Big grew to $3 million, the original product sales dropped to $1 million because the proper attention in the market for original product sales had gone down. Also the increased effort to get the additional $1 million from Mr. Big drained resources from the original product sales team. The first perception was, thanks for having Mr. Big and the extra $2 million in sales, but the bulk of the sales now were closer to the 10% margin.

As the second year wore on, it became too late to make changes to the operating expenses. As a result the second year results ended with $4 million in sales revenue and a loss of $25,000. The company was now at the edge of *the spiral to oblivion*.

Leadership—The Path to a Successful Leader

During my years of consulting for small company leaders, founders, or presidents, I came across many management styles. Although most were self-styled, almost all said they wanted to grow their company. One of the most difficult efforts in my relationships was to try to change the mind-set of the individuals to position themselves for growth. The closer the personal relationship, the more difficult it was to recommend changes. As I gathered experience, I found a method to help get the message across without demoralizing the client. The techniques I used were more directed to introducing benchmarks as opposed to battering them with criticism.

I developed a set of slides that we would take on one at a time to make sure the message was understood and had an impact. It covered information that I thought was common to my successful clients over a range of styles, whether their leadership was individualistic or by group consensus.

Much of the information seemed like motherhood, but it was proper in the context for someone wanting to change and improve. Keep in mind that at the beginning of our relationships, many of the people I worked with were near novices as managers, let alone leaders, but as I helped them and the company to grow, they went through the many needed changes in the company culture to successfully grow. They started to see the importance in criteria and priorities they had not previously encountered. It usually started with their "I" mentality and the mind-set was: "I am the only one with good ideas," "I am the only one that can solve the problems," "I am the only one who can get a sale." The first step usually was to convince each Number One that the employees were human assets that would be needed to help him or her attain a vision and successful growth.

The Number Ones had to present to their teams consistency, fairness, integrity, comfort, and confidence to gain respect as their leader. The employees expect the leader to define the priorities, review them constantly, and reorder them as necessary. At the same time, the teams did not want to be told how to do everything unless they asked for help.

As companies grow in size, new people had to be put into new leadership roles within each company. Not only did it make sense for each Number One to have broader management skills, but they also needed this to help

41

in the selection of new people for key roles. It became apparent when it was necessary to go outside to fill a very important job in a remote location.

As an example, the person selected to run an Asian operation I had started needed to meet the following skills before I left the company:

- common sense;
- a good understanding of the product, market, and product mix;
- a strong sense of responsibility and commitment;
- a proactive and discipline approach;
- market and customer sensitivity;
- a willingness to stretch and try things others wouldn't;
- honor;
- sensitivity to priorities; and
- passion.

There were Number Ones that I worked with who in the beginning suffered from the failure mode, and the company was doomed to stagnation if they didn't change. Many of the Number Ones I dealt with started their companies or inherited the Number One role in a company. Having very little accountability to anyone but themselves, they could play king and do it their way until they hit a road block in growth, or until I came along. The following list was a method to look at negative potential to avoid when evaluating themselves or other people for leaders:

- They don't communicate well.
- They don't utilize their staff and others for help.
- They don't have the energy needed for the task.
- They don't hire people who are better than they are.
- They demotivate staff.
- They don't set up proper controls or delegate enough authority to match added responsibility.
- They don't have a good reporting and follow-up program.
- They don't believe the customer is always right, until proven wrong.

By presenting the various lists to a No. 1, the idea was in getting each No. 1 to evaluate the pluses and negatives of their managers which indirectly made them see both the good and bad in themselves. By reviewing the lists, a No. 1 was able to see some of the behaviors common to them. This was a subtle way to slip in helping them change for the better.

In growing companies many employees run out of gas. In fact the third law in *The Laws of Management Physics* is, "A staff that stays together can't grow together." It is not realistic to expect everyone on the staff to have the same growth agenda including experience, education, networking, training and passion. The list below covers points to look for when leaders start to stumble:

- They focus on projects that won't involve any conflict in their lives.
- They aren't stern enough when their people stumble.
- They get on people's backs more often for silly reasons.
- They are moody.
- They constantly change their minds.
- They are influenced by whomever whispers in their ear last.
- Their attention always seems to be somewhere else.
- They force people to quit instead of firing them.
- They avoid tough customer problems.
- They stop returning customer calls.

This list helps a Number One identify those employees who won't grow alongside the Number One. It can also provide a basis for consideration to terminate people.

As most successful Number Ones grow and become more sophisticated, they recognize the changes occurring. They can then advance beyond some of the motherhood and now add strengths needed to continue on a growth path. These include

- decisiveness,
- good communication and listening skills;
- consistency in mood; and
- being upbeat.

When additional stakeholders (senior staff, investors, customers, suppliers) come into the company, Number One has to be held more accountable for performance and assessing the company's needs in relation to the stakeholders needs, and then communicate the results to everyone. A typical order of importance of a stakeholder list will look like this:

- Investors
- Employees
- Customers
- "I"

The order of importance in this list can be shuffled around depending on the nature and stage of the business as long as "I" is at the bottom. Such behavior will be true with a mature leader.

It becomes necessary as Number One grows to expect and get more from the human asset team. The need grows for Number One to better articulate tasks, define milestones, define objectives, define metrics, and define success. Early on during the "I" culture, successes could have been defined as taking as much money home as possible and praying things wouldn't change. Things do change, however, and the successful Number One must be able to cope with the changes. Number One now, with the help of the list above, expects accountability to enter the equation for his employees as well as for himself.

The bigger the company gets, the more Number One needs the support and growth of the management team to be on the same path that Number One is traveling. The interface with employees becomes more important, and Number One must learn to listen, provide feedback, and give credit. Hopefully by now, Number One has eliminated the "I" and "but" words. No more will you hear:

- Success—"I did it"
- Failure—My people screwed up
- "You did a good job, but … (STOP).

Number One now starts to realize that when it comes to building the employee team it is a must to

- allow failure,
- encourage teamwork,
- be supportive,
- lead by example, and
- encourage effective lateral communications.

Number One understands that employees want recognition and an understanding of how their contribution fits the company success. It is important to make sure to have employees understand they are a part of the destiny of the company. Number One now needs to provide a company for everyone that offers challenge, knowledge, and growth.

In today's competitive world, Number One must provide an environment that encourages techniques to generate innovation. Everyone will gain from this, and the company will become a company of leaders.

Managers Match

There are many styles of management with the best chance of success matched to a company's needs. Following is a list of companies in various stages. It is very unusual when a manager can be effective in all the following stages listed:

- Start-Up – Entrepreneur mentality needed
- New Division of a company – Seasoned manager
- Robust Growth – Vision and extreme pressure
- Flat revenue – Caretakers
- Turnaround – Ability to say *no* to a company that's in deep trouble
- Self-style – Owner mentality
- Big company – Budget Manager – to manage to numbers
- Small company – Businessman – to manage for results

Keep in Mind:

1. A manager great at caretaking is unlikely to succeed as an entrepreneur because they're not willing to risk their own personal fortune and/or work 70-hour weeks.

2. A manager great at robust growth with vision would get bored with caretaking.

3. A manager great at turnarounds, who can live by saying *no* to excessive requests might fail at high-risk situation.

4. A manager successful in a self-style business, with personal financial goals and family as a priority, could stumble where situations require customers' and employees' needs to come first.

5. Presidents or general managers who are successful in a large company by working to budgets may fail in running small company where cash is king.

Merger Fundamentals

There are numerous articles and books detailing the less than optimistic statistics that exist for mergers and acquisitions. It's estimated that well over 60% of the time mergers and acquisitions fail, while over 80% will fail to meet projected expectations.

Companies heading into a merger or acquisition are almost always doomed to fail. The major reason for this is a difference in cultures. Other contributors include poor planning and not having a dedicated team in place to help make the transition successful.

Although there are numerous check sheets and templates to be filled out by companies to accomplish the merger and acquisition, these often miss the basic requirements. In my experience, a lack of upfront analysis leads to an enormous waste of time, energy, and money. All this waste could be prevented by making sure four basic criteria are in place before starting any major effort. These include:

1. Making sure both entities share the same strategic objective.
2. Making sure there is a similarity of cultures between both entities.
3. Making sure there is compatibility before combining senior staff.
4. Having an agreement on the basis of and definition for the valuation of each entity.

I have found over and over again that if any one of these four points are violated, it will result in a complete waste of time, energy, and money. In one of my most recent consultancies, I observed eighteen months of futility after an offer was made to acquire a company; the offer was rejected, leading to a legal battle costing serious time and money. Fortunately, the deal eventually got canceled.

All this wasted effort could have been avoided by having the two parties put in place these four components. In this case, all four were wrong. If the merger had gone forward, it would have failed and been disastrous for both companies.

Mergers & Acquisitions—Beware the Inexperience

It is a historical fact that over 60% of acquisitions and mergers fail, and over 80% do not meet expectations. In many cases large companies can absorb a disaster as part of their business. For small companies a failed merger can be the start of their downfall into the spiral to oblivion.

Big companies can afford to assign resources to do the due diligence necessary before pushing the final button. The small company needs to use the existing staff that is already busy with normal duties. This leaves the due diligence completely to the inexperienced in the area of mergers and acquisitions. The alleged reasons for doing the merger or acquisitions in all size companies are similar; quick revenue growth, synergism to strengthen the market position, the potential for the combined organization to reduce significant costs. I have also seen in the majority of cases the ego of the top management come into play because they believe they can do it better than the acquired or merged company. A poor due diligence will leave the pre-acquisition conclusions to ill-fated perceptions.

Here is a case study of many of the things that can go wrong with the efforts of inadequate and inexperienced personnel trying to acquire a company. Company A was a computer memory company selling IBM compatible memory—with selling prices from $10,000 to greater than $100,000 per system.

Company B was a computer printer company selling printers to the IBM market from $5,000 to $20,000 per printer. Hidden under the pile of printers was their printer supplies business—paper, cartridges, ribbons—from which most of their recent revenue had come. Some unit prices were less than one dollar.

Company B was in trouble, and word got around they were for sale. The first perception was that sales were in the $10 million range. As it turned out this was at one time in the past. The second perception was Company B was even a bigger company than $10 million per year. This was one of many wrong perceptions. The reason for the image was that for years, Company B had an ad on the inside back cover of the leading trade magazine, thus creating a false image. Things were moving fast, and the pressure was on for the first company to make an offer to win. Unfortunately, when something bad turned up, the theme was, "It is such a good deal; we can overcome the trouble." My input from past experience in turnarounds was, "The longer something has been in trouble, the longer it takes to turn it around." Once again a wrong perception was that the trouble was recent. The advice from the company's outside CPA was, "Make an assets sale, and you can avoid all responsibilities for their past sins, whatever they were." Time didn't allow for a detailed financial analysis, and top-down numbers were determined and used for sales, cost of sales, and operating expenses. The consolidated financial statements looked great on paper. Discussions with customers were sloughed off on the basis that company A had similar customers and there was no time to explore this. This was wrong again on perception. The market was the same, but the customers were different. Company A sold to major brokers. Company B sold to small distributors.

But the worst was yet to come. It was concluded that the support people in Company B could be let go because Company A could absorb the accounting, shipping, and sales support. This was another wrong perception.

So Company A bought into a nightmare. The acquisition had problems, mostly in quality (as there was no quality control for six months), but more in commitments to their customers. Many of their customers were small brokers. The people who called in had problems like a unit not working so they couldn't be paid. Others had paid for a printer that was not delivered, and did not even exist in the inventory. To some customers a $15,000 or more cash outlay could affect their life style and existence as a company as they lived month-to-month on the profit they got for sales of printers.

The deal, as structured by Company A, was buying the assets. In doing so there was no responsibility to take care of past sins of the company. The sales manager almost became a basket case in talking to desperate crying people almost eight hours a day for four weeks until the calls started tapering off. The reality of the situation was that if Company A tried to make everyone whole, it would bankrupt Company A.

The sales from the acquisition were almost zero, because Company B had been an irritant in the market for months. Customers had to buy the supplies to keep the hundreds of Company B working printers in the market. The nickel and dime sales provided their only cash in whereas Company A's product sold for a minimum of $5,000 but closer to $50,000. Many supplies for Company B sold for less than $100. This created a negative impact on the company's system that resulted in a bundle of unhappy people that were never placated. For instance, for an increase of less than 10% of total Sales, accounting transactions were increased 40 percent. The shipping and receiving person, who was used to delivering a few boxes daily to the airport (on his way home), now had to wrestle with over fifty boxes of printer supplies every day. The extra effort not only put a strain on the support personnel, but hurt the performance of Company A's bread-and-butter products. The sales organization was ready to rebel because of the antagonism created by Company B's products with their end-user customers. In some cases, customers temporarily stopped placing purchase orders with Company A. So what seemed like a sweetheart deal became a nightmare. I believe Confucius first said, "If a situation sounds too good to be true, it probably is." What finally happened was that Company A sold the supplies line and phased out the peripherals, with a resulting loss in the thousands of dollars.

These are the lessons to learn:

- Make sure you do a due diligence on the target company—including talking to their customer base by examining all contracts and agreements.

- Plan the acquisition (or merger) to the nth degree, including how to announce the deal to the vendors and customers.

- Analyze the impact on the existing work load.

- Project the expectations of customers and vendors who may be so unhappy that nothing will keep them as customers or suppliers.

- Analyze the quality of the product being shipped; determine if there are warranties to be honored and what this cost will be.

- Make sure the cash flow needs can be met during the early transition.

In many instances, it is possible to hold back some of what is to be paid. This is to ensure that nothing will come out of the wall that was not discovered during the due diligence. Obviously, if a proper due diligence had been done the acquisition would never have been made.

Most important is to seek outside help, particularly legal and financial, to do the due diligence and help structure the deal.

Mr. Big—Dealing With

Many times the growth rate of a small company will be accelerated when a large opportunity comes along from a much bigger company (Mr. Big). The cultural mismatch between companies of different sizes can create real havoc. It is dangerous to want to do business as in the past with handshakes or without a documented agreement. First off, it should be clear that working without a document or contract is the worst kind of an agreement. When a disagreement occurs, there is nothing to fall back to such as a clear specification of how to resolve differences or what product delivery or service performance is required to justify payment.

Small companies often do not even have a documented policy for the terms and conditions for accepting a purchase order. Many times a small company is at the mercy of Mr. Big because of a lack of experience. Where this may be a completely new experience for the small company, it is likely Mr. Big does it every day in his world.

Here are tips on how to prevent a disaster from the cultural mismatch:

Legal

The first step is to get an attorney for your side. Don't expect a two-page agreement, as there are many conditions that may crop up that you would not consider and you need someone protecting you.

1. Avoid penalties for bad schedule performance.

2. Do not agree to give away the company jewels for nonperformance. Do not enter into a relationship that may cause you to lose your IP if the program goes sour.

3. Have strong cancellation charges if the customer decides not to go forward.

4. Try to avoid customer provided material, as that can wreak havoc with your efficient production flow when you lose control of your supply chain. Enforce payment terms. Try to get enough viability from the customer to build a cash flow (requirements) forecast. Keep in mind that if the relationship is successful and the customer increases the schedule, more cash will be needed.

5. Try to get a commitment to cover out-of-pocket costs like paying for the material up front needed to meet the customer schedule

51

requirement.

6. Build files to help cover all changes along the way in case trouble comes up.

Operations

1. Prepare to be the program manager even if you are the president.

2. Try to establish a single channel of communication so the customer won't overpower your people, who are most likely outnumbered, and are subsequently prevented from doing their basic jobs.

3. Protect your other business in case Mr. Big goes away. Be cautious of increased spending across the board and the neglect of the other customers. Try to structure the organization to split the business between Mr. Big and the other customers who got you where you were before Mr. Big showed up.

Sales and Marketing

1. Make sure the customer has a champion for you so you can continually get a fair deal. You can bet there will be someone in this big company trying to get your company replaced by one of their other contacts.

2. Maintain knowledge of the customer's product and market to insure no big surprises occur should the customer stumble and bring you down with him.

3. Analyze the impact upon the schedule and cost before agreeing to any changes suggested by the customer, and try to get additional revenues when warranted.

4. Don't fight the customer if he eventually decides to do the job himself, but instead support him, because it will take longer than he thinks, and this will provide you with continual revenue and a more efficient phase down.

Above all treat the relationship like a honeymoon—enjoy it while you can, but expect it to eventually end, and be prepared should this happen.

Be sure to be ready when a Mr. Big comes along. I have seen companies destroyed when trying to plan in the big leagues only to strike out.

Here is the worst example I can remember. There was a modem company selling $3 million in revenue a year and making hundreds of thousands of profit. A "great" opportunity came along from a big Mr. Big offering a potential for all their new planned modems and potential sales above $20 million in revenue. A program was put together and expenses were put in place at three times the floor space and several senior staff.

When the company got above $6 million in sales from Mr. Big, the world collapsed. Mr. Big was having problems in the new computer market he had entered, and since the project wasn't meeting milestones, he decided to shut it down. As you can imagine, this wreaked havoc with the small company, and by the time they reduced significant expenses, it wasn't enough. Within a year, they filed Chapter 7 bankruptcy.

Management Philosophy—One Liners

Businessmen manage a budget, Budget managers manage the numbers.

Sometimes it is easier to sell a bad product with good support than a good product with poor support.

Remember when they used to say, "You can't be fired going with IBM?" Now your boss will be upset if you do not look for alternatives to IBM.

When a company is struggling it's easy to make a quick impact by identifying the obvious: inventory is too big and unbalanced, collection estimates are too optimistic, market estimates are too ambitious, etc., but the difficulty is correcting them.

A company drifting down is like a marriage in trouble: if it took 3 years to reach a low point, it will take three years to get back and usually the people involved don't want to work at it.

A staff that got you in trouble most likely can't get you out.

In the early stages of a company's growth, an owner's mentality "drives" the company culture, but maturity occurs when leaders find they no longer can carry the company on their shoulders alone.

When trying to raise money from investors, keep in mine you eat, sleep, live your vision, but the investors have many opportunities—so you must first find ways to reduce the gap between priorities.

When you ship a product or provide to a customer that fails in their product or system even though it meets the agreed to specifications your attitude should be "we have a problem so let's fix it together."

For every action, there is an equal and opposite reaction, Isaac Newton: so for every new delegation there should be a control.

A customer's perception often can be more important than facts in their selecting a product or service.

Companies can suffer more from a lack of good management decisions than from bad managers.

You bet almost everything will take longer than you expect.

Death and taxes are inevitable, but I guarantee time will pass, so also plan your precious intelligently.

"For every action, there is always an equal and opposite reaction, or the mutual forces of two bodies on each other are always in opposite directions." Isaac Newton

"For every delegation, there needs to be a new control"

Outside Help Ignored

A big shortcoming with struggling mangers is their reluctance to ask for outside help, or any help at all.

A good example is the many times my clients have been hurt by second- and third-shift supervisors believing they could work out problems before making it clear that problems existed, or what those problems were. I have seen this reluctance at all levels of management and nationalities.

For example, one experience occurred when I was put in charge of an international organization for an American multinational company headquartered in Italy. A year-and-a-half prior to my assignment, the parent company made a big deal publicly about expanding their electronics component capability internationally.

Well, when I got to Italy the company was one step short from oblivion. To make the situation even worse, a communist union was putting the nails in the coffin by cleverly-organized strikes.

The problem: For over an 18-month period of time, the Italian staff was reluctant to ask for help from the big American, parent company. At the same time, the parent company was waiting for a business plan from the Italian company. The acquisition ended in complete failure, and the international company was ultimately sold (practically given away) to a local Italian business after experiencing millions of dollars in losses.

For startups, success can be enhanced by partners and advisors in the beginning. There are so many tasks to be done and even if the founder has the capability going it alone it will slow down the company growth and possibly miss the window of opportunity.

Paradigm Change—Not as Good to Be the King as It Used to Be

There was a time when Number One in a company operated like he was king and had no one to answer to. The person in charge made up the rules as he went along.

Words like OSHA, ISO9000, sexual harassment, compliance, and global competition were not in their business dictionary. Many companies were operated like the proverbial mushroom factory—kept in the dark while being fertilized. At the worker level, people were told what to do and when to do it, and if they were mistreated, they had no one to go to.

Local, state and federal laws in the second half of the twentieth century have changed the ground rules for operating. For instance in California, companies over a certain level of employees must have some defined classifications of employees who must take training on sexual harassment.

The relationship between customer and supplier also changed in the latter part of the twentieth century. Up until the changes were enacted, the customer was pretty much controlled by the supplier. There was a time in the industry I grew up in where the major supplier was IBM. They were able to tell the customer when it was time to change over their systems even if the old was operating okay. They had the leverage to stop supporting the old systems. Once you selected a computer system from a supplier you were basically locked in with the supplier's proprietary software and peripherals.

The advent of PC's made a big dent in this restriction, as the base system was now open architect, and many capable companies could supply compatible pieces of the system. However, the rapid growth of the computer industry followed closely by changing telecommunications industry left a lot to be desired quality-wise.

Such rapid growth is synonymous with compromise. It was not unusual for new products to be shipped unfinished in order to meet schedule commitments, and the design was then completed at the customer's site.

Unfortunately, this mode of operating spawned a generation of managers, promoted too rapidly and insufficiently trained, who then went into other, uncontaminated companies and perpetuated the style.

One of the real tragedies from this period was the way training became such a low priority. So many of the budgets I've seen set aside little or no money (investment) for training. Worse yet, I've seen some companies where accounting hadn't even defined an expense account for training!

The market has even a more profound change than losing the manufacturing quality to Asia. Major changes started to evolve during the 1980s, and upon entering the 1990s, the transformation to the customer becoming king had occurred. The customer now wanted as normal customization, short runs, frequent and instant changes to schedules, customer service on a 24/7/365 basis, compliance, and quality. This new pressure helped force many suppliers to look offshore for manufacturing of their products and the global sources responded to providing design, customer support, and more of the direct source for the product.

The global competition had hit small U.S. companies as well as large. I have been involved with some of the companies hit hard by worldwide competition. Some of the companies I work with offered engineering product designs, laser equipment, insurance service to companies, and manufacturing assembly. In years past, the presidents of these companies came to my monthly roundtable. We discussed changing employee relations, management information systems and how to market sales outside Southern California. Global competition wasn't even discussed.

Now these four companies have felt the hit from global competition, and so far this is how they have responded.

The assembly company does small runs and high quality assemblies for the military and medical markets. The laser company provides services for companies that cannot afford laser equipment. The insurance service company does seminars for companies to educate managers and employees to get the best protection on their retirement investments, and the engineering company breaks down the designs to utilize offshore software engineers while they maintain the program control, and make themselves available to their customers within twenty-four hours. The one common thread all four companies provide to their customers is flexibility and instant response, something not easily done by offshore competition.

Another paradigm shift was occurring in that entrepreneurial companies proliferated all over, with many lead by unskilled and inexperienced business men. At the same time, volume became the need of the day, and the country was not up to the task. The transistor radio and other communications products were already finding their way to manufacturers in Asia. I was sent to the orient by the company I worked for at that time to start a manufacturing company for cost reasons, but actually lucked out because we could not find the number of employees needed in Southern California to support our growth. We struggled to maintain a cadre of fifty assemblers in California. I had the great opportunity of setting up our first company in Hong Kong. When I left the parent company as president, we had over eight million labor hours off shore. I sit on a board today that has over forty million hours off shore. One thought, this era may have been the start of the phrase, "Jobs Americans don't want to do." ("Bye, bye, the song American Pie, this is the day American manufacturing died.") It is important to note that without Asian labor availability and cost, there would be no computer or communications industries as we now know and enjoy.

As a result of these failings, we are now faced with the task of undoing what's been done, unlearning what's been learned, and getting some long overdue efficiency back into the way we operate.

Without a doubt, changing a paradigm must start at the top. Number One must first ask, "What am I trying to do?" "What responsibilities can I eliminate?" "How can I work more efficiently?" Only then should Number One ask, "How can I get more from my staff and what do I need in human assets to go forward?"

Most importantly, Number One should look to the customers and vendors for their insights about the company's efficiency and attitude. This is a good time to really get inside the customer's head and make sure you're doing everything you can to get the maximum amount of business. The vendor should be a business partner, because they can minimize your purchasing costs and help you find ways to off-load tasks that can be done more efficiently elsewhere.

Setting goals is the easy part of the equation. Successful implementation, on the other hand, requires that you set, continually review, and communicate priorities. Over and over, I find that when a company is not operating efficiently, the senior staff does not have consistent priorities or they have not made them clear throughout the organization.

When priorities have not been made clear, employees will set their own priorities and agendas, perhaps believing that these are their boss's priorities as well. For example, the CEO of a $20 million dollar company was spending a tremendous amount of time selecting a dental plan for the company. He could have optimized his time by going through a broker or giving the task to a subordinate.

Good people can be the most dangerous when priorities have not been made clear, because they will go off in their own direction faster and farther than others. Number One needs to put the company's priorities in writing and make sure that the staff's priorities are aligned in support of the company's priorities. Number One must also make sure that employees are aware of each others' priorities. I have always told clients that one of a leader's primary functions is to set priorities and review them constantly as needed.

People also tend to confuse priorities with their desires. I once asked the Number One of a client company what his top priority was. He answered that his highest priority was to hire a national sales manager. "Well," I asked him, "why isn't there a line of people outside your door waiting to be interviewed?"

I then asked how long it had been since he had talked to the search firm and found out that it had been two weeks! Clearly, hiring a national sales manager was not really his top priority.

Number One must then determine if the top staff is up to the changes that need to be implemented. He shouldn't compromise with his staff or pay people to tell him why he can't make the necessary changes. In the past, I have told my staff that I could call in a wino off the street to tell me my plans won't work and it certainly wouldn't cost me as much! The staff should respond to the bosses thoughts or requests on how it might be accomplished. Let the boss decide if it is worth the costs, priority, time, resources, and risk.

Middle management as a phenomenon came into existence because the staff in place was not able to do their jobs efficiently. If staff can be made more efficient, there will be less need for supporting organizations. Staff efficiency is decreased by unnecessary meetings, excess reporting requirements, poorly defined responsibilities, and the continual distraction of "fighting fires." These types of inefficiency result in the addition of assistants, coordinators, administrators, and worst of all, program managers. In the commercial world, program managers evolved as a crutch because the systems in place couldn't get the job done.

To avoid all these problems, strive for efficiency. Define every position's responsibilities clearly, set and communicate priorities well, minimize meetings, streamline reporting, and give timely and accurate feedback. On the other hand, here's what not to do:

- Don't assign one person to do a task and five others to nitpick and second guess her. Give her the ground rules and specs, and let her do her job.

- Don't require three bids and twelve signatures to buy a pencil. Keep decision-making authority at the lowest possible organizational level. For example, in one of the companies I worked for, purchase orders required six levels of approval. When I went back and talked to these people, I found that everyone who had signed the purchase order had assumed that the person before them had analyzed it, so they had not analyzed it themselves. Even worse, we gave the vendors copies of all the paperwork (with all the signatures!), and they usually thought it was pretty funny.

- Don't undermine your sales staff. I have seen situations where there is so little trust in the sales staff that, when they are dealing with a customer, they have to go back to management over and over just to get the price down an inch. However, if sales people are to be your interface with the customer, you have to give them some decision-making authority. Instead of handicapping the sales staff from the start, hire the right people and train them to do the job the way you want it done. Make sure they understand that while they represent the customer, they work for you.

- Don't go overboard trying to satisfy a customer. In one company, I found that out of thirty employees, eight were working on a problem that required finding twenty-five cables to meet a weekly shipping commitment. Obviously I had impressed upon them how important pleasing the customer was, but I had certainly not made it clear who was responsible to solve the problem.

- Don't do it that way just because you've always done it that way. Too often, we accept things the way they are. It is natural to review all the systems and processes of a company in trouble. After all, what they're doing now obviously isn't working, right? I was once with a company where I attended quarterly progress meetings. One general manager complained for several meetings in a row that he couldn't meet goals because he couldn't hire enough senior engineers. When the CEO assigned someone to look into the problem, it was found that they could solve the problem by getting study assistants to work as gophers for the senior engineers, relieving them of mountains of paper work. They had to change their strategy, to do it a different way.

When all is said and done, the most important part of changing how you run a business is to improve efficiency. Knowing this, how do you go about improving efficiency?

- Do it right the first time. This is, by far, the best and most effective way to improve efficiency.

- Define roles and expectations. In my consulting practice I've found that, more often than not, top staff members do not have a position description. I still find that more than half of the executives I deal with don't get a written review.

- Define Responsibilities and Authority.

First, do the obvious: Match the authority to the responsibility. In fast-growing companies, responsibility and authority change so rapidly that it can become unclear who is supposed to be responsible for what and who can authorize what. This can create inefficiency and duplicated efforts.

I have found two effective techniques for clarifying responsibilities and authority. The first I call "one-liner policies." It often takes too long to set up and maintain a formal, detailed policy and procedures manual, but one-liners can be zapped out instantly to those involved. For example, if a new VP Marketing has been put in place to control travel, you could make a new policy, "All travel must be approved by the VP Marketing."

The other technique for clarifying responsibility and authority also effectively maintains the checks and balances that tend to get lost in the chaos of a growth situation. In this technique, you set up three categories for tasks such as signing checks, signing leases, pricing, and setting terms and conditions:

1. a person responsible for approval,

2. a person who must be consulted before the decision is finalized, and

3. a person who must be informed.

For example, let's say all top staff has the authority to approve travel for their staff up to 200 miles. The CFO is running out of patience with a customer who isn't paying on time and makes plans to send the person in charge of receivables to visit the customer. The VP Marketing must be consulted, because they may be working on a major opportunity with that customer that makes it an inappropriate time to shake things up. If it is still okay to send the person, then the regional sales manager must be informed, since he should know about any visits to customers in that territory.

1. Streamline Reporting

Top staff should report to the CEO weekly with a short list of one-line updates. This will save multiple phone calls and meetings in the hallways, but still give the CEO the input he needs. These reports should contain five to ten brief items such as, "There is nothing new from IBM," or "Engineering is still adhering to the latest schedule," or "The audit looks like it will take one more week than planned." If the CEO wants additional information, he can contact that person at his convenience.

Also, accounting and MIS cannot determine what reports are needed to run other departments. The heads of accounting and MIS should sit down with the staff, both collectively and individually, to find out their reporting needs with regard to content, form, and frequency. Too often, piles of unneeded reports accumulate on the desks of people who don't read them, and then they feel guilty every time they look at the pile. On the other hand, I have lost count of the manufacturing managers who have complained, rightly so, that they don't get the information they need.

2. Shortened (But Focused) Meetings

Meetings are the cancer of an organization. They are usually too long, have too many people, and are not focused on the topic. Often, few of the action items discussed get accomplished.

First, the meeting shouldn't start without an agenda. When I was the boss, I walked out of meetings before they got underway because there was no agenda. Second, someone has to be in charge to keep the meeting focused, to stop unrelated small talk, to write the minutes, and to follow up. Third, copies of the minutes should be given to all participants' bosses, because they are the ones who set the priorities of those attending. Finally, people should only attend if it is really necessary, and the person in charge should enforce time limits to make sure everyone makes their points quickly and concisely.

3. Priorities

Set clear priorities, review and revise them frequently, and keep everyone involved up to date on what they are. If the CEO has done nothing other than set priorities and make sure they are adhered to, he has done a good job.

Priorities can be a tricky area, because setting them doesn't mean that they will necessarily be adhered to. I have often found that when you give someone the third "top priority" in one week, the first one tends to get lost. Also, too often priorities get spit out with no follow-up. Many times managers fail to recognize when their staff is already overloaded, so a new priority will not have any impact. In this situation, the manager needs to make clear which other priorities can be downgraded.

The results of all this newfound efficiency can be mind-boggling. One CEO found that they were able to reduce the beta testing times for their new products from twelve months to three months. Imagine what could be done for the company with the nine months of creative energy left over! The importance of efficiency cannot be underrated. That's what all the fuss is about!

The emerging growing company can benefit by the following principles:

- Do what you do best, and outsource whatever you can for efficiency and cost, but never, never outsource your core competency.

- Make sure to put the infrastructure in place to keep up with the growing sales.

- Overhire personnel to be positioned for the growth as it occurs.

- Make sure all projections for planning resources give high priority for the human asset needed.

- Be wary of spreadsheets that can make can make or reject plan changes with the push of a key while most likely not factoring in the human element.

- Surround yourself with employees who have the stomach for rapid growth. We used to describe a company I worked for as like working in a match box that is moving toward a lighted furnace

- Keep your employees informed of the continual changing directions to keep up with growth opportunity. Move from the mushroom factory to an open kimono. Keep them informed and let them know their role is vital to the success of the company. Listen to them and give them feedback.

- Find vendors and suppliers who are willing to have a partnership mentality and are willing to grow with you while taking some risks.

- Maintain and retain an outside cadre of experts such as legal, finance, and marketing to help take you through all the new barriers along the growth to the top of the mountain. Try to put an advisory board in place.

- When you ship a product that doesn't work in the customer's system, even though it meets specifications, your attitude should be,

- "We have a problem. Let's try to fix it together."

- Make sure someone in the company is assigned to stay on top of the worldwide trends, particularly in your industry.

Pricing—Not Really Rocket Science

Early on in the product cycle, pricing the product is done more from a gut feeling rather than from accurate information provided by the accounting personnel. Admittedly, success is relative, and I have seen many small companies operate successfully for awhile without ever understanding standard costs or inventory control systems.

It gets down to understanding the material costs in a manufacturing system or the cost of an hour of labor in a service system. Beyond that, it is important to understand the cost of the added value—all costs in place minus the material or product hour to make a sale. If Number One or whoever does the pricing has a grasp of the added value in place for the month, they can be sure that when they price something, it covers all the added value expenses after materials will be paid for. Usually one sale won't cover it all. The price-setter must have a great feel for the business and always keep in mind how the timing of the shipment affects the added value in place. For instance, if the added value is $50,000 a month, the sales and margin (after costs) must yield $50,000 to break even for the month.

In manufacturing, when it is clear that the period is covered, any extra sales that can be delivered in that time period will create a margin above the added value in place and go directly to profit.

I used a technique for years when being pressured to squeeze the price. My response was to ask for a higher delivery rate to increase margins above the added value, because costs do not go up as volume does in the near-term period.

In my consulting experience, I have often found a situation wherein the company priced an item for fear of not getting the order. I have lost track of the numerous times that my advice to set a price at your comfort level, then double it, was questioned. First off, I believed the potential customer must have an interest in the potential supplier, especially if the bidder is a small company. If the buyer believes the supplier can do the task, and feels the price is high, he will negotiate rather than run away. Many of these companies never lost a deal based on price, so why not try for more. It is almost impossible to increase the starting price in a negotiation as the supplier, but there is almost always pressure to push it down.

As companies grow, the product offering expands, and competition gets more prevalent, more sophisticated accounting systems become a necessity for defining profitable pricing. There is a danger here in that accounting systems start to introduce reserves and accruals, and the system is usually based on numbers, not common sense. For instance, I ran a $12 million division in a multibillion dollar corporation. All the products were customized for the OEM customers. We had a standard cost system based on standards for yield, purchase material, and inventory write-offs among other criteria. The standard for the cost of the product was based on the capacity of the facility, said to be $20 million, and projected prices for purchased items. Every month at the group operation meetings, I spent more time on explaining all these variances of the standards and little on the market and strategy. This variance occurred because our revenue was under $20 million, purchased item cost had different prices, the product yield was different than forecasted, and the product mix that varied monthly used different quantities of material.

I kept my sanity by falling back on something close to a combination of the added value and the projected cash we would spend every month until I got corporate accounting to abandon the standard cost system and change to a system based on job order.

Quality and the Real Cost of Problems

When a product fails in the process or in the field, there is a tendency for the supplier company to increase testing in the manufacturing process. While this cost is easy to account for, it is far from the total cost needed to make it right.

When there is a product complaint, in many cases, the basic problem originates in a poor design. Rather than pursuing the most direct solution of redesigning it, which adds time and expense to the process, some managers will pass over this option, choosing instead to minimize costs, all the while risking the possibility of future failures. This could be a doomed perception.

The clichés we have all heard associated with failure include: "Do it right the first time" and "You cannot test quality in a poorly designed product." Both are very true. Some companies will try to correct a defect with a "band aid" mentality. Unfortunately, just fixing a specific defect can create other problems that you would not encounter if you were to look for the actual cause. This is particularly true if it is a software problem.

Over the years, I have come across many situations where nagging problems occur because the time was not taken at the start to correct problems; instead, compromises kept preventing a solution from being found.

Whenever I start with a new client, be assured that they will have a "customer from hell" in their portfolio. Many times, I was told that "the customer from hell" was to blame for complaining about a problem, when in fact, the problem was due to poor product quality. This lack of responsibility wastes valuable time and drags out problems longer than necessary.

It is dangerous when management has chosen to accept the risk of poor quality to save time and costs. For instance, if a printed circuit board assembly has over fifty known defects, you can expect that there are probably others that were missed in the testing. In comparison, if a unit has only two defects, you can bet that those two are problems will be the only ones. These must be treated differently, and the chances of a poor design or process are increased with the first board.

But testing and repair are not the only costs involved when a product has defects. Depending on the magnitude of the problem and the importance of the customer, there could be quite a few "extra costs" that managers commonly fail to take into account:

- Extra time spent on inspection and retesting;
- Management time for discussion and meetings;
- Redesign;
- Repair costs;
- Handling customer complaints;
- Overtime;
- Warranty claims;
- Consultants;
- Scrap and waste;
- Necessary reports;
- Downtime from the manufacturing process;
- Loss of revenue from the dilution of not working on other orders; and
- Loss of time and future revenue dilution of engineering tasks.

When a product's quality is poor, it will impact the company's financial performance from the cost of late deliveries and lost opportunities to its perceived weakened image and lost business due to poor product performance.

Costs can also mount as a result of management taking a negative attitude toward the parties responsible for a product's poor quality. An excellent way to solve this problem is to assume that you, the supplier, are wrong when there is a product problem: Try very hard to prove this theory and when you can't do so, then you will know that it is not your poor performance.

Never forget: a customer will eventually forget high prices or late deliveries, but they will constantly be reminded of poor quality and a negative image of the supplier.

Ready to Sell, Wait!

There are significant issues to understand before you think it's the right time to sell your company and plan your future thereafter.

Like all major transactions, before you jump, you must have a plan. The plan to sell will be like a program to sell any product, where in this case, the company is the product. It includes dressing up the pitch by featuring all the positives of the company, deciding how to reach potential buyers, and deciding what the valuation will be so you can be prepared to negotiate an offer.

The basis for this will be mostly financial schedules in nature, but it is important to first determine the assumptions to develop the schedules. It would make sense to seek outside help to make the plan. An investment banker can help, especially if you will give them a contract to find a buyer. Lawyer and tax specialists need to be added to ensure you will get not only the maximum value of the company, but the maximum cash out. These two can be very different. As an example, a company value of $1,000,000 can be so decreased because of taxes that what is left for you can be a real shocker. The expert outside help determines the valuation of your company and how you can realize the most net value by how the deal is structured. For instance, the upfront money may be modest, but the deal also includes a ten-year consulting contract, which may be more to your liking. I have seen a deal where the buyer was motivated by emotion rather than logic, so he chose a million dollars cash for the company . After paying maximum taxes the seller was in tears.

After all this, are you now ready? The answer is, Wait!

Accept that this in an emotional situation and that it may top anything you encountered in your life before this. Even more important than being prepared financially to face the world is the more important preparation for the ensuing emotional experience. There are several issues to consider and these include the following to ask yourself.

Do you have an alternate passion to replace running the company after all the years in business? Don't expect sitting around the house or playing golf every day to come up to the ego satisfaction of running a successful business. You should have an alternative such as a lifelong dream of starting a new company, donating your time to charity, making up for all traveling you wish you had done, or starting a new life with a new marriage.

Do you understand what the ongoing income needs to be in order to continue the life style you and your family enjoy? Be careful on your estimate for the cash you need to live on. I have heard often, "I only take $100,000 out of the company," not realizing all the personal expenses that have been charged to the company through credit cards, the annual trips to Europe with your wife charged to the company, all the health care expenses for you and your family charged to the company, and all those years the children were on the payroll to cover their college expenses charged to the company. I had a client who thought $3 million was a lot of money for the sale of his company, but when he realized he was spending $500,000 a year, he started looking for a job.

Can you live without the power, independence, and daily respect you had all those years in business? The power of running your own company is hard to duplicate in any retirement role. Don't underestimate the leverage you have as an owner with all that power and how important that power is to you. Don't underestimate how your ego thrived with daily success or from playing big brother to your employees.

Do you understand the tax commitments that can leave you with far less cash than you expected? Are you ready to be disappointed with a lower valuation and the restrictive terms and conditions for payment than you hoped for, and are you prepared to accept such changes? Keep in mind the value of the company has nothing to do with the days you painted the building and swept the floor or went without a pay check. Most likely the valuation will be based on getting a suitable return of an investment on today's performance and the projected value.

Are you prepared to be locked into the company for a period of time that can range from months to years? This will occur if it is perceived that the day you stepped out the door a big void will occur. This will be very true if the new buyer is not from the same technology or market. In the preparation for the sale, work hard to develop the staff and all the necessary documentation to give the buyer comfort with your leaving. On the other hand, most times the committed length of a perceived need to hang around doesn't occur because the new Number One will eventually want you out long before the contract ends. This will allow you to negotiate with the new owner wanting to end the contract.

The point is, before you start a negotiation, make sure you are ready with a plan to make a deal and most importantly, that you are emotionally ready and prepared to go through with the deal.

Sales People are Human Also

It is possible sales people can also be successful in other management disciplines such as marketing and operations, but other personnel in non-sales functions are not likely to be successful as sales people. Sales personnel have unique personalities. To get most from a sales staff, look for people who are passionate, motivated, pushy, unconventional, and competitive.

I had an interesting experience in my large corporate days. One of my sales people lost a major sale for over $100,000, and sent a letter to the customer's board of directors complaining and trying to salvage the situation. It happened that the CEO in the multibillion dollar company that employed me was on the customer's board. In the culture of my company, the CEO put in a call to my boss, but there was no way my boss would return the call, expecting abuse. He gave me the task of returning the call. Since the CEO was characterized as a hard, cold person I did not look forward to making the call, and I actually started thinking about my options in case this killed my career. I made the call, and after listening to our CEO questioning the intelligence of the action for about fifteen minutes, he paused, giving me the opportunity to ask, "Am I to reply?" He replied in a very stern, voice, "I am waiting." All I could think of, "What would you have done?" I was a little frightened at what he would come back with, and I was really surprised and amazed when I heard laughter. I hit the right spot, and I knew why he was the CEO. After some pleasantries, he gave me one recommendation and that was, "Keep your eye on that guy as he may become my boss one day."

In that company culture for sure, only a true sale person would have used that method to try to turn the situation around. I did keep my eye on him, and eventually during my time in the company moved him into a regional sales manager position.

It is easy to have a love-hate relationship with sales people. This is because it is hard to agree with their style and lack of logic, but at the same time, they usually have a loving personality, and above all, they bring in the orders.

Stagnation—The Wrong Path to Growth

There are many signs that indicate robust growth is not in a company's future. Companies reach plateaus in their growth, and then are often held back because they don't recognize the importance of culture. Below are ten signs, common in stagnant companies, that a company is more inclined to be stagnant rather than growing.

10. There is too much talk about changes and not enough about actions.

9. Decisions take too long, creating dilutions as the "indecision bubble" expands.

8. Staff's expectations are too low, so they don't support or give a high priority to change.

7. They don't have enough champions to promote and focus on new programs.

6. They lack the superstars needed to grow through to the next plateau.

5. Employees at all levels are not held sufficiently accountable for their decisions.

4. The company lacks a sense of urgency, particularly in product development.

3. The tempo of the company is too slow.

2. Change is the exception, not the norm, and the rate of change is too slow.

1. The president doesn't have the hands-on style and cheerleading ability to produce a high growth rate.

Most companies with which I worked in my career had in their minds that growth is the major indicator of a good manager. Once I convinced them that making profit is another great measure but that making profit can be fun, many of my clients changed their perception.

In many situations, I had to convince the manager that he did not have the stomach for robust growth. It helped him sleep better because he could count the money in their bank account rather than sheep, and they fell asleep much faster, not worrying about being a failure as a manager.

Strategic Alliances

Strategic alliances are agreements, general between two parties with the same strategic goals. If not, the odds of success will be disappointing. The ultimate agreement occurs from an acquisition or merger.

A business strategic agreement, alliance or contract can take many forms, (e.g., a marriage to a multibillion dollar company or equity transactions with another company). In business, there are many different agreement transactions that can include investors with money combining marketing organizations, outsourcing manufacturing, and buying or merging with a company to gain a larger market share or accelerate growth.

Relating strictly to business, I believe an alliance or partnership should be explored at the very beginning of a start-up company. In my years of reviewing business plans, I have seen many good ideas as opportunities that do not result in a successful enterprise because the founder-entrepreneur insisted that everything be done his way *only*. A goal is always to get the investors—be it the founders' or outside investors' money—a return on their investment (ROI). My point is that with an alliance the founder can get there faster through jointly concentrated effort and with far less stress and personal risk. The reward may not be as big as the dream; but if successful, the founder of the first effort can use the financial reward to exploit the next dream or concept.

In reviewing my investments, I look for market need, a company to match a specific need and, most importantly, how to penetrate the market to gain the forecasted sales that made the start-up and investment attractive in the first place.

In reviewing my investments in the last 15 years through the angel investment organization to which I belong, most of my investments in start-ups doing it alone are now over 10 years old and are still not providing a ROI in any form.

Not all alliances are a sure thing. There are numerous reports that over 50% of all acquisitions fail and over 75% do not meet expectations. I had an experience on the board of directors of a $500 million revenue company where we made an offer for a foreign company, but before the agreement was finalized, the company I was with decided we wanted out. In the U.S., you can walk away from a deal like this, but you cannot do so in a foreign country.

Interestingly enough, I believe that to make a deal like this you must first have and meet four basic requirements: (1) a similar strategic goal, (2) compatible cultures, (3) an understanding of matching the need for the senior staff (e.g., you can't have two CEOs), and (4) a valuation formula to be agreed upon up front. In the example mentioned above, we failed on all four.

Because a strategic alliance goes far beyond customer/vendor relationships, the purchasing department of a company is not normally involved. In fact, during my early outsourcing experiences, the successes with companies outsourced to were more like partners.

The best approach for an agreement is to start with the two parties, individuals or companies, reaching a general agreement, LOI (Letter of Intent or MOU (Memorandum of Understanding) and then giving the result to attorneys so that they can then fill-in and finalize the remaining details. However, no matter how much a lawyer pours black paint over an agreement (and perhaps they should), it's still the responsibility of those at the heads of the company to decide if any action they take is worth the risk. It is an attorney's role to present the potential risks to the client and explain what can be done to lessen those risks.

In my experience with small company presidents, I came across many agreements that were done naively, based only on the ultimate intention for success. There were no default clauses (or what are called "what-ifs" – the protection if the plans go awry) or what would happen if one party didn't live up to the agreement. These clauses are put in to define what action must be taken in the event of failure.

Achieving growth in any company requires money and good marketing. In a start-up or small company looking for investors, it is wise to investigate the backgrounds of the potential partners. There are many reputable angel groups and venture capital companies that may wish to invest. Be aware, too, that there are a myriad number of brokers/ matchmakers that may not have the depth/experience required. It always helps to explore investor portfolios to determine if they specialize in an industry or market like health or high tech, which could be beneficial to a start-up or small company.

In dealing with an agent or broker to help find investors, make sure those seeking investments understand the fees or commissions involved before wasting too much time on an agreement.

In my past experience with engineering designs/designers, the customer base included many large companies that were looking for alliances through which to obtain products or technology. In a company I ran at one time, our customer base included Cisco, Symbol, and Lockheed, who came to us for their initial product designs. Because there was so much give and take, there had to be more than a customer-vendor relationship due to the unknowns involved during the process of developing a new product. Therefore, in this example, the large companies could have lower costs and a more expedient amount of time during which to market their product by soliciting the assistance of outside engineering firms.

When outsourcing, based on the discussion above, you can now see how much can be gained—not only in time but especially in the cost advantages with an alliance or partners. A key to growth is that it makes sense to keep identifying gaps in the organization and the processes required while looking for outside alternatives.

Peter Drucker, management icon once said, "Many CEOs of big companies make deals to satisfy their egos." In my experience in one multibillion dollar company, the parent company bought an international company. In my new role, I was supposed to straighten out the businesses (and this was 18 months after the acquisition!). In that time, the Big Company was waiting for a business plan while the Little Company was waiting for direction, guidance, and help. There were numerous definitions in all the legal acquisition documents but not one saying what each side was expected to do going forward. During the next 18-month period, it made more sense to put the various products back into the America divisions. We then ultimately sold the foreign company to local businessmen. In this deal, there was a lack of conducting a proper due diligence before the deal was made. (*See the chapter entitled "Due Diligence" for further discussion in this regard.*)

Many of the failures I come across that do not meet expectations suffer from poor due diligence. It seems one party or the other is anxious to make a deal and pushes to do it quickly.

In summary, strategic alliances can fill voids in one of the potential partners and accelerate growth in revenue and expand breath in the product base to help expand market penetration.

Turnarounds—Before It's Too Late!

I have done several turnarounds in my career. By definition, a turnaround situation is a company in trouble, losing money, bleeding cash, and operating under an old strategy with a lost direction.

I have developed several rules for cleaning up turnarounds. I chose to help some companies by directing their staffs before it was too late and before outside forces were brought in. There are times when a company with great potential has gotten off track by poor cash management. It turns out that 10 to 15 percent of my assignment could have been carried out by Number One, with proper support.

A company in trouble is like a marriage in trouble—it will take just as long to get out as it took to get in. Many married couples do not put the energy to work at resolving problems when they consider the marriage too far gone. An exception can occur if a traumatic situation develops, such as a seriously ill child. The couple may use this occurrence to pull together again.

On more than one occasion, I asked Number One, "Do you want to work at this, and if so, I will help rather than take over." On most assignments, the company got in trouble from trying to grow too fast, trying to be all things to all people.

The most important initial step is working and changing the top staff. The first step is to create the trauma mentioned above and adhere to the following:

- A staff that got the company into trouble cannot get it out, or they would not have gotten you into trouble.

- You need dramatic changes quickly, or like a sour marriage it will take as long to back out as it took to get in.

- Interview all employees to get a good idea of the basic problems and who are the good people—find the contributors in management and supervision. Employees live with the problems and possibly know better than management about what is broken, and they may even have ideas on how to fix the problems.

- Don't expect to change the culture immediately unless you replaced everyone—which is most likely not feasible

- A technique I used was to evaluate the staff to identify the six to ten people being paid the top salaries, and let half of the other go immediately. At least it neutralized the culture by bringing in new thinking and by starting to make changes. It forced each company to move faster to solve problems—many times a staff will believe that doing nothing is better than something; therefore they will have little concern about things getting any worse. Because they were already surviving in the present environment, there was little incentive to change the status quo. The input from the employee interviews can help do the evaluations. This will also be the first step to improving morale.

- Meet with all the key customers and vendors even though it will be painful—tell them the truth about how it is—after all they probably have been given many unfulfilled promises.

    - Example: after my sales manager was burned out from so many bad calls, I took a call in his office and had the customer tear me up and down for over forty minutes and even called me a couple names I never heard before. My sales manager said, "Wow, I guess we will never see that guy again." I said, "Wrong. He could have told me in ten seconds, "I never want to see your face." Forty minutes of his valuable time means he needs us." In time, the customer turned out to be our second largest customer as we got well.

- Keep in mind you may only get one more chance to make a new promise or commitment, whether it's for banks, vendors, customers, or your own sales people.

- Expect to change most or all of the sales people, because they have become the customers saviors and bitter against the company for being let down with too many bad promises and inadequate reactions to their needs.

- Be wary of the top financial person in the company who has come to believe his loyalty to the bank is more important than the company—he's thinking ahead about changing his job to the next company. The finance people and sales people are very sensitive to the customers and banks, because they need these relationships when going to their next jobs.

- Expect to use the word No for quite a while, until you get your get your arms around things. Make sure those above understand that the odds are high that things may still get worse before they get better from the clean-up being planned.

-

- Consider the staff personnel who keep giving reasons why any change can't work to be in the first group to go.

Of course Number One has to have some competence and the willingness to make a major change in the direction he or she has been driving the company.

One reason for considering utilizing some of the people in place is because good or bad, they probably know more about the business than a stranger brought in to drive the changes. The trick is to separate the good from the bad.

Underpaid, Really?

Are you constantly debating whether or not your people are being underpaid because of a continuous increase in job responsibilities? It is natural, in a rapidly growing company, for employees whose roles and responsibilities increase to have this growth outstrip their compensation. The increasing profit is needed to fuel the high growth, but it would lessen the potential for success if everyone's earnings increased proportionally with growth on a continual basis. Companies compensate for the earnings shortfall in different ways; some use titles and others use perks and ad hoc bonuses.

Trouble develops when a key member of the team is enticed to leave when given a better compensation package from outside the company. At the same time, during the company's growth period, there is a need to go outside the company for more skill and experience. The problem manifests itself when attempting to hire outside personnel for existing job functions. Employees in a job for quite some time, though reasonably paid along the way, may be nowhere near what the competitive salaries are in the broader market for those positions.

This creates a problem when comparing the personnel in place to comparable positions in the market. It is okay to compare position pay scales to the market, but the inside people should be compared to the requirements of what is needed in the positions for continuing company growth. The need to go outside is generated because inside employees do not have the potential for what is needed going forward. Most often, in a high growth situation, the key roles get filled along the way with personnel that have been inside the company over time. Many are in the biggest job they have ever been in and have had no time for increasing individual personal growth with university education, attending seminars, networking, and trade shows. Their past experience gained from these roles is insufficient to take them to the next level. The experience has been narrow in scope with the same type of responsibility, even as the company grows, but at an increasing scale, and there is no way to predict how these inside people will perform in what lies ahead.

In many cases in rapid growth, people in key positions are so busy chasing the company priorities they have little more to offer. The people coming in offer experience in the future needs, further education, contacts, networking, and the potential to innovate. In the final analysis, if the people inside can't take the company forward, then they are not underpaid based on their loyalty and function title.

Will the Real Inventory Please Stand Up & Be Counted

Inventory is one of the largest out-of-pocket expenditures for a company and can have the greatest after-the-fact impact on profit performance.

As important as inventory is, the financial report packages supplied to directors and shareholders seldom if ever go into detail about the kind of inventory on hand or even provide an analysis of inventory-related details. Whenever limited definitions of the inventory are given, conclusions on value and product turns are usually misguided. In the face of such vagaries, inventory discussions just die away while the problems persist.

The evaluation of an inventory is greatly aided by accurately defining the key categories that make up that inventory.

It has always amazed me how some manufacturing companies can fit their sizeable inventory into limited definitions. In my experience, accountants seem reluctant to have too many categories. Perhaps that is because the greater the breakdown, the more work for them. If left to his own, Andy Accounting would assign only three classifications to inventory: **Raw Material, Work-In-Process (WIP), and Finished Goods (FG).** In fact, I have found that the fewer the categories, the more the manufacturing manager is blamed for having a bloated inventory or one that is out of control. The fewer the classifications, the less likely an analysis will provide a true measure of his performance. Such a limited breakdown does not reveal the effect other departments have on the overall inventory figure or reveal their responsibility for creating a situation that is entirely beyond manufacturing control. **Poor inventory accounting practices can destroy a company without management knowing what is happening.**

Inventory items spread far beyond the manufacturing floor—to engineering, vendors, marketing, and customers—and the more it fans out, the less chance of its utilization at the original cost or value. Since Max Manufacturing has no control over these items, manufacturing performance should not be measured on the turnover rate of the entire inventory. It is a gross error to divide the entire inventory dollars by the inventory used in the cost of sales (COS), and hold the head of manufacturing accountable for inventory turns.

In order to define and quantify the total cost of the inventory, it is necessary to go far beyond the production run rate. Inventory planning requires more than just looking at revenue projections. Many issues are often excluded in operating plans. Consider these needs: demos for marketing, products for evaluation, spares and maintenance support, customer returns due to defects, and samples for engineering evaluation.

The first question to ask is: What investment in manufacturing inventory will support the sales level?

Accountants are proud of their systems when they manage to get the book value close to the physical inventory, but, as I have already pointed out, this is short sighted. Poor inventory accounting can destroy a company without management knowing what is happening. The danger comes when inventory numbers on the balance sheet are believed without question. Accepting the global figure without substantial and detailed breakdown is suicidal. No one can ever know how well the company is actually doing without knowing what makes up the inventory, what elements can actually be used, and what values can be assigned when the bits and pieces are turned into finished and sold product.

The lesson: real manufacturing inventory must be segregated from nonmanufacturing inventory and evaluated properly before anyone hammers the head of manufacturing for nonperformance.

My best advice: call together the heads of the various divisions—marketing, manufacturing, accounting, engineering—and introduce them to the following concepts and categories. The following list of inventory classifications is not exhaustive, but the categories are common to most manufacturing businesses. Those elements not under the control of manufacturing are indicated by an asterisk (*).

Raw Material: The components and parts waiting to be used in the production of finished goods. Although raw material is under the physical control of manufacturing, parts are normally ordered based on a forecast provided by Mike Marketing, which is not controlled by manufacturing.

When questioned about it, Max's defense is: "I am a good soldier and order parts in line with the forecasts I am given, but I have never had an accurate forecast since I have been with the company."

Work in Process (WIP): All material between raw material and finished goods. The better the scheduling system is, the better control of WIP inventory.

Although Max isn't guilty of overusing this ploy, this is an area manufacturing managers can use to make their overall performance look better. If labor and overhead are added to the value of WIP, the ongoing periodic manufacturing costs are minimized. (*See the chapter Spiral to Oblivion in my book The Laws of Management Physics: A Handbook for Hands-On Managers about really "Dirty Maxes!"*)

Finished Goods: This is where products are stationed until sales orders allow them to be shipped.

Many companies with direct shipping to customers can have finished goods in inventory just long enough for a cup of coffee. Poor handling of data entry plagues this category. Products can be shipped physically before they have become Finished Goods on paper. This drives an accounting system crazy.

Max's reply to Andy's complaints: "All data entry is done in a timely fashion because I recognize its importance."

*Material not on a BOM: The BOM (bill of material) includes all the parts and components needed for manufacturing a given product. Engineering is responsible for producing a bill of material as part of the product definition provided to manufacturing for making the product. In heavy engineering-oriented companies, the material purchased, but never actually used in the manufacturing, tends to accumulate in inventory.

This becomes an inventory problem in rapidly growing companies with evolving product lines and companies whose heavy engineering orientation includes a product mix with product development revenue. In developing a product, engineering buys material, and whatever is not used ends up as excess material in inventory. In addition, engineering departments may make initial material purchases for production, but material intended for manufacturing can be rendered obsolete by design changes before production even begins. Either case creates extra, unusable inventory items.

This category would allow Max to run a report showing material not in a BOM. His point is, "If it isn't on a BOM, how can I ever use it in manufacturing the products we are selling?"

Who can argue with that (*See the example on "Company E" at the end of the chapter*).

*Obsolete Inventory: Everyone is to blame for this category but no one takes responsibility.

Max says, "Sure we may create some obsolete material at times, but the biggest cause is the discontinuing of products by marketing. Engineering is a close second, changing part numbers with little concern for good parts that still exist in my inventory, which then become doomed for obsolescence in inventory purgatory."

Then, to get his nails into me, Max asks "Why doesn't management write off obsolete material when it is identified instead of holding onto it forever?"

He strengthens his point by showing me components in plastic bags that have turned yellow from aging. My poor defense is, "Because if they throw away the obsolete inventory and take a write down, it will hit the bottom line in a negative way. It reduces the asset base, thereby reducing the net worth of the company."

Max adds, "Management likes to believe the obsolete can eventually be sold at or near costs, Hah, what a pipe dream. In my experience offers of one cent on the dollar are common." This is sad, but unfortunately true in many cases.

*Surplus Material: These are components and parts heading down the path to obsolescence. They accumulate because of overly optimistic forecasting by marketing or from a company downsizing its product sales.

Max points out that in order to get a price break, purchasing agents get carried away with overordering. He got red (or I should say green) in the face when reminded of the 1000 years worth of green paint used for terminals sold to Sears that ended up in his inventory. It seems that Max's overzealous purchasing people believed marketing's blue-sky forecast and got carried away because of a great price break. Low and behold, tons of green paint was purchased for a particular customer who never used it.

By using a sophisticated computer software system and a reasonable forecast, managers can easily identify surplus inventory. Max may admit that poor planning and purchasing under his control can develop surplus and obsolete items, but still claim the problem occurs more from engineering and marketing decisions than his own.

Max will then ask, "So I've identified it, will management write it off or at least set aside the reserve?" Naturally my answer is, "No Comment." As a consultant I have no intention of undermining management's authority, even though I agree with him.

*Marketing Samples and Demos: The number of samples and demos held in this category depends on the nature of the product, ranging from a $1.00 floppy disk to an operating system worth tens of thousands of dollars.

A sloppy accounting system might keep demos and samples in manufacturing inventory only to watch the value deteriorate. Even if they are eventually sold, the value of samples and demos will be far less than a product sold new.

Max, who cannot control the need for demos, is right in demanding, "Don't use the cost of these in my inventory performance measure."

Expensive systems dragged around by Sammy Sales from show to show throughout the year are still considered for sale. A smart Max will serialize all products manufactured. This helps his position when someone decides to analyze the inventory. Then he can demonstrate what has been given to marketing for their disposition and never returned. Why should he be punished for items still sitting on the books but out of his control?

*Customer evaluations: Product sent to customers to evaluate can be out of the physical inventory for months at a time and still be counted as available for sale. I have seen a number of policy statements limiting the time product may be held for evaluation at a customer site before obliging them to pay. I have also seen few of these policies fully implemented.

Aging plays a role here. As deals age, product may be offered at lower prices that the customer can't refuse. This has an adverse impact on sales expectations and inventory dollars when the cut-rate deal is made.

*Material Returns Authorization (MRA): Rejects do occur, and field replacement is necessary. In some business cultures, replacement products are sent to the customer before the unwanted product is returned. What is the result? The returned unit floats somewhere in limbo, maintaining its inventory value, but without a use to Max. The reality is that once the customer gets the replacement and it works, there is no urgency to send the original back. Max gets hit in a second way by being given the responsibility for getting the product back, even though marketing and sales have the customer contact.

*Material Review Board (MRB): Components or finished products may be rejected for no apparent reason, or because changes or modifications have made the item unacceptable. A component or system can be rejected anywhere along the line, at incoming inspection, while in the production cycle or by customers. The urgency for disposition depends on the need for the item by one department or another, or the customer's pressure for delivery. Instead of facilitating the disposition of material, the MRB can become a pigeon hole for collecting inventory due to the lack of interest of the parties involved and their failure in making a timely disposition decision. Since all departments in the company have a vested interest in the rejection process, a good MRB should have representatives from quality control, manufacturing, engineering, sales, accounting, and marketing.

*Inventory in Engineering "being evaluated": Engineering is great for taking parts and systems off the floor for evaluation. Some get returned, but many end up in cabinets and desk drawers or test beds. Engineers are notorious slackers when it comes to paperwork, so nits and bits disappear from manufacturing inventory without a record. Enterprising engineers, in the desire to resolve issues in off hours and in need of a component or part will not be deterred by a lock on a door or cages surrounding inventory.

Max comments, "Engineers hardly ever put things into inventory, but like to take out with no transaction record." Yet Max gets blamed and is measured by paper dollars on the books and empty slots in inventory.

*Maintenance Service Spares: In order to make service and repair quickly available in the field, companies often provide spares at field sites or, even better, at the customer's location. If these are considered as part of the inventory dollars Max is responsible for, he gets hit for things he can't put his hands on. Accounting can lessen Max's headache by considering service spares as material to be capitalized, removing it from the active inventory and treating it as a fixed asset to be depreciated.

*Customer Service Spares: More emphasis is being put on customer relations these days, with Customer Service departments springing up under Marketing divisions and handling customer return problems. This is all well intentioned, but Customer Service has become a graveyard for unused material in manufacturing. This organization may work well, but all the inventory-related parts and components should not be carried in the manufacturing inventory.

Of course, Max says these people are string savers and will justify holding onto tons of material as long as one of each product from day one is still in the field.

*Inventory (Equipment) not for Manufacturing: This is a technique used by companies in buying capital equipment. The equipment needs a part number before it can be received into the management information system. Before being delivered to the department or office that ordered it, equipment is assigned a number, and it is added to the inventory.

Max says it is just another dollar number he doesn't have access to. Fortunately, if anyone remembers to take it out, it isn't in inventory for long.

*Trade-Ins: Companies that take trade-ins from their own products or even at times from competitor's products seem to arbitrarily assign them inventory values. Max claims the odds of this stuff being resold out of inventory are between nil and zero, dinging him again for dollars beyond his control.

The lesson?

Before knocking around your manufacturing manager for an apparent inventory disaster, establish the proper categories and do a thorough analysis. What I have said all along should be clear by now: The odds of turning the entire inventory into product and revenue are very, very low.

Do not compare the total accounting book value to the level of inventory being shipped. It will not give an accurate picture of the performance of inventory usage. There are numerous factors and categories not related to inventory usage in the cost of goods sold. The above breakdown should raise the proper concern to look further into particular circumstances.

For those companies who do not break down the inventory beyond raw material, WIP, and finished goods, I guarantee a big surprise in their future.

Some Inventory Examples

Company S is a start-up, high-tech systems company. In one year, their total inventory expanded from $450K to $1 million. The cost of goods was running at $150K per month. The accounting system only accounted for two categories; raw stock (material) and finished goods.

The manufacturing manager was called in to explain the growth and the large inventory, seven times the monthly COGS. Thanks to the records kept by manufacturing, including serial numbers and disposition, it was shown that $450,000 was under the control of marketing. As a result, only $600,000, or four months of inventory was under the control and utilization of manufacturing. The calculated manufacturing turns ratio went from 1.8 to 3.

Company E is a high-technology, engineering-driven company with rapidly changing products. The total inventory was $500,000 and the cost of goods shipped was $120,000. The president demanded, "Why is the inventory so large, over four months worth, and not even three turns a year?"

An analysis was done to identify material in inventory that was not on a BOM. The result found $180,000, was essentially unusable manufacturing inventory. The manufacturing inventory exclusive of non-BOM material was $320,000 or 2.66 months of COGS, which yielded a higher turns ratio of 4.5.

Company D is an aging, high-tech systems company with several changes in products and reduced sales. The total inventory was $1.2 million and the monthly sales required $100,000 per month. The company had been continually downsizing its number of employees, but the inventory in place had not been analyzed on a continuing basis.

A first-pass analysis revealed that obsolete inventory—material not used in production for two years—was $200,000. The next pass found material not used for a year and yielded another $150,000. The last pass, based on the level of shipments in the past six months, indicated that $175,000 would be surplus after the next year's shipments. The total suspect inventory was $525,000, reducing the useful inventory to $675,000.

This took the turns from one per year to near two turns per year. Worse yet, it reduced the net worth of the company $525,000. In this case, the impact was one third the net worth of the company, a real blow.

Section 2

Advisory Boards—The CEO's Secret Weapon

During my career I have served on several boards of directors, both private and public. I have seen many changes in the complexity of running successful companies that encountered significant changes in the market environment due to the advent of the Internet, the increase in global competition, increases in legislation for compliance, and increased interest in watching over companies from the company stakeholders.

All of this has resulted in the need for more participation from the company directors. No longer can a private, growing company rely on directors who are relatives and friends. Directors need to have expertise that will help the company grow and the experience that will help the management face what lies ahead. A company's management's lack of experience created by the new barriers tend to block growth.

The Sarbanes-Oxley law brought a dramatic change to the requirement of public boards which has temporarily changed the priority to be on governance issues rather than company strategy. A famous academic guru on board of directors expressed this at a seminar. He said he was on a board of twelve directors for a Fortune 1000 company. He said at most, only two had an understanding of the market the company was in, and he wasn't one of them. The days of celebrity directors are coming to a close. Unfortunately the residue from all the corporate scandals creates a guarded Board atmosphere that usually causes board discussions to include such statements as, "How it will look to our lawyer or the outside consultants that monitor public companies?"

Even though the pressure of change caused by Sarbanes-Oxley is easing, the end result is that public company directors have seen an increase in the need for specialization as well as an increase in time and energy needed to keep up with the new laws. Additionally, companies need to acquire more knowledge in governance, audit, and compensation issues. Ironically, surveys show that the desire of directors on public boards is that they do want to be more involved with company strategy, but with all the new activities there seems to be less time for strategy. A director recently remarked to me in a board meeting, "It seems the time we use to discuss the future of a product's needs is now taken up for discussion of future directors and officers insurance." Directors on public boards are now adding time to their duties to include outside education classes.

What then is the answer? An advisory board can consist of individuals who have specific experience and expertise that will support the company's strategy and major growth operational issues. This can be the answer for more detailed help. I call advisory boards, "The CEO's secret weapon."

Advisory boards can be made up of people who are not influenced by shareholder responsibility rather than having directors who are only concerned with a fiduciary responsibility to all stakeholders. The members can provide specific help, skills, and time that have become more and more limited to the board of directors.

Public companies have the leverage to form advisory boards, because they can probably afford to pay cash compensation or publically traded stock to the members. Private and particularly small companies tend to fight off the effort because they say, "We can't afford it," even though they haven't even tried.

The most often asked questions offered as rebuttals are:

1. Why would experienced people want to do this?

2. Who would be interested?, and

3. How can I find people to join?

I have had success forming advisory boards for public and private companies and I will try to answer those questions to develop a degree of comfort and commitment to form an advisory board.

Here are reasons as to why these experienced and talented people want to get involved with an advisory board. Many are looking for a chance to contribute by giving back the help they receive along the way.

- Many are looking for networks for business and social requirements.

- Many expect to enjoy the peer involvement with challenges and even new knowledge.

- Many are out to save their marriage by getting out of the house and off their wives nerves.

- Many expect to get psychic rewards and even ego satisfaction.

- Many see this as a step up to public company boards.

When it comes to who these people are and how to find them, I would start with what I call the "White Hairs" and "No Hairs." I have found many candidates with "White Hairs" and "No Hairs," many of whom are retired or semiretired. You can usually find several in any business community.

You need to look for people who are or were in your market, technology, or industry. Retired and semiretired ex-managers and executives are a natural base from which to start. The best place to find these types of people are in networking and referrals. Referrals can come from contacts such as your legal firm and accounting firm. The market is a good place to look as customers and venders probably know good people they have worked with. A potential venue is watching the newspapers and trade media for people you think might help. The point is, they are out there, but you need to work to find them.

The important issue no doubt is how to compensate people at the level you are seeking. Assuming they have one or all the reasons above, then compensation may not be so important or even a deal breaker. The candidates want to explore whether or not they can make a contribution before even bringing up the topic of compensation.

Here are examples that indicate possibilities.

My first example is that I was able to get an engineer to serve on an advisory board for free until the owner/president took money out of the company. When that happened, we developed a table with a step function so that every time the President would increase his annual take home by $25,000, the advisory board directors' compensation would also go up.

Second, one of my clients and I offered a modest quarterly cash-based compensation and a modest stock option in a public company to a leading icon in the computer storage business. The "white hair" was the head of marketing in a company that recently sold to a Fortune 1000 company. What we thought was modest at first was an insult to him. He said he made more in one hour from his newfound wealth than our offer. We replied that there was no amount that would satisfy him. After thinking about it over a great bottle of wine, he agreed on being available on call as needed to three people in the company, the president and our marketing and engineering managers.

Third, I had an experience for a company called NUCO that wanted to change from an OEM supplier to a product company. We were able to build an advisory board that comprising marketing type from the new market, a systems/network engineer, and an ex-CEO of a chip company trying to do the same application the company was going to do with a new approach. This group was together for over a year and the company was able to make the transition.

There are several methods that a company could use to attract the talent and expertise needed to succeed. Members can be offered a stock option, a modest retainer, consulting tasks that might develop and a success factor if the company is sold or reaches a level of positive cash flow.

It must be agreed that advisory board participants will give you a reasonable amount of time and continue to be effective. One advantage is that there is no long term commitment to members since a company's needs and priorities will change with growth. This change may occur when a company takes a new direction and the timing of and emphasis on help in marketing, human relations, accounting, or revenue production becomes crucial. No doubt help could come from some of the board if their time would be available. Consultants could help, but they usually require expensive hourly or program fees, and they only give one viewpoint. When members of an advisory board get together they play off each other and positive sparks can be generated on ideas because they are being challenged.

There is a serious downside in that directors will be sensitive to what they consider outsiders. Although more involvement with strategy and risk is desired by many directors, I believe their lack of time available and dilution of their duties is not a good fit. For me, strategy needs to be lived, and a group of directors meeting four to six times a year to cover a multitude of topics in their meetings doesn't get it. In robust growth, management is faced with many new experiences beyond fiduciary requirements and strategy, such as expertise in planning, human relations, sales, cash management, and keeping up with the infrastructure.

The results of contributions from boards of directors or consultants can border more on advice that is based upon logic or motherhood rather than sound advice based upon experience and detailed knowledge with the situation. Counseling is needed to help management, which is advice that can be done with the resources available within the system. This requires help from long-term, specific experience and expertise that an advisory board can focus and provide.

Banks—Equity Is Not in Their Vocabulary

The first thing to understand about dealing with banks is that they are not investor and that they want to deal in the short term not and the long term. They recommend you use other sources such as insurance companies for long term loans. Too often, borrowers get frustrated and disappointed when the bank is not caught up in their dream. The bank makes money on the loan money; they do not speculate on the future. Generally, banks will not lend funds for the borrower to make acquisitions or develop products for the future. They want evidence that the borrower can make payments from two possible existing sources the day the loan is given. Usually in small companies one of the sources has to be guaranteed by the major owner. They will fund needs for working capital, including inventory and accounts receivables, and they want proof of collateral now.

In dealing with banks, approach them with the following in mind:

1. Banks will not usually tell you why you have been rejected. Today, they can hide behind "the regulators," using them as the bad guy. The excuse for turning down a loan isn't always logical. They will also use the lame excuse, "I tried hard for you, but the guy downtown shot the loan down." Someday I would like to meet that invisible guy downtown.

2. I believe loan officers would take a little more risk if bank management put more emphasis on their need not to lose business opportunity. It is too easy for a loan officer to reject a loan rather than stand up in front of his peers weekly to report on a loan performance that made him nervous going in. If rejected loans were analyzed more carefully, more risk might be taken, with greater rewards for all concerned.

3. It can help to look for banks that allow loan approval by an individual rather than by committee. With a committee, you are relying on your loan officer to make the pitch to his committee, and this is scary. In that situation, it pays to make sure the loan officer (interface to the loan committee) is knowledgeable about your business and convinced that you are successful. The more informed the bank is, the greater your chances of getting the loan.

4. It is worth the effort to present your business to the bank officials

you are dealing with and to try to get above the loan officer.

5. The business financial cash flow projection must include a line specifically for payments to the bank. You should point out to them what actions and alternatives you plan if in fact the business doesn't go quite as you planned. An impressive report will show what can be adjusted, if necessary, in order to ensure that the bank gets theirs.

When you make the presentation asking for a loan, make sure you do the following:

1. Include a business analysis. Make sure your bank contact understands both your request and the nature of your business. Make sure they feel secure about what they know.

2. Make sure the bank feels comfortable with your management team. Get them to meet as many people as possible and convince them that the company is strong enough to withstand the turmoil of key management staff leaving the company.

3. Make sure the bank feels sure that the company will survive a downturn. Show them a disaster plan under which the company could withstand a 20% drop in sales and still be able to make payments.

4. Make them believe that the company has liquidity, good performance, and adequate cash flow.

5. In any presentation to the bank, make sure there is always a line showing when and how the bank gets their money.

6. Always be prepared to offer collateral.

Remember, the bank will only lend you money if they believe you can pay back the loan on time.

Banks are trained to require two sources of repayment, cash flow from the business and collateral. The primary source for short term loans is cash flow, for long term loans, earnings. Repayment plans need to be supplemented by some form of collateral, such as accounts receivable, inventory. Banks are the happiest when receivables alone can cover the loan. Even when the loan is covered by receivables, the bank will also have first claim on all the assets. Then, if something goes wrong with the original plan, the banker will always have something to fall back on.

Now, here is where the banks become hypocritical, because after saying they only need two sources repayment, cash flow and collateral, they say, "Oh, by the way, we would like a personal guarantee from the majority owner." This guarantee is almost universally required of small companies, so this talk about only needing two sources of repayment is bunk.

The banks say that the personal guarantee ensures that the borrower is committed psychologically to the business's success. Banks may even force the lender to take a second mortgage on their home to provide a payment should the lender be in default. They don't expect a great deal of security from the personal signature and say that they may not even go after the individual. What they want is that individual's total support and dedication to making the business successful. The loan officers are reluctant to risk the bank's money if the borrower is reluctant to risk his or her own. In other words: no guarantee, no loan.

Keep in mind that the bank is always comparing the risks to the rewards. Since they work on a small return on assets (ROA), they have to be right 99% of the time. They need several good loans to make up for one bad one. Therefore, they also need to be convinced that you are in command of your business and will respond appropriately to any downturn. They also do not generally lend in high leverage situations, and might use 3 to 1 as the upper limit (the ratio of all liabilities to the tangible net worth). Anything above this ratio will probably scare them off. Banks are limited in the risks they can take from both a business and a regulatory viewpoint.

Since banks do not like surprises, keep them informed, especially when you are having trouble with the business or the loan. Banks can also give far more help than just credit. Use their services in other financial matters. For instance, if you plan to go to international markets, seek the advice of your banker.

1. It is important that you build a good relationship with your bank, and there are several ways to create and maintain this relationship:

2. Communicate with them in a timely manner, even when you have bad news.

3. Stay off the "bad" lists, like the overdrawn account list, the late payer list, and the personal exception report.

4. Keep the bank informed of trends in your industry and your goals for the company.

5. *Pay them on time!*

Today, most banks will only lend money when (1) the company is profitable, (2) the debt to net worth ratio meets their criteria, and (3) the borrower is willing to guarantee the loan. It's true: Banks will only lend you money when you really don't need it. Therefore, prepare ahead of time by developing a good relationship with your bank and demonstrating your commitment to repaying them.

There is one requirement that can let the bank call a loan even if you are paying regularly on time and it meeting the covenants. As part of the performance guarantee, the bank will include criteria related to various balance sheet items like net worth and working capital. Banks need to keep the pressure on the borrower, and many borrowers will tell you they were failing the covenants even before they get out the front door when signing for the loan.

Board of Directors—Adding to the Human Assets

No doubt the vast majority of companies in our country do not have a board of directors. The many small businesses usually use family or friends to compose their board of directors. At best their contribution may be in investing or providing moral support.

The law requires federal public companies to have a board of directors and even defines the mix of insiders versus outsiders. The purpose for this is to insure the shareholders are getting a fair representation whereas insiders alone can and do cause conflicts in decision making.

A growing company needs to put a board in place as soon as possible to gain the experience and wisdom of people who have already been where a growing company wants to go. As I have noted to most of my client Presidents along the way, every day they show up for work, they are running the biggest company ever. This means they will face new challenges they never knew even existed. So why is there a delay for adding this valuable resource? It fits with the reluctance for hiring outside resources like consultants, lawyers, or accounting services.

One reason is that Number One doesn't want anyone looking over his shoulder, and second, there is a perception that no one would be interested in their small company, or if so, they would be too expensive to hire. This is so wrong, but the inexperienced person doesn't know this. I have lost count of the number of private companies for which I have served as a director. I can say in many situations that for myself and most of the others who served, there was a lot more interest than actual financial rewards because of the unique experiences from being part of a growing new company.

Number One must be serious about robust growth to know that there is a need for change and that the future requires more talent and experience. Number One also knows that it is hard to keep up with the resources inside. As a result the mind-set opens and the need to find help moves up the priority ladder.

The challenge then becomes how to find directors. The most likely path is from referrals. The task is to make it clear what is expected of Director's to family, friends, suppliers, investors, trade shows, education affiliates, and all networks aware of the desire. Like any question, if you don't ask it, you get no answer. Therefore when you find someone who strikes you as a qualified director, ask if he or she is interested. The worst thing that can happen is getting a no answer. In your forward thinking and planning, decide what experience can accelerate your growth and what voids in the company need to be filled.

This could include someone with experience in raising capital or a distributor, a lawyer, or someone with experience in your market. I have had experiences where it made sense for a single decision maker to mull over with whom to start. I have recommended considering people to bring them financial, marketing, legal, or spiritual help. Directors don't need to commit indefinitely, because the balance of a board will change as the company grows and changes. It disappoints me that the formation of a board has changed in recent years with new pressure for compliance to the laws starting with the Sarbanes-Oxley in 2002. I believe that in the growth of the industries I have served, computers and telecommunications, success was heavily influenced by starting a board of directors who could contribute more toward the business needs and less because of legal pressures. Ironically, many directors on public boards state the desire to be more involved in company strategy.

But why doesn't this happen? Because the emphasis overwhelmingly falls on governance to insure that the company is complying with all the new regulations in recent years. I don't say governance is wrong, but what I get from seminars and presentations is that the director's top priorities are:

- care,
- loyalty, and
- disclosure.
- Fortunately I still enjoy serving on Boards of private companies where the Directors provide
- oversight,
- strategy,
- guidance,
- experience,
- mentoring,
- and most of all, *wisdom.*

Directors on a formal board are like members of the family, but they have a fiduciary responsible to all the company stakeholders. They will get involved with all aspects of the company from strategy and planning to meeting compliance to the laws and certainly the financial performance of the company. I once joined a board of a small company, and for a while the majority owner was embarrassed to show me the company bank account because it was so strong and mostly his.

No doubt the laws for public companies will eventually get to apply to all sizes of companies, so there is a need to have directors who ultimately can cope with the similar public companies needs. The wise Number One will push for the expertise and involvement experienced directors can bring.

Breakeven—The Threshold for Success

Every company should have an understanding of its financial numbers that are required for survival. The first two Laws of Management Physics explain this clearly.

Law#1—"The goesinnas need to exceed the goesouttas."

Law#2—"Profit is muscle, cash is blood."

The financial analysis to find the survival numbers is called breakeven. Breakeven is the minimal sales required to cover all the costs, including overhead, to reach that sales number. There are typically two breakeven sales numbers. One relates to profit, and it defines the necessary sales needed, including the margin that results from the sales of product or services, to cover all the costs in place to end up with zero profit. It sounds like a circular nightmare, but it is easily determined. And one related to cash, which is determined by cash items only.

First, management should know the fixed costs (i.e., overhead) in place at any sales level. Second, management needs to know the variable costs of manufacturing the product or of the labor needed to perform the service. There is a simple example below to illustrate breakeven analysis. Still a big circle? Start with the fixed costs in dollars, and then determine the gross margin by subtracting the variable costs in percent from the sales at 100 percent. The variable costs are normally a fixed percentage of the sale price over a wide range of sales values. In many small companies, labor is practically a fixed cost because no matter what the shipments are, the same labor force will get them out, so we will consider labor costs as part of the fixed costs. In this example we will use material as the only total variable costs. Subtract the variable costs percentage from 100 percent to get the gross margin, which is equivalent to the added value percentage. This yields the percentage of sales revenue that will be left over to cover all the other costs, including fixed costs and profit. Considering that the breakeven point is at no profit, divide the fixed costs by the added value percentage to get the break-even sales number. The formula looks like this:

$$B = \frac{C_F}{\left(\frac{P_W - C_M}{P_W}\right)}$$

Example: Fixed costs (C_F) equal $60,000. The difference between the wholesale price (P_W, or price-to-market) and the variable material cost (C_M) to manufacture each item divided by the wholesale price yields the margin percentage. For this example, let's use $100 as the wholesale price and $40 as the variable material cost to manufacture each item. This results in a margin of 60%, or 0.6 [= ($100 – $40)/$100] The breakeven sales number (B) is $60,000/0.6 = $100,000. At a price-to-market of $100, this means the company would have to sell 1000 units to break even. At that point, management would have to decide if the company's current resources could handle that level of production and distribution at the level of fixed costs.

The sales that would be needed to cover the fixed costs and variable cost to manufacture the product at zero profit is $100,000. In this example labor was considered fixed because in this company, like many small companies, the labor is already hired and in place and will get paid no matter what the level of sales is. The target to breakeven, then, can be called the sales needed to cover all the costs of the company, which includes the fixed costs and the material costs, with no money left over for profit. Theoretically a company can survive with zero profit.

If the company did $110,000 in sales, the margin at 60% would be $66,000 and for the fixed costs at $60,000, there would be a profit of $6,000. However if the company only did $90,000 in sales, and the margin at 60% would only yield $54,000, not enough to cover the fixed costs, resulting in a loss of $6,000.

For small companies with no reserves and little money in the bank it is best to consider cash breakeven. It is hard for some business owners to imagine how a big company reporting a loss of $1 billion can survive. This is where profit and cash separate. The bigger you get, the more noncash items start to occur, including depreciation, reserves, and accruals.

It must be expected that in a rapidly growing company, the profit will most likely be insufficient to support the growth because of the necessity of increasing the working capital. I have seen presidents run companies literally from a clip board, getting information during the day on what shipments went out the door so they could project cash available from the customer when paid. They also do a daily input tracking of money in the bank. Although this might not give the manager an immediate answer on profitability, he could recite chapter and verse on cash. In doing cash breakeven, the fixed (added value) costs need to be recalculated removing the adjustments for noncash items. The costs added get adjusted for profit items that do not require an outlay of cash, such as like depreciation and accruals. The math occurs in a similar fashion, using the adjusted cost numbers minus noncash items. This yield the same margin derived from the sales and the variable cost margin in the direct cost of the product. For example, the added value fixed costs would be $56,000 after taking out depreciation. On this basis, the breakeven cash sales number would be $93,333, which is $6,667 less than the profit breakeven number.

Once the breakeven numbers are clearly understood then, with any planned cost increases, the breakeven sales numbers can be calculated to project the sales number needed to cover the added costs. In the early years of a start-up or the early growth period of a company, it is extremely important to break even before the cash available expires, or there will be no future.

Busting $10 Million—The First Significant Barrier to Overcome

Ten million dollars is symbolic of the approximate revenue level that a company needs to achieve in order to make a major change in its culture so it can bust through that barrier and to continue its growth.

Here are many of the changes that need to be made to "Bust $10 Million" in revenue:

- Hiring people who are challenged by the situation;
- Hiring subordinates than can be better than their bosses;
- Trusting subordinates by giving them equal authority to go along with additional responsibility;
- Removing the "I" mentality from the number one leader;
- Having new products in addition to the original entry;
- Making people accountable for their performance;
- Using outside help to supplement the weaknesses in the company and people;
- Introducing planning to the method of operating;
- Adding the capability for cash management;
- Paying people fairly;
- Increasing the emphasis on processes, methods, and procedures;
- Adding a program to allow all the people to share in the rewards;
- Making sure the company is compliant with local, state, and federal laws;
- Defining a vision and mission, and making those clear to everyone in the company;
- Creating a challenging environment to attract and keep talented personnel;
- Understanding the importance of priorities, review them often, and reorder as necessary;

- Improving communications by letting the staff know the leader's strategy
- Empowering the staff by allowing them to communicate their approach to achieving the strategy.

Focus—Beat the Statistics for Failure

Two of the most frequent failures of growing companies are

1. management trying to be all things to all people and in particular, to all customer requests; and

2. cash management.

Trying to be all things to all people can be the death-wish of a company. To help counter this fault, the word focus should become a part of the management vocabulary. A company determined to accelerate growth can try going in all directions at once by chasing every potential opportunity that arises, but it is too easy to go off in the wrong direction when numerous opportunities are hitting you from all sides.

Even many Fortune 500 companies learn from time to time that the lack of focus hurts. IBM, the giant computer company, for instance, learned very much that they could not be all things to all people even as great as they were. For years they were by far the leader in mainframe computers, dominating 85% of the world's market. Yet when they tried to get into personal computers they failed to be anywhere near the leader. Going from one end of the spectrum, at mainframe computers to business-based customers, to the opposite end at personal computers to consumers, they stumbled and staggered for years before they finally gave up. The result was selling their PC business to a Chinese company.

It is difficult for small companies to say no to customers for anything if they see a big potential jump in sales. Always keep in mind everyone in a small company is already overwhelmed and hard-pressed to take on more responsibility. The answer, to avoid disaster, is being disciplined with respect to the company focus. This is where focus is so important for success. Know where you are going and stick to your discipline in making decisions.

All companies should beware of jumping too far onto new paths. A bad situation I have often come across that is guaranteed to derail a company is prematurely jumping into a new market with a new technology and a new product. This usually occurs when a company has great success, but became arrogant and overconfident in jumping in. The failure comes when the company wants to do the jump with their same marketing people, same technology, and same products, all unfamiliar to the new market needs.

The answer is to continue to do what you do best, and then, when diversification makes sense, plan in detail what new skills will be needed. Once that has been determined, begin the process of putting those skilled people and required technologies in place before making such an important move.

Gross Margin Alert

I lost track of how many times I have heard "My gross margin is greater than 40%" in a proud fashion, ignoring the real world for a great gross margin—whereas the real dollars of gross margin can be far more important. You can have a gross margin of 90%, but so what if the revenue isn't high enough to cover the expenses needed to be covered by the gross margin.

In a manufacturing company, the gross margin equals the revenue minus the cost of manufacturing the product. Whereas in a manufacturing company direct labor and material to produce the product are easy to identify. In a software company there may be very little material or direct labor or none. In the pricing structures, a manufacturing company may get by with gross margins as low as 10% to cover all the supporting costs and profit, but a software company may need at least 90% margin to cover all costs and profit.

High-Performance Superstars

Start-ups and businesses pivoting for more rapid growth must look ahead for personnel with experience and talent required to support anticipated growth. It may be difficult to identify loyal personnel who may top out, but growth can also provide opportunity for lateral personnel movement.

Alert LOMP # 3: "A staff that stays together cannot grow together …at the same rate."

Once I joined a company as Employee #60; one of my peers was in charge of manufacturing. When I ultimately became president, there were eventually three people between us in the reporting structure. As we moved manufacturing to Asia, my friend became very important in the logistics of the organization.

In small-growth companies, at least two superstars are required to bust $10 million in revenue; to pass $20 million, five superstars would be necessary.

Following are several of the characteristics to look for in a superstar:

- Passion
- Intelligence (Street Smarts)
- Self-management
- Leadership
- Networking
- Teamwork
- Organization Savvy
- Sense of Responsibility
- Ready to Fill Vacuums (Voids in the organization)
- Flexibility to Run New Programs
- Potential to Grow

Of course, if someone had all of these characteristics, plus a multitude of others, it might be something for *Ripley's Believe It Or Not*. Nonetheless, always be on the lookout for superstars.

Hiring Smart—The Selection

I believe that it is very important that the final candidate's future supervisor do the reference checking personally. This is too important a step in the overall process to delegate to others. He or she should be asking questions about the candidate's reactions under various conditions, not about whether they work hard, are loyal, or other minor concerns. Obviously the referenced person is often on guard to avoid saying anything negative, so that is why the questions need to be more open ended. Don't ask simple yes or no questions. Most people will not make negative comments about a candidate even if you prod them that the candidate cannot possibly be perfect.

One technique that often works is called wait time. Ask an open-ended question or a leading comment, and then simply wait silently for them to respond. If they offer a very terse response, just say, "I see," or "Yes…" and then wait some more. The person on the other end of the phone will most likely feel the need to fill the silence, and end up saying much more than he would have otherwise, or more than he would have in response to a directed question.

You would also be surprised what you can learn by listening "in between the lines." I personally do not like to acknowledge negatives in my role as a reference check, in fear of the obvious possibility of a lawsuit, but the caller can draw a lot of conclusions by responses such as, "My daddy always told me that if you can't say anything nice about someone, you shouldn't say anything at all." Even in today's litigious society, this might also draw a lawsuit.

Before beginning the search and interview process, my hiring personnel need to believe that they are the best game in town. One objective in the hiring is to find the best person available—the superstar. Therefore avoid putting a financial cap on the position. After the person with the "right stuff" is found, a suitable compensation package can be determined. If there is a need and the candidate can meet the need, then a gap between what is offered and what is desired should be closed. Closing this gap will soon be forgotten after the hired person gets established in her duties. If the hiring person is truly looking for the best possible person, she should expect to find one that needs to be pulled out of her current company with her present employer holding on and screaming. It is normal to expect the candidate's current company to make counteroffers and produce creative incentives to try to get the candidate to stay.

Finally, I tell my clients that if they're the best game in town and they want me to help them find a superstar, they need to buy into my hiring biases.

1. *Don't hire someone who is currently unemployed.* While this won't sit well with the millions of unemployed, remember, we are looking for a superstar. The person has to be in demand. If laid off due to unfortunate circumstances, the person in demand will have no trouble walking into another position.

2. *Don't hire someone who has jumped from job to job too soon.* Instability is a drawback in any position.

3. *Don't hire someone who has followed his boss from job to job.* You will seldom find a leader among those who have followed someone all his career. The superstar is a leader, not a follower.

4. *Don't hire someone who isn't focused.* This person is generally responsive to any job and doesn't make it clear what he is interested in. He doesn't really know where he is going.

5. *Don't hire someone who made more money in two previous jobs, and don't hire someone who will take a significant pay cut.* There may be some sound reason the candidate wants to join the company, but if you are paying less than in two previous jobs, the mind-set of your candidate is wrong. Someone who isn't ambitious on his own behalf will probably not be ambitious on yours either. Anyone should be able to see that this is not a good fit.

6. *Don't hire someone who has done no research on the company before the interview.* Why hire someone who is not interested enough in the company to find out something about it?

7. *Don't hire someone who has not been with a winner.* Once a person has had a taste of being on the winning team, nothing else will do—he must get there again.

8. *Don't hire someone who doesn't seem basically intelligent or who has no common sense.* It is amazing how good a person sounds when he knows all about the specific jobs he has done. However, you need to make sure that he can walk across the street without jeopardizing traffic.

9. *Don't hire someone who has failed to achieve success in his previous (current) company.* Do you really want to hire a CFO from a company going bankrupt? Or an engineering manager who hasn't released a newly designed product in years?

10. *Don't hire someone who will accept any job available—barber to brain surgeon.* This just demonstrates how dangerous a person is.

11. *Don't hire someone who was fading or being put aside in their previous company.* In the reference check, find someone to decode all the fancy titles that may indicate this condition.

12. *Don't hire someone who has worked in the industry for several years, consistently earning far below the norm.* This strongly indicates that the person has a problem you'd be crazy to inherit voluntarily.

Searching for someone to fill a key position requires patience when it comes to personnel. Having nothing for an extended period of time is often better than settling for something much less than what is needed. Remember, it is important for this person to hit the ground running, and not require training—or rehabilitation. If you conduct an intelligent and patient search, you can find a superstar. And finally, and most important, at the top of my list is to look for people with passion for the position.

Hiring Smarts—The Interview Process

The chemistry of how the person would fit into the organization is crucial, and the early meetings should cover this issue. It's a very good idea to introduce the candidate to the staff, who will work as peers with the candidate and to those who will be the candidate's "inside customers."

During this phase, you should explore the candidate's capabilities and complete the reference checks. The better you get to know the candidate, the better you can assess how well he or she would fit into your organization. Phases one and two can both be conducted more successfully if they take place in a relaxed atmosphere, such as over a meal or in a hotel lobby.

The final interview process should include several meetings with you and the candidates and selected key people in the organization. This process is very important to both you and the candidate, so don't apologize if it becomes tedious for both sides.

During phase three, it becomes important to make sure the candidate gets to know all the subtleties of the position and all the cultural issues that will affect his or her success. This is the time to explore all the issues and doubts you may have. For example, the candidate from an important big company position with all the fringes might have trouble making the change to your "do-it-yourself" environment. It is extremely important to be candid in the interview phase, and it is needed to direct much of the conversation as if the candidate is already in the job as you envision it.

On the positive side, if the candidate is the potential superstar, then try not to let the relationship break down over compensation issues. Bear in mind that if there is a real need for someone to fill the position, and if the candidate is the right person for the job, then yielding to a few dollars difference will be long forgotten before very long. The new hire also presents a good opportunity to change the culture if this is needed. Hiring a strong, new key person with an entirely different viewpoint will expand the company's operating style.

On the down side, make sure that this person is far more capable than any candidate inside. I have seen in large companies where a good inside person who is competent, loyal, knowledgeable of what is needed, and potentially successful was passed over because those making the hiring decisions were aware of and only focusing on the candidate's weaknesses. However, because the outside candidate is unfamiliar to them, they are not aware of the outside candidate's weaknesses. This hiring decision then becomes a morale problem when others in the company realize that the new employee was selected from a two-page résumé and a two-hour interview.

Interviewing those who make the short list can have at least three interview steps:

- Does the individual meet the criteria?

- Does there appear to be good chemistry among those involved? And

- Have you gone over the role in more detail and searched to see if there is a specific fit?

Hiring Smarts—The Search

Clients have often asked me to help interview candidates for key, senior positions in an organization. This can be a good idea, because I will usually look for different things in an applicant than they would. I have different experiences, and I am not under pressure to hire someone in the near term. However, before I accept such a task, I make sure the client understands that I will expect certain things of the process and that I will have a number of biases right from the beginning. I will be very selective. This is particularly true when hiring superstars.

Search Firms

To begin with, I recommend using a professional search firm, even though at first, my clients usually think they are too expensive. "After all," you might ask, "who can do a better job of finding and interviewing than those with a vested interest?" What you may not realize is that looking for referrals or advertising in the newspaper cost far more in time, energy, and hidden costs than the out-of-pocket costs of a search firm. The winners you are looking for are rarely the kind of people who read the want ads, and in fact, one of the tasks you should give the search firm is to go after specific people (give them names!) who are doing a good job for competitors or have a great image in the marketplace. You are out to hire someone who may have to be pulled away from his or her present job and expect their present employer to do everything possible to keep them.

A newspaper advertisement will bring in all sorts of résumés, each of which must be read. Additional time is then spent making the phone calls to check references, and all these things are taking your time away from your main duties. This is doubly wasted time when the search firm is better equipped to do the reference checking than you are. Newspaper advertisements for senior positions often bring hundreds of responses, but out of these will usually come only two or three candidates worth talking to more than once. Meanwhile, you have already spent many hours and considerable expense—even before you've started looking closely at those two or three. Newspaper ads are being phased out in favor of Internet services Monster.com. But here again a significant effort needs to be done after desirable applicants are identified.

I insist that, before anything else is done, the position and expectations be well-defined. Often the written job description and the actual job responsibilities are very different. The search firm can help you define the role this new person will play in the organization, listening to what you say you want and then playing it back to you in written form. Once the search firm clearly understands your needs, they will most likely present you with several candidates that all meet the established criteria and leave it up to you to select the one that would fit best into your organization and where the chemistry feels good.

In addition to their basic role of finding candidates, the search firm can then serve as an excellent go-between when you've gotten down to the negotiating phase. Unlike newspapers, search firms can provide candidates that are currently employed by competitors, and therefore good sources of enemy intelligence. The search firm can then help you access that information, either from their data-gathering efforts for the candidates or from direct interviews by them or by you.

It is important to understand that in most cases, the new hire should be an upgrade in the position. You can expect outside search firms to recognize the need for culture changes. It is possible the inside interviewer with his or her own agenda can chase good applicants away.

Lawyer is not a Dirty-Four-Letter Word

No doubt the frequent lawyer jokes, putting lawyers down, and misunderstanding the cost of having legal expertise prevent many companies from calling on a lawyer until they get into trouble.

With the business environment getting more complex because of new labor laws and the expanding need for compliance, a company's management resources must have ready access to legal know-how. More companies are getting in trouble for lack of skill in the legal needs in human resources as well as the broad area of operating a business in today's environment. Part of the problem is that management does not know when this expert legal support will be needed. Small growing companies tend to utilize the president's assistant as a human resources manager or even a clerk in the accounting department.

Both small and large size companies go as long as they can without a lawyer as part of the team, but the trouble is management in a growing enterprise doesn't realize when the time has come for a lawyer join the team.

Even today in a growing company, with a first-time president, I come across problems that should have been rectified years ago. For instance, employees are paid as a consultant without covering payroll taxes, even though the person meets all the requirements that define an employee. In my last famous survey of ten, three companies were guilty of this infraction. Then there is the case of illegal firings—again two out of ten. And sexual harassment known to members of the senior staff had occurred in four out of ten companies surveyed.

Legal expertise covers more than people problems and manifests to needs in dealing properly with customers, vendors, and landlords. One of my laws of management physics states, "No Contract Is the Worst Kind."

I have come across several companies in my career that believed a handshake to close an agreement was a sign of good faith by participants. There is a naïve belief that all the positive things in the agreement will happen. Even when there might be something in the verbal agreement to define what should happen if the agreement doesn't go right, this will be forgotten when problems arise and bitterness starts to develop.

If lawyers had been used, they would have formalized the agreement with a contract, and the contract would include defaults, situations that would define what would make the agreement become invalid. The contract would also include a bunch of "what ifs" that would define what happens if items in the agreement do not happen, as when the product is not delivered on schedule or one party in the agreement goes bankrupt.

Sadly I have seen many business partnerships become bad enough to end up in a court for a lack of a partnership contract. In this situation, strong friendly relationships are destroyed, and many times even the company employees have split loyalties, causing the company to dissipate while the equal partners are battling for control.

I have experienced that the biggest reason for small companies' failures while growing is poor cash management and trying to be all things to all people. I have not kept details regarding the lack of legal expertise in such a team, but I do put it in the top five reasons.

Management Lies—A View From the Top

Often a manager will make statements in the heat of the moment, usually under pressure, in an attempt to satisfy his boss or get someone off his back. You'll often hear such statements at board of directors' meetings, when managers are thinking, "If I get through the next hour I won't have to worry about these guys for another three months!"

Everyone has heard the now infamous, "The check is in the mail." If someone who owed you money said that, would you believe it? Management tells lies, too—both the ones we've all heard and new ones that are a tribute to the creativity of the American manager. Below are some of my favorites.

CEO

The CEO says to the head of a company being acquired, "Don't worry! Things will be the same as they have always been. I want you to run the company as always. Think of this as a marriage." Just remember, on a honeymoon, somebody always gets screwed!

In front of a customer or the board of directors, the CEO says to his staff, "No problem! I'll make sure you have all the necessary resources." Unfortunately, when the audience leaves, so does the offer.

The CEO again: "Don't worry. I wouldn't think of making an acquisition without talking to the board first." 'Nuff said.

When the time comes to replace a top level person, the CEO sometimes comments to anyone within hearing distance, "I will hire the best person available regardless of sex, color, or creed." At this point, at least half the people within hearing distance are rolling their eyes.

A CEO is raising money. "I have investors beating down my door." "I always have someone ready to put up $2 million. I just have to let them know." Sure. If you believe that, you probably also believe that Michael Jackson's only had two operations on his face.

When he turns the company down for a loan, the CEO will hear the bank's loan manager say, "I thought we had a good case here, and I really went to bat for you, but the guy downtown turned it down." I am still waiting to meet that guy downtown. Personally, I doubt he even exists.

Management Staff

The management staff is being questioned by directors, and responds with, "You don't understand my area," or "You don't understand my market." In their minds, this solves the problem and ends the conversation. Ironically, the bad results the manager presented make it clear that it is they themselves who don't understand the situation.

A board member recommends that the management staffer call someone for help. The reply, "I tried several times to reach Joe." What he forgot to mention was that he called at lunch, or at the very end of the day (as if he really wanted to talk to Joe, right?). The same thing happens when Joe is an irate customer; the management staffer never seems to be available.

Finally, when things are bleak and the situation needs some creative solutions, it's the guys who got the company into the situation who will tell you, "Trust me." Be wary of anyone who says that. That's almost as good as the guys who say, "Well, to tell the truth ...." If this is the truth, what was I hearing before?

Manufacturing

"I don't have an inventory problem," says the manufacturing manager, when the walls of the storeroom are bursting and the cash flow has dried up. After all, it's not his money at risk ... And on the flip side, a director insists that "Inventory turns should be at least six," because other (possibly unrelated) companies such as the flower shop around the corner are doing six. He makes these demands without regard to the nature of the business or the current competition.

"The revenue is in the bag." I marvel at how a revenue forecast given the 30th day of a month can be missed on the 31st day of the month.

"Next month we will have linear shipments." What this means is that when it's the 30th day of the month and only 20% of the product has been shipped, they will be shipping 5% of the target each and every hour through that night.

You'll hear this one from either the sales or manufacturing manager. "We will be back on schedule next month." This is often said when it would require an all time booking or manufacturing record month to come anywhere close to the schedule.

Marketing/Sales

The sales manager, when sales are low, can be heard to say, "I will pack a suitcase and go on the road until I get bookings." This sounds dramatic and committed, doesn't it? However, weeks later, the situation has worsened and his suitcase is still collecting dust.

Be wary of the salesman who uses words like "good for business" or "margins."

Ever heard this one? The salesman says, "If we don't lower our prices, we will go out of business!" More than once I've been told this, but even several months after we held absolutely firm on prices no salesman ever produced a report on the business lost as a result.

Or how about this one: The salesman says, "We got this job even though we were the highest bidder." Believe this and you probably also believe "I'm the only one that was given the competitor's prices." And talking about naïveté, how about the salesman who says, "I get more insight because the customer is my friend." I cringe when I hear this because the salesman probably believes it himself. How often salesmen fall for the old Maxwell Smart trick: "I will be out of the room, and if you can read upside down, you can see your competitor's prices."

The marketing manager, on the other hand, might tell you, "Our pricing formula guarantees a 20 percent pretax profit." I've always wondered what happens to that elusive 17 or 18 percent, because more often than not, the actual profits are two or three percent. How often does anyone ever make twenty percent pretax?

How do you know a salesman is lying? His lips are moving.

Personnel

The employing manager says to the candidate for a key position, "Don't worry. Join the company, and within 30 days we'll work out a bonus plan and tie up any loose ends." Promises, promises. There are at least three companies where I'm still waiting on that plan. Candidates have to realize that they have their best leverage before the agreement, and it only goes down from there.

General Manager

The general manager is explaining something, and the subordinate says, "I understand." But so often, the employee really wasn't listening or really did not comprehend. The flip side of this is just as confusing. The manager says, "Okay," meaning by that, "I hear and acknowledge." The employee hears, "Okay," meaning, "I approve."

In a cash crunch, management says to the board, "We will shut down the dock and stop all material coming in." You can check the shipping dock days later and find that they never heard about this, and the material keeps coming in.

Haven't we all done this at one time or another? The general manager says, "If sales don't improve by (fill in the date), we will be making some cuts in personnel and expenses." I could grow a beard waiting for this to happen. Unfortunately, from this time on, all kinds of energy is wasted in misguided attempts to delay these actions, even as the situation is crumbling around them.

Engineering

Sometimes you'll hear the engineering manager say, "Trust me. The project will be completed on time and within budget." However, if left to him, it would never be done. You could even double the engineer's estimate of the time and cost for a project, and it would still come out late and over budget.

Quality Control

And this one from the quality engineer: "We don't have a quality problem. It's the customer's system." Often, this is said before the quality engineer has gathered enough facts to realize that the product was DOA at the customer's site.

Management Information Systems

MIS has its own set of lies. "With this new (and undoubtedly very expensive) MIS system, I'll be able to close the month in four days and get rid of all kinds of people in accounting." Then, when the system is on line, the head count just grows and grows.

The MIS manager again: "Although it normally takes several months to make a system conversion, we are organized to do it by (fill in date)." Several months later, the system still isn't online, and everyone is up in arms.

Implied Lies

Be wary of the implied lies in answers from subordinates to questions from personnel above them in the organization. The same question might very well receive multiple answers, depending on who's asking. A worker on the line will give different answers to the president, their immediate boss, the engineer from a different department also responsible for the product, the quality engineer, and their fellow workers.

Asking a second question can help you fully appreciate the answer to the first question. This is especially important in dealing with people who do not volunteer information. For example, a general manager asks a manufacturing manager, "Will there be any problems meeting the revenue forecast for this month?" The answer is "No." Or even better, "I will guarantee it."

Sure enough the job gets done and this month's revenue forecast is met, but the next month's revenue is disastrously low, ending up hurting the company. When the general manager complains to his manufacturing manager, the answer he gets is, "I had problems last month, and had to pull in from the future, but you didn't ask about futures!" The general manager should have asked the second question, "And how will it affect futures?" Given all the facts, he or she may have been able to avoid irritating a customer by adjusting some priorities and lessening the problem's impact.

President

After guaranteeing that the firm will buy someone's company, the president says, "The board will go along with whatever I request." Months later, the poor seller is still waiting to be acquired while he sees his assets going down the drain.

When they are having quality control and yield problems, presidents have been known to say to the board, "I will stop the line if necessary," when in reality, everything that is not tied down or breathing will be shipped for revenue.

The president tells you, "I can always get an accounts receivable loan." This is generally followed by, "I can go to the bank if I need money." Obviously he never figured out that banks only lend you money when you don't need it.

"I don't care if our salesmen make millions on a commission. I would welcome it. After all, the company benefits from it, too." says the president. And then, at the first hint of a "bluebird," the word processor is directed to change a number or two in the salesman's compensation plan.

The company is rapidly outgrowing the president, and he says, "I'll know when it's time to step aside." Right! And Magic Johnson knows when to retire! Power that puffs up one's ego clouds judgment. With that comfortable salary, the retirement program, and the thrill of control, why quit voluntarily?

The president tells you, "I can fund my growth from my profits." What he doesn't realize is that the more successful the company gets, the more cash it requires. And this same president will probably not welcome investors, because giving up any real ownership is giving up the company's control. It amazes me that people with years of business math haven't figured out that 5% of a $100 million dollar company is a LOT more than 100% of nothing.

Finally, here's the one that has deprived me of the most sleep over the years. The program managers and engineering personnel are missing major milestones, and they'll tell you, "Don't worry!" I really hate that. I never did understand how a delay to meet the next major milestone can be longer than the total program planned.

Or worse yet, the cutesy version: "No need to worry!" Then, for sure, I worry. And I can't sleep at night.

Managers Over Their Heads

There are times in a manager's career when he can get in over his head. Most often, it is because the job grows faster than he does. What can help prevent this from occurring is if there is unity in the work force. However, it must be recognized that a staff that stays together cannot grow together at the same rate.

Despite the best of efforts to work together, there will always be factors that cause differences. These include differences in personality types, educational levels, networking strategies, and personal agendas. Unfortunately, in most companies, it usually takes far too long for management to recognize problems and even longer to make the necessary adjustments. In most cases, subordinates recognize the situation far sooner than management.

Some warning signs that indicate a problem in management are the following:

- A manager avoiding a project that might require facing and dealing with conflict;
- A tendency to change directions when making tough decisions, basing his final decision on who last whispered in his ear;
- Moodiness that affects the workplace environment;
- Inattention to matters at hand or a lack of follow through;
- Avoidance in dealing with difficult customer problems;
- Aggressiveness toward staff; getting on peoples' back more often;
- Communication problems: Inability or unwillingness to communicate;
- Poor decision-making; decisions made that defy logic;
- Decisions made based on the fear of failure or avoidance of losing face;
- Unclear or unstated priorities;
- Tendency to force employees to resign rather taking appropriate action to terminate them;
- Engaging the boss in interactions with irate customers;

- Blaming mistakes on others;
- Discomfort with change; taking actions that actually slow down needed changes;
- Avoiding meetings with unhappy, internal salespeople;
- Delaying meetings with superiors;
- Reneging on promises to staff.

When you determine that someone is in over his head, the next step is to find out what is causing the problem, and then see that your manager gets straightened out. If this doesn't work, it is time to make a change in personnel.

Keep in mind, when a problem of this sort is finally recognized, usually it is already too late. Taking an action, even if it leaves a temporary void, is better than taking no action. So don't delay in making any necessary changes if the manager no longer fits the job requirements.

Market Sizing—The GPS Approach

Growth companies will eventually reach barriers that require more market information beyond the present customers' base to help them estimate their future growth rate. This frightens companies, because they may not know where to go for more market information. The Internet can provide a massive amount of information once it is clear how to find it. In addition there are many outside services to complement what you can get from referrals from your suppliers and customers. There is also a subtle method to gather G.2 market information by interviewing candidates in your market for marketing and sales positions.

In essence there are three approaches in accomplishing the data desired.

Macro/Big Picture

1. Analyze the size of the market your product goes into and estimate the percentage of sales that your product is in the customer's product. A company had a sub-assembly that went into a computer peripheral. A trade magazine provided reasonable estimates of the total peripheral market. This was backed by interviewing purchasing managers in the customer base to get the similar material purchased as a percent of the customer's sales dollars. An estimate of the potential market then could be calculated from the total sales of the customer's market. It turned the product was roughly was 4% of the customer's product, and from this knowledge and knowing the percentage of the market this particular customer shared, the percentage of the total market could be projected.

Available Market

2. Analyze the total requirements of your potential customer base to get your available market. It's getting easier to find the revenue numbers for the players in a market. It's also possible to project from a few customers. For instance, a small company was dealing with three big customers who represented 60% of the market. It was easy to project the total from this base. By analyzing their growth rate it could be assumed their suppliers could grow at the same rate.

Micro

3. Analyze the total sales revenue of all your competitors. This information can come from trade magazines, trade shows, or trade organizations as well as public information on public companies.

If a company is projecting robust growth, it first must understand the market it is in and this market growth rate.

The danger in getting and using total market numbers is not knowing the mix of product that relates to your segment.

I inherited a division in a multibillion dollar international company. There were over 100 divisions in the company. The previous general manager survived a couple of years by projecting growth to $100 million from a base of $10 million. Investments were provided by the parent for a couple years to support the projected growth little growth, but time ran out and the GM left the day before he was to be fired. The product was commercial multilayer printed circuit boards. After analyzing the market, it was discovered that 50% of the demand was done "in house" by the customers themselves, 50% of the remaining available was for the military, and 60% of the commercial nonmilitary was for single layer boards. Since the division business was in commercial multilayer boards, all that was available was $300 million from this very large market. The task to grow 10 times to $100 million revenue with over 100 suppliers in this relatively small market put the potential for growth in the proper perspective. I assume the previous general manager thought he was going to take market share away from competitors as they stood by and cheered him on.

I have encountered numerous business plans where the entrepreneur says, "Don't you believe we can get at least 0.001 percent of this $4 billion market," and most often the answer was "No." There is much more to a market definition than size. There was a hi-tech company that grew to $5 million in sales with high-speed logic elements and was looking for big money to invest in a foundry. One question slowed them down, "Has any customer ordered a second time?" Unfortunately the answer was "No," because everyone (most likely engineers) was only sampling and wouldn't necessarily buy big production quantities.

Robust growth requires high risk and guessing the future, therefore to lessen the risk more effort has to be put into the marketing function to understand the market available.

Marketing Tips for the Non-Marketing Staff

For the non-marketer, common sense can effectively create the balance necessary to match the marketing mentality. Keep in mind that marketing is more perception than fact. Being better than Mr. Big when competing doesn't always win for you.

Years ago, a famous cliché was, "You won't get fired for picking IBM." Today with the massive amount of competition and choices, many people now say, "You may get fired if you don't consider alternatives to IBM."

Checks and balances on the marketing personnel are essential because they aren't always right. If you find a situation presented by marketing that is "too good to be true," it probably is.

It is good to understand that what you see isn't always what you get. It is possible to take advantage of a negative situation and turn it into a positive customer experience. I had an experience in a takeover role where none of the marketing group wanted to take calls from a customer, because most likely the customer would be irate. While sitting in a marketing manager's office, I decided to take the customer's call. The customer beat on me for forty minutes and slipped in a couple of abusive names to call me, which I hadn't even heard in the military service. When the call ended, my manager was quick to say, "Wow, I bet you are glad that is over." I said, "Wrong, it is good to know that the customer really needs us. If not, he could have said in ten seconds, "I never want to see you again." The ultimate result turned into a $2 million per year customer.

Challenges can create opportunities, so don't be quick to turn against an opportunity because it doesn't easily fit. I believe every good customer must have started out small; on the other hand, however, don't mistake an "opportunity" for a "business." I have seen too often marketing create an excitement for something new, management gets caught up in the emotion, and as a result neglects the existing golden goose that keeps the company going. On a priority basis, expanding the market you are in usually is the easier way to expand sales. The knowledge of the market and its idiosyncrasy goes a long way in adding features and products to your existing product/services offering. Beyond that, taking your products and technology to a new market turns out more difficult than perceived. The most frequent failure criterion I have heard is "We didn't know it would take so long." But going out with new product/technology into a new market can be disastrous. Being new, often the resources are not in place that know the market and products. New is great, but the end of a product life can be a very profitable situation if properly planned and executed.

And finally there is a need to believe that some of the best deals are the ones you walk away from. You can actually win by losing what could have seriously impacted the company in a negative way. The longer you chase a deal, the more likely it won't be good after giving up more and more to stay in the chase.

To provide a check and balance for a marketing push, the marketing personnel should adhere to the following concepts to be more effective:

- In negotiation, avoid trying to be all things to all people.
- Make the task of verifying a plan's assumption a high priority.
- Use titles for the marketing personnel to your advantage with the customer.
- Keep your frustrations with the customers from employees.
- In negotiations, push for "Your price, my terms," or "Your terms, my price," and avoid giving in to both.
- Avoid letting your ego enter in product decisions, especially if it needs to be killed.
- Don't let too many management layers build up between the company's top management and the customers.
- Sell to the highest possible level in the customer's company.
- Treat manufacturing reps as direct sales personnel and support them.
- You can drive a customer away gracefully by raising prices when needed.
- Prefer step pricing to volume pricing for large quantities.
- Always be aware of how the customer uses your product and what (if any) alternatives they may have.
- Consider that the customer likes to deal with Number One in the market and personnel in a company.
- Too much backlog can keep you from making competitive deliveries.
- One person only should be responsible for setting pricing and delivery schedule priorities.

Mindset—The Proper Combination of Perception, Perspective, and Priority

Recently formed business companies are most often small companies usually run by one person with an "I" mentality. I have seen such companies grow as high as $5 million in revenue with one person "doing it all" when it comes to managing the company, but thereafter the company typically becomes revenue capped. The revenue-capped level depends on the nature of the market and the product mix. For instance, if revenue depends on more of the same to grow, the successful growth can be at the top of the available market and have the highest-end customers. But if a company grows by expanding its market and enhancing its products or service, more of the same way of doing things will hit a barrier.

I have found $10 million in revenue to be the first major barrier, but I have seen barriers at $50 million and even experienced a company hitting a wall at $500 million. The numbers here are not exact, but are symbolic of the range for what can happen, depending on the specific company's products and market. Growing beyond $10 million revenue is where most companies will hit a barrier, unless there is a significant change in mind-set and the culture of the company. Somewhere past $5 million in revenue, competition increases, profit margins get tougher, personnel max out and there are not enough hours in a day for the "one-person" band to do it all. For the first time, Number One's inexperience in robust growth most likely will cause him to struggle to keep up with the continual changes that occur running a bigger company. In reality every day Number One shows up for work, he is running the biggest company of his career. Number One can get spread out so much that even what has been previously accomplished will start to suffer.

For a company to grow, a major change in the mind-set must come about. Mind-set is the proper combination of perception, perspective and priorities. Mind-set is also a significant part of the company's culture. Here is a comparison of two stages of a company to illustrate the change needed in mind-set.

A. The company run by the "I" mentality and organized to top out in their growth typically applies to the small and new start-up companies.

> Perception—The president's perception includes an "I" mentality, which means no one else has good ideas, no one else can do it

better, no one else can solve the problems, and no one else can make strategic decisions.

Perspective—No one is to be trusted with authority to match any responsibility even as it keeps getting broader. No one is allowed to approve pricing or make proposals to customers. No one can make commitments to customers or suppliers.

Priorities—All priorities are kept in Number One's head and are subject to change constantly without communicating the changes to the employees who need to know, and often then calling the employee incompetent. Number One spends the time to get involved in the simplest of tasks. I have often sat and watched a Number One, while I was getting paid as a consultant for my time, sign every check, without scrutiny, as a rubber stamp.

B. The company poised to grow and bust through $10 million in revenue:

Perception—Number One believes he can trust people and realizes that he must go outside the company to hire experienced personnel.

Perspective—Responsibilities are delegated with supporting authority. He is even comfortable hiring people who may be better than him. He has scheduled staff meetings particularly to keep the team involved and opens the books to help motivate the staff.

Priorities—Priorities are continually reviewed and changes are made clear to those who need to know. Follow up is needed to insure that everyone has priorities in line with Number One. Planning enters the vocabulary, and it is made clear that to make the plans happen, priorities must be defined and executed for the success of the company.

If A is okay to run a self-styled business and forego growth, more power to him. but clearly B is on the right track to build a growing, successful company.

Mindset—The Heart for Successful Growth

Many companies succeed! Many companies do not.

Most companies achieve at least some of their goals! The rest do not!

Since success is relative, even successful companies often do not attain their full potential.

Why is this true? Most company management personnel understand the theory and mechanics of management. Managing isn't all that complicated, and new theories and techniques are written about constantly. With all this education and preparation, why don't all companies have the best possible success? Why do companies with successful periods have to suffer through down periods? Why do companies manage to survive for years but never bust through that next revenue plateau to become big and profitable?

I believe the answer is related to management's mindset. When managers don't have the mindset to run a business at peak performance, the company will suffer.

What is mindset? Mindset is a combination of perception, perspective, and prioritization in decision-making. It also helps to have patience and skillful planning to go along with that mindset. Mindset is a major part of the culture.

I have seen companies grow to as high as $5 million in revenue with the "one person" mentality "doing it all" when it comes to managing a company. The revenue level depends on the nature of the market and the product mix. For instance, if revenue depends on "more of the same," the successful growth can get to the top of the revenue range. Robust growth beyond that is almost impossible without a major change in the mindset.

Robust growth requires change, and this requires the continual effort to review the mind-set to help bring about that change. It is the inability to grow beyond $10 million revenue where most companies will hit the first major barrier unless there is a significant change in mind-set and culture. Somewhere past $5 million in revenue, competition increases, profit margins get tougher, personnel max out, and there are not enough hours in a day for the "one person" band to do it all. Everyone gets spread out so thin that performance starts to suffer, and the company will be doomed for failure unless management changes its mindset.

Cash

Profit is high on everyone's list of important management words, but cash is more important than profit. Cash is perhaps the most important thing to keep track of in running a company. A company can survive without profit, but it cannot survive without cash. Profit is the muscle of a company, but cash is the blood.

Company Management must understand cash management. Statistics show that most small companies fail because they run out of cash due to poor cash management. Most start-ups fail, even with dynamite ideas, for exactly that reason. Large company unit managers would perform better if they were cash-driven rather than budget-driven. If cash were king, there would be less chance of ending up with too many employees or too much inventory.

One of the biggest misconceptions of growth companies is that they believe profit will support the capital needs, whereas in robust growth companies, the more successful the growth rate, the more outside cash is needed beyond that provided by profit.

Priorities

The setting of priorities is one of the most common and serious problems in poorly performing companies. This is also the weakest point in poor managers: they do not know how to set and communicate their priorities well. When a manager's staff is not performing to expectations, often it is because they have their own set of priorities that are not the same as the management's. The best boss I ever had used to sit and patiently listen to my goals and priorities and look for mismatches as a basis for making changes.

Whenever I have been asked to work with a struggling client's staff, I usually find that the boss's priorities aren't clear. Priorities should be written down whenever possible, and the manager must take the time to make sure they are understood. In fact, it is a good idea to have employees state what they understand the priorities to be to make sure the employees' priorities are consistent with management's priorities. We very commonly mix up the priorities as stated with what we would like them to be.

For example, I once asked a CEO client what his top priority was, and he replied that his absolute, number one priority was to hire a national sales manager. I then asked him why, if it really was his priority, there weren't candidates lined up outside his door waiting to be interviewed. Further research disclosed that he had not even talked to the search firm he had hired for two weeks. I believe the reason for the lack of follow up to hire someone was that he enjoyed playing the acting head of sales.

In the final analysis, the manager who makes everything work is the manager who establishes priorities that fit everything together. Setting and reordering priorities is the most important responsibility of the person in charge. Priorities should be monitored constantly to ensure that they are consistent with the company's evolving goals and objectives.

In several of the troubled companies I advised, there was a big gap between what the management wanted to do and what was happening. It was my job to analyze what was the reason for the gap. The management knew what needed to be done but couldn't pull it off. The majority of the time it related to poor priority setting.

Perception

The availability of cash can get lost in a growing organization. Accounts receivable (A/R) can be like a gold mine. More emphasis on collecting them will provide found cash. A/R for collateral to borrow money is natural in a successful company.

But too often it is assumed that an accounts receivable credit line will automatically be available, and at least 80% of the receivables' value can be borrowed. In reality many times only 50% of the value can be borrowed. This is because there are discounts related to the mix of customers. There are restrictions and limits related to a heavy concentration of one or two customers, government and international customers, and overdue accounts that will reduce the borrowing potential.

It is better to emphasize that using A/R collections as a money source can be more effective and cost far less in interest than if receivables are used as collateral for a loan. New companies often fail because they counted on an accounts receivable loan as a given. It is not a given that a bank will lend money against receivables, because many other factors related to the condition of the company come into play. Banks are not investors. They are against lending money unless a company is profitable, because they assume profit will yield some cash. The most important issue with a bank is that it insists that customers have two sources of cash available to pay back the loan. This is why it is almost a given in private companies that the largest shareholder must personally guarantee paying back the loan if the company cannot.

Perceptions relate to more than cash and can be a part of the culture of a company that is driven by Number One. If priorities are not clear, employees will perceive what they believe the priorities are, and this can be in conflict with the company priorities.

135

The worst example of poor priority setting and perception management I've seen in recent years was a case where it was alleged that bricks (literally!) were shipped to customers instead of disk drives. Only a poorly directed management signal to the troops, "Revenue must be met at all costs," could have possibly caused such an irrational action! The pressure came from the chairman of the board who had not been around when the shipments were made. He did end up in jail, however, as a result of the actions of his employees. It was his pressure that had employees cheating, because they believed that is what he wanted.

Planning, priorities, perspective, and perception add up to focus, a key to successful management. Making a company work depends directly on the definition and implementation of priorities, and meaningful priorities depend on sound planning, accurate perceptions, and ensuring that all personnel involved have the proper perspective. Often, to deal effectively with employees (or customers, for that matter), you must realize that you have to deal with their perception of the situation, no matter what the facts are.

Building and implementing a good plan require that the perceptions and perspective of the team are clearly understood. The best-formed plans will go astray if everyone isn't aligned—if they aren't seeing things the same way. In making plans and decisions, listen carefully and look for what the perceptions are, then respond accordingly; do not rely on fact and logic only. Also, make sure everyone has the same perspective and will support the plan with enthusiasm. This is why it is so crucial for a company to have a mission statement: it's the tool that gets everyone's perception and perspective aligned.

Perspective

Two experiences I had with the same client company illustrate the importance of focus. This client was forming a joint venture with a Japanese partner. The Japanese partner's priority was to seize the opportunity to break into a major segment of the U.S. computer industry.

In dealing with the Japanese early on, I was confused by how long it took for them to make a decision on a new venture or relationship. I eventually learned that they were spending all this time getting everyone to be involved in the program aligned in the same thinking—aligning perception and perspective. This was to ensure that everyone who would be involved would support the new program with the same enthusiasm and priority once the start button was pushed.

In the joint venture, they were commissioned to build a new point-of-sale terminal, and the negotiations for the specifications seemed to go on forever. When their team finally agreed on the specifications, the tempo picked up significantly, and when we got the first prototypes, they were actually better than what we would normally consider production quality.

The design and manufacturing was accomplished in four months, in time for major trade show. It would have taken our team six months longer, and many of our people would have fought it all the way because it wasn't their idea.

While I was employed by the American partner, a multibillion dollar conglomerate, there was more than one occasion when I watched the company make an acquisition that failed miserably. Their only approach was to send the group merger acquisition team out to make a deal, and then to jam the new acquisition into an operating division that was not part of the original decision-making process. There was no attempt to align priorities or work the perspective on the deal with the people who carry it forward. The first time the division manager heard of the deal was after it had already been closed. It was doomed from the start, and largely because it wasn't the division manger's idea.

Another example of how perspective can warp judgment: I may have lost yet another friend because I used my right to disagree. He founded and owned a small, successful company, and one day we had the following conversation.

"Dick, I am going to sell my company, and I would like your help."

"No, you won't."

"Why do you say that?"

"Because the last seventeen guys who said that didn't sell, and since I am a consultant who relies on my experience and statistical probabilities, I would bet that you won't sell."

"Well, you're wrong. I don't need your advice anyway. I will go find someone who agrees with me.

Why did I tell him that he probably wouldn't sell his company? There are several reasons. Mine were based on my experience and the "sellers'" personality. His were based on naïveté. The result was that we had very different perceptions and perspectives.

1. Exploring a sale is often only an ego trip for the owner or founder, who needs to see that someone out there thinks his company has value.

2. The company has become a way of life for him, not just a job or a business, and it is hard to give up.

3. The owner finds, as Mel Brooks once said in a movie, "It is good

to be king." Since he answers to no one, why risk a change?

4. Even if he starts to get a little serious, the owner's perceived price includes all the blood, sweat, and tears that went into building the company, and his price will be too high for an investor looking only at the economic return on his potential investment. I have seen many deals collapse at the last minute, and I did not want to go through that again.

5. At some point in the process, the owner usually realizes what is happening and begins to worry about what he will do after his company is sold. He asks, "Where will I go Monday morning if I have no company?"

My advice for someone who really has the desire to sell is that he should first find another activity that will replace the intensity of running the business and give him the same satisfaction. Before the exercise to sell even starts, an owner should get into the correct mind-set for being a nonowner.

Conclusion

Planning, priorities, perspective, and perception add up to focus, a key to successful management. Making a company work depends directly on the definition and implementation of priorities, and meaningful priorities depend on sound planning, accurate perceptions, and ensuring that all personnel involved have the proper perspective. Often, to deal effectively with employees (or customers, for that matter); you must realize that you have to deal with their perception of the situation, no matter what the facts are. I have heard more than once before a planning session. "Here we go again with something that won't happen again. Can't we call this off?" My recommendation has been not even to start the process if that is the attitude.

Building and implementing a good plan requires that the perceptions and perspective of the team are clear and well understood. The best-formed plans will go astray if everyone isn't aligned—if they aren't seeing things the same way. In making plans and decisions, listen carefully and look for and respond to perceptions; do not rely on fact and logic only. Also, make sure everyone has the same perspective and will support the plan with enthusiasm. This is why it is so crucial for a company to have a mission statement: it's the tool that gets everyone's perception and perspective aligned.

Money Really Doesn't Grow on Trees

Growth from zero revenue or accelerating present growth rates requires capital, and the higher the revenue growth desired, the more cash is required to support it.

Don't be fooled by the cliché that there are millions of dollars out there searching for a place to be invested and make more dollars. Certainly there are many worthy companies and individuals who need cash. Why are there so few actual transactions? Why are so many winning ideas lost for lack of funds?

This is the number one issue among start-up and small enterprises wanting to grow faster: "How do I get the cash I need?" Unfortunately, these potential borrowers often start out very naïvely, believing that once they announce their business opportunity to the world, the investors will be standing in line for a piece of the action. They soon become hardened after several false starts and rejections, but they still have trouble learning that the money is not yours until the check is cashed and the funds are in the bank.

This naïveté is illustrated over and over again in business plans I am asked to review. They all assume that an accounts receivable loan will miraculously appear as soon as it is shown needed in the spreadsheet. Of course, very few loans occur as planned.

And why is it that some companies find private investors (angels) who are virtual strangers? Why is it that some businesses can successfully do public offerings, even with poor performance, low sales, and negative profit, while at the other end solid, established businesses with a great plan or a history of profitability and good financial performance can't even get a line of credit?

In my opinion, the key difference is the "storyteller," the person leading the company's fund-raising efforts and the presentation. There are some people out there who can get lenders to commit just by announcing that they are thinking about starting a business. While some of it is trust earned by past successes, but more often it is the storyteller's personality and charisma. Most of all, it is a storyteller who knows how to tell a good story, and knows how to handle the particular audience.

Each category of investor has a different agenda. Here are my perceptions of debtors and investors, which I hope will help approach the task of raising capital more knowledgeably.

Investors—An Overview

To begin with, the famous complaint, "Banks will only lend you money when you don't need it," is often true. Its corollary is, "Plan ahead and borrow money when you don't need it."

Another saying, "Investors want to own you," is also not far off the mark. There is a reason why venture capitalists are often called "vulture capitalists." If you accept this, and approach the fund-raising process with a healthy dose of cynicism, it will help you deal with the heavy hitters more effectively.

Before you commit yourself, you must know how lenders and investors think.

Friends and Relatives: The easiest place to borrow small amounts is from friends and relatives, but is it worth the aggravation? They will haunt you to your death with questions like, "How is our money doing?" or "When can I plan to use the money for Joey's college tuition?" Many a friendship has ended over borrowed funds.

Angels: These are usually sophisticated investors willing to risk $50,000 to $250,000 on a stranger with a dream. Unfortunately, angels will most likely deal with the CEO/President as if they are dealing with a child and hurt his effectiveness.

Venture Capitalists: Venture capitalists are well-organized and have an organization that will sit on you. Their goal is to dominate a situation, and they will try to structure the deal so that they either have a majority ownership going in or will eventually get it. Their experience can most times help in growing.

Banks: Banks always want a sure thing, and they'd take your firstborn as collateral if you let them. They will structure the deal so that you've already defaulted on at least one part of the agreement before you even get out the door.

Finance Companies: These are companies who will charge interest rates several times what a bank would, but what might be the alternative? Probably nothing.

Senior Debt Lenders and Asset Lenders: They'll start by saying, "We're really not in the equity business," but somehow they manage to work stock warrants into the deal while you aren't looking. Be careful, because if you stumble, you will be amazed at how much ownership they end up with.

On the positive side, these investors are the people who write the checks. If you don't get them involved, your dream will evaporate and die. Keep in mind they are looking for comfort in the investment, and this comes from trust and credibility.

Motivation—Through the Back Door

If you do a Google search for motivation on any given day, you will get over ninety million references. In addition, there are thousands of books and articles written on motivation every year.

When you search Google for the definition of motivation you get, "The wants and need that drive a character."

No doubt on a short-term basis, one of the most successful motivators in business for a company's staff is a bonus, but my favorite benefit for motivating people through the years is to give them recognition of a job well done in front of their peers. The rewards can range from anything that provides a person material rewards to some form of spiritual benefits.

But whatever technique that is used to motivate staff, it can lose its effectiveness over time. Even money can lose its impact when it becomes expected and considered an entitlement.

So the question is, can you keep the motivation going as time moves on? The answer is yes, and this is done by what I call "the back door method to motivation." The power to motivate key personnel can be done by removing demotivators and situations that irritate people. For instance, the biggest demotivator of all time is when a manager gives an employee responsibility without the authority to accomplish the responsibility.

I have seen managers demotivate their staffs without realizing it. As an example, the manager who starts every sentence with "I" does not realize how this wears on people and demotivates by not recognizing the contribution of other individuals.

Then you have a company president who lacks honor with an attitude that says "I created success" and refuses to share the success, but when things go wrong he is quick to "say my staff screwed up." To top it off there's the typical expression you find in strategy sessions from the President. "I am the only one who can solve problems."

I believe that senior people who are self-starters do not need all the effort at motivation, because they have the strength of character to do what's needed to be successful. The key is not to find ways to continual demotivate them.

The following is a list to show how many ways people can be demotivated.

The De-motivators

Staff members who are chewed out in front of peers.

Staff members who have their dignity taken away.

Responsible person is not part of the meeting.

Staff doesn't get feedback on suggestions.

The boss is not available when needed.

Staff is always told how to do things and is not asked how they would do it.

Staff is put down when they ask for help.

Staff is not given feedback on performance.

Top management lacks integrity.

Trivial policies are pushed on senior people.

There is a lack of honesty in one-on-one meetings.

There is a double standard among staff members.

Unrealistic goals are set or required.

Boss goes around his staff to get things done.

Boss fails to communicate company objectives and priorities.

In many exit interviews I have conducted through the years the person leaving usually ends the conversation with a list of the de-motivators. They weren't necessarily the only reasons for leaving, but seemed to have a heavy influence on the decision. De-motivators create frustration, and the person who never accepted calls from search firms starts to listen to them when frustrations grow.

I strongly recommend that the person in charge look to avoid demotivators and start with one-on-one discussion with the staff to weed them out.

Motivation—For Better Productivity

Productivity depends heavily on employee motivation, including:

- Survival
- Knowledge
- Self-Esteem
- Wisdom
- Recognition
- Self-Image (which can be enhanced by a shared vision and purpose.)
- Meaningful Job Rules
- Authentic Mentors
- Positive Coaching for Development
- Job Security
- Rewards for Results
- Recognition
- Growth Opportunities
- A Fair Environment
- Consistent Management

Motivation—Key Personnel

Motivation doesn't always require money, culture of fairness, or challenging job and environment, recognition of employee contributors can go a long way.

The best way to motivate senior personnel is to remove and prevent those things that destroy motivation:

- Boss gives responsibility without marching authority.
- Boss's style is to compartmentalize the team.
- Boss's lack of honor ("I do well, but my people screw up").
- Boss thinks he is the only one who solves problems.
- Boss tells successor of new duties before he tells the incumbent person they are being relieved.
- Boss starts every sentence with "I.'
- Boss gives negotiating responsibility with no decision-making authority.

Start-Up—One Liners

A demo is worth a thousand pictures.

Customer Validation of the product requires getting an agreement they would pay for the idea.

It is not the plan so much to help, but it is the planning process.

Start with assumptions to your strategy and review constantly for validity.

A large part of marketing is based on perception of the customers more so than on facts.

You must want to make money to interest an investor.

Major reasons for start-up failure: poor cash management, lack of focus, and trying to be all things to all people.

Advice can border on motherhood, whereas counseling is advice that can be done in the system.

It doesn't matter what the facts are, it is the perception of those you are dealing with that are really important and must be addressed.

Naiveté—Beware

A good manager must have a bit of cynicism as part of his portfolio.

I've seen managers believe over and over in something even when they say, "It is too good to be true," and it usually is.

I've seen agreements poorly written because they are written only with success in mind. They are absent of any failure conditions or "what ifs." "What ifs" are defined as what should happen if the original assumptions and expectations do not occur.

Operations and Growth

Be aware as you grow, one of the dangers of having operating personnel with specialties is that the individual handling shipping, for example, on a full-time basis, can hurt the company if she/he gets sick or leaves the company abruptly (I refer to such people as "one-ofs"). To prevent this from occurring, it is recommended to cross-train employees to "cover their backs" of the "one ofs." I have seen a company, when acquiring a company, hurt by not having employees as back-ups. It was assumed, for instance, that an individual in accounting could absorb the additional work required, even though that individual was already working a 50-hour week.

In many cases, cross-training can be a big help—but only if the culture of the company supports this concept, because many employees do not like this kind of activity and unions will balk against it in union shops and prevent it from happening. Since cross-training isn't the only answer, planning manpower for growth needs to cover the company's eventual requirements.

But beware of spreadsheet planning as just one click can expand the manpower needs in numbers without regard for the nature of the environment and the various skill levels of all personnel involved/required.

Accurate figures of merit are important when planning for personnel that will be required as the company grows: like how many lines of code the software person can write weekly.

As an example of a terrible misunderstanding over people proficiency, I was in charge of a printed circuit board manufacturing company. Engineering was headed by a superstar named Pat. Every customer order was individually customized. It was the job of engineering to develop all documentation to place orders in manufacturing—which was a key role in the company. I thought it would be a good move to promote Pat to head operations with all new responsibilities. As it was, Pat had been able to process the equivalent of $1 million in orders a month Pat did a great job running operations but, as it turned out, with the changes that took place it took three new engineers and six months to duplicate the same $1 million level.

Personality Changes Along the Growth Path

A company reaches maturity in its decision making when its decisions are based on financial (economic) and marketing considerations. However, a high-tech product start-up company can take a considerable amount of time to reach this point. During the company's growth, each operating discipline takes over control of the company for a period, dominating the company's decision making. Eventually growth slows until the next function takes over. These time periods can be shortened if management recognizes what lies ahead. The following describes the typical evolution of a high-tech start-up enterprise.

Phase One: The Entrepreneur

Usually, individuals who start companies are technical entrepreneurs. Their management skills are limited, if they have any at all. Too much energy is wasted on new experiences, such as dental plans and building leases. Whenever the entrepreneur learns a new management technique, it is like a new toy, and he tries to apply it to every situation.

This person often makes agreements and deals unilaterally with employees and customers, and establishes precedents that will come back to haunt the company. The customers relate to the one man, and he must be everywhere and on top of everything. His great ego creates the illusion that he can do everything better himself. He no doubt believes that he will become a financial expert, and nobody can tell him anything different.

His expectations of his staff are also generally unreasonable. With the limited numbers of staff, everyone is forced to wear several hats, and soon important matters start falling through the cracks. He judges his staff according to his own skills and abilities. His attitude is, "If I can write 1000 lines of code by Friday, why can't everyone else?" The staff gets very little mentoring.

Phase Two: Engineering

Eventually sales reach the point where the company has to build more than one of each product. At that point, engineering has to direct the company. There is little or no documentation or complete designs, so manufacturing is directed from sketches, red-lined drawings, and verbal instructions. Engineering ends up running the testing as well as performing the quality control functions. They make hourly decisions, with no checks and balances, and no one does anything without asking engineering.

In this phase, proposals and manpower loading are done poorly, with no concern for yields or labor inefficiencies. Everything is programmed for success, and no contingencies are included.

The results? All vendor questions get directed to engineering, and they must handle heavy customer interface. Product designs are often finished in the customer's facility. Unfortunately, this situation can't last for long.

Phase Three: Sales

With product available and the organization growing, the company desperately needs to secure orders beyond the original customer contracts. Sales must "feed the dragon," and it tends to do so with unilateral decisions on schedule commitments and continual pressure on the internal organization for lower pricing.

Sales pricing philosophy is based on large volume orders that often show up in small releases. The priority given to customers is based on the "loudest squeaks." Since sales doesn't know how to lose, they try to be all things to all people.

This is a dangerous phase for the company, and it can lose its focus grabbing at everything.

Phase Four: Manufacturing

As organization and revenue grows, revenue becomes key for both profit and working capital. Sensitivity to customer needs drops as manufacturing takes over. Too much is expected from sales in getting orders and deliveries exactly as needed for planning purposes.

Manufacturing tends to optimize revenue dollars, ignoring the prototype and small dollar items. This can hurt the company down the road.

Under the continual threat of "falling off the cliff" (the end of the backlog), manufacturing makes all kinds of schedule promises in order to get orders, but the company doesn't have the material planning and production control skills to make it happen yet. Manufacturing tends to overorder material, build unneeded inventory, while the organization isn't yet ready to implement cost-saving measures or industrial engineering, dangerously leaving these to the design engineers.

Phase Five: Quality

With a growing volume of shipments and limited controls, customers start to get unhappy with the poor quality. A quality control department gets established. Quality control becomes a major decision-maker, getting involved in just about all shipping issues. This includes becoming the customer interface. Quality control also decides the revenue schedule.

At first, this department is assigned to the manufacturing manager, who has a basic conflict of interest because he wants to ship anything that isn't tied down.

Soon, the "I'll stop the line if I'm not satisfied" attitude prevails, and "quality" gets overdone. It becomes a negative force without quality engineering and corrective action skills. Fortunately, this is usually a short phase in the cycle.

Phase Six: Marketing

The marketing department evolves from internal technical people and generally starts with a heavy applications orientation. It includes poor listeners who talk down to customers. They have a "never lose an order" mentality, and sacrifice margins for volume. They believe that the solution to every problem requires a meeting with scores of people. The constant threat of a customer bailing out is used to win internal support. The customer becomes god, and all kinds of things are given as incentives such as free samples and field service.

As commitments get bigger, orders start coming in under poorly written contracts. The importance of planning is finally recognized, but while the company isn't doing this planning, the mistakes get bigger and bigger and the negative impact on performance increases. So does the disillusionment of the senior managers.

Phase Seven: Finance

The organization starts to get heavily involved in financial decisions with little historical data, but everyone still expects precision. Engineering and manufacturing can't wait for accounting to respond to their needs, so they start up their own accounting functions out of frustration. Products planned because of engineering's ego fail to meet adequate expectations of sales return on investment.

Finance starts to make unilateral decisions, getting the other departments up in arms. The emphasis on numbers increases, instead of the emphasis on credibility, and there is little concern for contingencies. Sensitivity to customers drops, and collection pressures create stressed customer relationships. A new MIS system is pushed through, but since the organization is not ready for this, the costs, time expenditures, and frustration grow proportionally. Finance has the initial responsibility for MIS and seems to do this in a vacuum, ignoring the needs of the other departments. The lack of timely financial information related to cost/price relationships puts the company at high risk.

Fortunately, throughout the cycle, improvements are taking place, and good leadership can force the company through these phases faster. In spite of all the hazards, many companies survive this process, and eventually go on to great things!

Planning—As Exciting As It Gets

One the biggest reason for a company's inability to sustain growth is the lack of a planning discipline. Fortunately some companies can become successful to a certain level without ever documenting a strategic or tactical plan, but then they hit a wall as the market environment changes as they grow. In my experience with new clients, at my round tables and in seminars, whenever I would go around the group and ask what comes to mind when I say the word planning, the majority of the audiences say, "Boring!"

It takes a while but I have been able to convince many of the people with whom I work of the importance of planning by making the plan a completive challenge and demonstrating the satisfaction that can come for the resulting success.

The four most important aspects of utilizing a plan are that:

1. plans are born to be changed;
2. the planning process is often more important than the plan;
3. the preparation to make something happen; and
4. the foundation for the plan and adequate energy are assumed to define the plans.

There is no way to overstate the importance of assumptions. There are times or situations where more energy should be put into the assumptions than in to the plan. The effort in the assumptions forces the management to think out a much better plan. Assumptions can include competitive information, pricing expectations, resources needed, yields in manufacturing and product life expectancy.

Assumptions need to be reviewed periodically to see if they need to be changed, and if so, it is necessary to go back and make appropriate changes to the plan.

The better and more complete the assumptions, the easier it is to make changes when unexpected obstacles occur. It is also important to get the participants in the plan to understand and agree to the assumptions.

There are Plans and there are Plans.

Everyone has a plan on a daily basis—not necessarily a written one, but one used to set the priorities for daily activities. Companies can have a multitude of plans for a number of aspects of their business, including budgets, bank dealings, internal issues, forecasts, objectives, cash flow, departmental issues, production, and operations.

Even an operations plan for the year can have versions depending on what it is used for. The same plan used for internal compensation goals can be modified when presented to the board of directors, the bank, or the shareholders. The internal plan can be the toughest, as it defines the actions, in detail, for the tasks and priorities to meet the company's objectives. The Plan given to the bank is the most conservative, because it's dangerous not to perform to what you tell your banker for fear they will call your loan off.

The best way for jumping on the planning bandwagon is to eliminate the myths that exist when it comes to planning,

The biggest drag on changing a non-planning culture relates to myths, which, if believed, will provide the rationale for never starting a formal plan. And unfortunately, it is tough enough even without myths to do your first meaningful plan.

The following are common myths that will hurt a company's growth until they can overcome their belief in them.

- *I can't figure out where I will be next week, let alone forecasting five years from now.* I have heard this so often, it is a cliché. I must admit that talking about multiyear plans does frighten people. The key is to understand where you want to be and not how many years are needed to get there. Once your objective is clear, you can then start defining what has to begin today to reach that objective. Here I am, here is where I want to be, and here is what needs to be accomplished to get there. (Who knows whether it takes a month, a year, or several years to meet an objective? Multiyear plans are losing favor in big companies because technology and global markets are moving so fast it's difficult to predict more than eighteen months).

- *Formalized planning restricts flexibility.* Wrong! Flexibility is often mistaken for hip shooting, a decision made in a quick fashion, with little thought given to it. Actually, the more planning a company does, the better they are positioned for flexibility in their altering course as changes occur. Planning creates an awareness of what a company is capable of—hence it makes being flexibility in decision making more easily understood and implemented.

- *We will get to $40 million because it's there.* This must be the worst reason for counting on meeting a goal, but I have heard it over and over in my career. "Because it's there" was fine for climbing Mount Everest, but can you imagine the extensive and detailed planning that goes into climbing Mount Everest? This quote has shot down many business plans with sophisticated investors for lack of intelligence in the plan.

- *Business is short term therefore planning ahead is a philosophical exercise!* This is the basis for stagnation! See two case histories.

  ⇒ Small company "Stagnate"—Owner Sally Stagnate's philosophy is to only buy material for the job after a sales order from a customer is received. Deliveries to customer then are based on the availability of material and collection time of money to pay for it. In almost all business, there is a competitive time required, and it is not based on the convenience and risk-free basis from the supplier. The only planning is the manufacturing cycle and not for meeting the customer need. This is superconservative and almost risk free. This philosophy can be okay if the company is a way of life for the owner with no desire to grow or be competitive as long as she takes out enough money to support her family.

  ⇒ Small Company "Grow"—Owner George Grow wants to grow and become more of a competitive force in the market. He recognizes that competitive delivery times are shorter than lead times to receive material and collect funds from customers. Because of this, he knows his inventory and accounts receivable will need to grow. He knows to get a bigger piece of the market, he needs to be competitive and must take the risk of buying inventory ahead of time and thus risk obsolescence. He may even have to risk having bad debt by extending credit to customers on a broader basis. Therefore planning becomes essential.

- *Only the Big Need To Do Planning.* Wrong! Many big companies have backup and reserves to cover mistakes; therefore they can tolerate weak plans. Small companies can go down the tube with one significant mistake, making planning even more important to prevent this from happening.

Here's where the first two Laws of Management Physics prevail.

Law #1—The goesinnas must exceed the goesouttas! (Refers to cash.)

Law #2—Profit is the muscle of company, cash is the blood!

Cash availability should drive all planning in growing companies.

- *Let's set the goal high enough to make sure if we miss it, we will make the real goal.* Tell this to short guys like myself, that in my wildest imagination, I never thought I could slam-dunk a basketball, so I never wasted any time or frustration on it. This myth is one of the great demotivators of all time. Give a staff or team unreliable goals and they will give up before they start.

- *I don't need a formal plan, because I have it in my head.* The greatest chance for success of a plan is to have full participation of those needed to make it happen. It's easier to commit a plan to paper than to have the staff walking around with a hammer and chisel—to get it out of Number One's head.

- *Don't you believe I can get 0.1 percent of a $4 billion market?* No, not unless you show me the details on how you plan to do it. Just because a market is big doesn't mean you can get even the smallest sliver of the pie. This is also a deterrent in getting investors for your company who recognize the importance of having a plan to penetrate the market effectively, let alone getting 0.1 percent of the available market.

- *Planning is boring.* This is the oldest myth of all. I have found most successful business people are highly competitive. Since many of us, for various reasons, can't follow their dream (my reason—no skill to participate in professional sports), what better way than to use the business and the market as the playing field? Sports require a great deal of strategy and planning, and you will find professional football teams have detailed game books for each game. Business in this sense is much tougher because far less is known about the competitors or customers than about an opposing sports team regarding their style and capabilities. To me there is no greater satisfaction than planning something and then making it happen. I have several friends whose greatest satisfaction is trying to beat their best golf score several times a week. So why not a plan? Meeting a plan should get the juices going full bore, and many times meeting a plan can be highly rewarding to self-esteem and to financial well being.

Where Does It All Start!

A plan can only be developed if there is a purpose, like laying out a sales strategy or a production run. For a company, it starts at the top, and there needs to be a vision and a mission. My first encounter through the years with many new clients was the same. "I have no mission or goals" was the usual statement. These were people operating companies with some degree of success, therefore they had to be operating with more than magic, and they inherently had a goal. It only took one lunch or dinner to pulse them, to develop a list of objectives that, amazingly, they could achieve in so short a time. And from this list we could define in writing their goals, objectives, vision, and mission. To me the vision is the dream, and could be, as examples, "to be the best," "the richest," or "the leader." The mission follows the vision and has enough meat in it so that it can be used as the basis for a plan. Here is an example of how the vision and mission tie together.

Vision: To be the best most profitable manufacturer of bathroom fixtures, and be known around the world as the "King of the Crapper."

This is like a dream, but the question is how do we make it happen?

Now let's see how we build on this mission.

Mission: To provide premium innovative bathroom fixtures utilizing a new technology for flushing to the leading construction companies in the international market.

This information gives the substance for building the foundation of a business plan.

We now have the:

- Product—bathroom fixture
- Market—international
- Customers—construction companies
- Differentiation from competition—innovative flushing mechanism
- Type of company—manufacturer and/or distributor

There are enough objectives in the Mission Statement to start to plan the details to make the items in the mission statement happen.

It is wise to keep in mind that whenever you discover a bad situation and the need to make a change, it is already too late if you don't have a plan.

Priorities—The Base for Making Goals Happen

One of the most important aspects of managing priorities are setting and implementing the priorities, reviewing them periodically, and reordering them as necessary.

 In addition make sure that your priorities are consistent with your goals, and do not mistake desires for priorities. It is also crucial that everyone in the company knows the priorities and that you have communicated them in such a way to your employees that they are all on board with them. Obviously, as the market and the company culture change, you will need to be flexible and change the priorities as necessary.

Without Priorities to make things happen all the planning in the world will not work. I have participated in numerous planning meetings wherein the team participants at the end of the meeting are charged up and ready to take on the world's market and the competitors. But many times after a meeting on strategy and planning, the meeting ends up without establishing priorities and tasks to make everything happen. The excitement of the meeting is doomed to dissipate without assigning priorities, tasks, and accountability.

It is necessary to hold follow up meetings to review the progress and reassess the priorities. Management and employees will guess at what they think the priorities are and work on them accordingly if the top person doesn't have clear priorities. This can be dangerous to the unity of the company.

Risk—Nothing Ventured, Nothing Gained

One dictionary definition of risk is "facing some kind of peril, jeopardy, hazard or exposure with a chance of injury or loss."

With any plan or commitment comes risk. The trick is to understand the risk when working the plan and watching for troublesome red flags so that you can react quickly to minimize or eliminate the impact of those problems.

Robust growth involves risk, and the nature of growth requires putting resources in place before there is any guarantee the costs will be covered by additional cash.

It is important to have the correct attitude when taking risks. The rewards of risk can far outweigh the costs, so make sure to analyze the risk/ reward factors carefully. At the same time, if the major decision maker is against risk, he just needs to call enough advisors until one is against the risk. He can use this as a supporting justification for not taking the risk action

Risk needs not to be thought as gambling, if an understanding of what risks and plans are developed to control the risk. Be careful not to believe that sharing risk reduces the danger, because two wrongs will not make a right.

Exercise caution by not taking on too much revenue too fast, not trying to break any records, or prematurely pushing a new product into the market. Once you have analyzed the risk, don't add new and different activities that could alter the formulation of the risk. Don't focus on satisfying your biggest customer, but consider how you can establish some new ground rules that will help you reap the rewards of the risk.

There are probability estimates that can help evaluate the difficulty for doing something different regarding a new direction for the company. When entering a new market, finding a need is the least difficult task. Developing a match for that need is ten times more difficult than identifying the need, and penetrating the new market with that match is again ten times more difficult than developing the match.

In the same way, getting products to market has a similarly exponential difficulty depending on the combination. Expanding Present Products in the Present Market (PPPM) is the easiest, and thus serves as the base line. Bringing new products to a present market (NPPM) increases the difficulty by a factor of ten. The next step up, again by a factor of ten, is taking present products to a new market (PPNM). Finally, a thousand times more difficult than PPPM is taking new products to a new market.

There is a specific danger with the unknown for a NPNM choice, and it should not be pursued without drawing on people with marketing and technology experience from the new market.

The characteristics for all risk decisions should include the following:

1. Accept the uncertainty;
2. Know the potential gain;
3. Know the potential loss; and
4. Determine the significance of all before proceeding forward.

You can minimize the risks by:

1. Minimizing the impact of playing hunches;
2. Making sure facts support the information given, but be prepared to back down if not;
3. Describing your hunch to people you trust to get their experienced input;
4. Test-marketing the hunch;
5. Filtering the negative "black paint" input from those who are not risk takers; and
6. Most of all, not letting too much emotion prevent you from giving up when it is time to do so.

There is an axiom for risk taking that goes like this: If it can hurt, but can't help, run from it; if it can't hurt, but might help, try it; if it can hurt, but might help, continue to consider it; and if it can't hurt, but will help, go for it.

Conclusion

With the changing business environment and increasing global competition, old tried and true methods of planning and risk taking may not do it. Planning today requires innovation and breaking away from the limited skills of the team. Do not hesitate to get all the outside information you can in making such an important decision.

Remember that not taking a risk is taking a risk.

Selling the Positives

Fred Founder is always pleasantly surprised when Mary and Sally bring home a winner that Fred considered a lost situation. It's like he throws them a lost cause, and they turn it into a sound and winning strategy. For instance, in recent activities, Growco won four contracts against strong competition.

After assessing all the inputs, he voices his concerns or worries and throws out his concerns:

Fred worries: "But we're such a small company!"

Sally replies: "We'll pitch the 'personal' touch."

A small company can stress the personal touch against a much bigger competitor. Being able to put all your top management in a room with the key customer personnel can give the customer a level of comfort not usually available from a large, tiered company. The customer, facing all the key decision-makers in your small company, can overcome the idea that he or she is facing the often illusive "they" encountered in big companies. The effect of beating up on a regional sales manager of a large company, when necessary, can be diluted by the time the complaint reaches the top, even if the complaint or request never gets to the top management. Being able to pick up the phone or send an e-mail memo to a top manager in a small company can get instant response.

Fred worries about the limitations in the design: "It has fewer features?"

Mary: "We designed for cost and simplicity."

Fewer features can weaken a competitive situation; therefore all the negative or useless bells and whistles of the competitor must be exposed. If the total capability of a software program is never utilized, all the features may not be needed. In many cases, the less complex approach can be more user-friendly, and your product can be pitched as having been directed to meet their needs. Sally's favorite retort in this situation is, "And all the extra sizzle isn't really needed."

Fred worries about the bottom line: "There's no more 'give' on our side!"

Mary: "We sell a complete package."

It may be difficult to overcome a competitor's lower price or costly additional features that time will not allow to be added. In this situation, modest features such as dressing up the manual or jazzing up the packaging "at no extra cost" might be a dealmaker. I have seen an order turned around by a supplier offering to package the product in a form that was conveniently used by the customer to ship direct to their distributors.

Fred worries they can't afford to add any new features: "How can we look special without substantial investment?"

Mary: "We will be their fall-back alternative."

Sally: "We talked about adding the packaging at no extra cost."

In today's market, specifications and features aren't the only criteria for selection. More often than not, Mary has had more success offering the customer a weak product with strong product support than with a good product and poor support.

In Mary's mind small companies do not have to have it all. Buyers wouldn't even be talking to Growco if they didn't want them to be a part of it. The key is to search for a positive sales pitch that can give buyers a degree of comfort when defending their supplier selection decision to their bosses.

Buyers can take the seemingly safe route by going with a "big" supplier, but that solution can be painful now. There was a time when it was said that purchasing personnel wouldn't be fired by going with an IBM image and IBM-sized company. Fortunately, purchasing people today face a real risk of termination if they do not consider a company other than IBM.

Mary Marketing and Sally Sales, old pros that they are, have been doing all this for years. They know that much of marketing is based on perception. In dealing with customers, the phrase, "What you see is what you get," must be influenced by another phrase, "What you perceive is what you buy." The ability to "sell what you have" is the mark of a strong marketing and sales function. Competing on a features-only basis and a one-to-one measure can lead to many defeats against a stronger or bigger competitor.

No matter what your competitive position in the market, you can always find positive attributes to pitch and sell. The trick is to get the customer to perceive there are other factors that you can bring to their needs.

Superstars—When Needed

As the company grows, the need for superstars grows. Superstars bring you passion, experience, and exceptional growth potential.

Many start-ups begin with limited management experience, and in many cases, the lack of management depth beyond the founders. For example, with an engineering founder/president of the company, what can he bring to his personnel in sales, marketing, manufacturing, quality, and finance?

Superstars should have the ability to handle the various roles they are requested to hold and have the growth potential that allows their career to go in different directions as needed by the company. It is refreshing to have people like this in a growing company banging on the president's door and continually requesting the president give up more responsibility. They are there to help define what is needed for every new idea and to let the president decide whether the cost, resources, and risk are worth it.

A company with a growth rate that exceeds the growth rate of the individuals needs to plan on finding personnel with more experience and skill than the position requires. In fact, any hiring activity should be driven to overhiring people with experience because of the growth potential the overqualified person can bring to the organization.

Normally the new needs of a robust growth company cannot be met fast enough from education and training of all the existing employees. Many with a lack of growth potential will max out and get so overwhelmed to a point that they will operate on the edge of having a nervous breakdown.

Mixed in with the new hires, there is a need to find and hire superstars. My experience says you need to hire superstars and have them in place to break through the revenue barriers along the way. For example, two superstars are needed to bust the first $10 million barrier, and up to three or four are needed to the bust the second $20 million barrier. This assumes that the president or founder driving the company may not be a superstar. The quantity of superstars depends on the nature of the business. If the growth can be done with more of the same, the need for and time to bring in superstars can be put off, but if the growth gets into new markets or products or technology, then you need to get them in sooner than later.

When it comes to hiring superstars to be part of the team, it can be easier than you think to eliminate the ordinary applicants to get to the finalist. One of the most important attributes I look for in an applicant is passion, not only in new people, but in all the employees across the scope of the company. A physical attribute I use to screen for an applicant is to look for is "leaner," but I also try to avoid a "slumper." I look for those people who lean forward, particularly in making their pitch or point in the conversation. I even like it when they override what I am saying to get a response in before I finish my sentence.

I always chuckle when I think of an experience I had hiring a security company in Hong Kong. I admit I kept the gentleman waiting in the lobby for a while. When I finally did go out to the lobby he was slumping back and dozing with a pipe in his hand. As you might imagine, it turned out to be a very short interview because he was obviously a "slumper."

Refer to the section on "Hiring Smart" above for the twelve personal characteristics and experiences to avoid in hiring a superstar.

Terminating Personnel—Alert

When terminating personnel, a more important concern may relate to the remaining individuals still employed rather than those being terminated. No doubt there's concern about how the terminated personnel are going to be affected, but if their termination is handled badly, those employees who still remain could quite possibly become "de-motivated," wondering/worrying about whether ultimate termination will happen to them as well.

Time Management

Managing the important things needed to be done in the time available.

The biggest time management myth that immediately comes to mine at this writing, is, "But I don't have the time," which can develop from poor discipline in *using* valuable time (e.g., spending too much time on easy, enjoyable tasks rather than recognizing what tasks are more important or, even more relevant than only those that are considered urgent*). No matter what language is used to say it, "There are only 24 hours in a day," so regard them as precious time to be used as efficiently as possible. (*Often times, the word urgent is overused in business primarily because it's based on emotion rather than on actual and/or already existing priorities.)

In the past, when trying to help a workaholic, I concluded that a typical day for him included:

- Job-related tasks—13 hours
- Sleeping—6 hours
- Eating—2 hours
- Traveling—2 hours
- Shower, etc.—1 hour
- Family—0 hours
- Self-Improvement—0 hours
- Entertainment—0 hours

To get the most out of this particular workaholic's time, we started with the following:

- Analyze—What important tasks need to be done?
- Organize—Prioritize the time by importance, and the plan to schedule it.
- Plan—Make it happen with the discipline that's required and necessary.

We agreed that family time was important and *had* to be added to the list. There are numerous examples of time management, but the one I came upon most often was with small business owners and presidents. I was getting paid by the hour and would often times sit and watch them signing a stack of checks; even though each had detailed attachments that were ignored. Since the alternative was much easier and far more efficient for the executive, we established a signature approval level that allowed small amounts (i.e., a vast majority of all checks generated) relating to operations and within budget, to have two signatures: those of the department head and the head of accounting. Checks over a certain (higher) dollar amount were to be signed by the president. Additionally, we defined the requirements for the detailed back-up that authorized the check—a change that required the president to trust his employees.

Following is a list of time killers:

Procrastination—continued to delay of decisions; way too much time spent rehashing the same discussion over and over again. (Example: the salesman racing into the president's office proclaiming: "If we don't give Company X a ten percent price reduction, we'll lose the order!" Since this is the biggest customer, Mr. President, of course, knows in his heart that he has to do this—yet, before agreeing to do so, he initiates two days of circular discussions, unnecessarily tying up key management personnel who could be spending their time accomplishing more important tasks.)

Reactive Management—priorities for the day start with the first phone call or another type of office intrusion. Being overwhelmed, urgent gets distorted and often creates way too much wasted time. What's important is to have a management team that's proactive in order to save significant time so the owner or president do not feel compelled to cover every "urgent" matter themselves (e.g., one answer is to train all levels of personnel in order to empower/enable them to handle a majority of the "so-called" urgencies.)

Lack of Delegation—the topic directly (and appropriately) follows the paragraph above wherein managers *must* learn to delegate as much time as they can to subordinate levels of employees, which is a natural characteristic of good management. It is, however, also important to keep in mind that every delegation requires compatible control until full and complete trust is developed and established.

Interruptions—I have found that accounting people working on those long columns of numbers can suffer greatly from interruptions. I have also run into this problem myself. The simple answer is to convince accounting managers to let everyone in the office know that they are going to close their office door for a specific period of time every day so that they are not interrupted. (**Note:** seldom will there be a request for help that can't wait for a short period of time.)

<u>Duplication Responsibility</u>—as you can see, bad time management is also just plan *bad management*. In a high-pressure situation, under-pressure management often times gives duplicate assignments to their employees, which not only waste time, but can even have a "de-motivation" effect on employees involved.

- Operating time on all levels can be wasteful and occur from"
- Bad meetings
- Long phone calls
- Saying "never" saying no to a request
- Easy distractions
- Too much small talk
- A committee decisions mentality
- And my all-time favorite: <u>Doing it wrong, the first time</u>. I have never ceased to marvel at how often I have seen it believed there wasn't time to do it right the first time, there always seems to be time to correct the problem from not doing it right the first time.

<u>Timely Tip for optimizing your effective time</u>, in addition to killing the <u>time killers</u>, can significantly help when planning and managing time. Always start with the most difficult task first (or you may never get to it), and then improve your personal efficiency by planning your days, weeks, and months in advance.

In other words:

- Determine the goals.
- Establish the priorities.
- Practice discipline.
- Utilize peers and associates to optimize your time.
- Learn the difference between urgent and important.
- Getting to the important tasks might make urgent tasks easier by starting with the elimination of all time killers.

<u>Always keep asking yourself: What's the best way to use my time?</u> It is often said that taxes and death are inevitable—and we all know that to be the case. However, I can also guarantee you that time will pass, so plan it wisely in order to avoid facing the same problems or unfinished tasks months in the future. (*See a big list of "Time Killers" in Appendix B*).

What is this Thing Called Innovation?

The president has a vision to build a concrete monument with the company name on it at the top of the hill for everyone to see.

He is pulling a wooden wagon with wobbly wheels up a long steep hill. The wagon is loaded with sand and pebbles, and the load is uncovered so that sand and pebbles are spilling out in all directions through the slatted sides. There is no road, and the path is pocketed with holes and rocks that cause the wagon to buck and roll from side to side, forcing the president to follow a zigzag route up the hill. For every move upward on the scarred terrain, there is a half move backward. The struggle is almost unbearable, but the obsession of this vision drives him on.

If only the staff would share his vision, the task would be made easier. "Sally Sales" would run ahead and put up a sign to let everyone know that the wagon is coming. "Andy Accounting" would separate the load and put a cover on top to keep it from blowing away. "Max Manufacturing" would repair all the leaks and strengthen the latch on the back gate. "Ed Engineering" would find a way to put a motor on the front and ease the pull. It might still take days to reach the goal at the top, but at least the president wouldn't kill himself, and he could spend his time planning on how to best utilize the monument after it was completed.

But in today's highly competitive market, a shared vision is only half the battle. Someone may beat you to the top. How great it would be if he could also rethink how he should do things, and, with open-minded discussions, come up with a better idea. This is where "Mary Marketing" starts to shine with her thinking and creative planning mentality. She is quick to grasp the need for getting there first and also optimizing the resources. Her thinking goes outside the so-called box. Her response to the situation above is, "let's hire a helicopter and lift the load and all of us to the top of the hill and thus accomplish the task in less than half an hour."

Changing the culture in today's business environment is a necessity, but after sharing the vision, new and better ways must be found to pull away from the pack. This is where the need for innovation to drive change takes over.

Word Games—Are These in Your Dictionary Yet?

Accountability—is similar to maturing when it becomes necessary to hold employees accountable for their performance. I used the expression for years, "Say what you will do" and "Do what you say."

Advice and Consulting—Advice comes from all directions based on logic. Motherhood alone can be harmful to the recipient, whereas consulting is advice that can be done within the system, with the resources available, and usually is helpful.

Assumptions—the necessary foundation for any plan. They force management to think about what needs to be accomplished, and provide a basis for reviewing any changes that might be needed.

Balance Sheet—a powerful tool that often is not considered a part of the company's arsenal—it contains the vital signs of a company, provides a snapshot of the assets and liabilities, and serves as a foundation for running the company.

Burn Rate—covers the costs in place and the cash that would be needed to cover all costs in place monthly if there were no income from the sales revenue.

Cash Flow—is derived from cash in and cash out and from a timely projection of the future operation of the company.

Comfort—is required by those above you to provide the support needed and requires honest and timely communicators to develop trust and credibility.

Communications—requires sending, receiving, and listening. It falters whenever it is one way.

Communication Above—is allowing those above you in an organization to talk to your people as long as they do not chew them out or influence their priorities resulting in unwanted change.

Controls—should be married to delegation. Controls can be in the form of limits, reporting, and the definition of responsibility and authority.

Creativity—goes beyond imagination as it requires a solution within the resources and values of the system. A salesman can get the order if he pays the customers real estate taxes—dangerous imagination. A salesman can get the order if he takes the customer to an enjoyable museum—

creativity.

Debt—comes in many forms of liabilities from the obvious bank loans to the more subtle, vendors and suppliers delivering with a delayed payment. An up to date Balance Sheet with an understanding of the various liabilities and can help control debt.

Delegation—is the method to develop Trust to get away from an "I" culture. Delegation requires giving up responsibility but, to be effective, authority must go with the responsibility.

Global Competition—used to be a foreign word but with the Internet and developing countries providing competition, it is now on our shores and needs to be watched and factored into the company strategy.

Hands-On-Management—is operating within the systems and resources that are real and not to a text book—it is differentiated from micromanagement which is telling someone what needs to be done and when to do it. Hands-on-management is telling someone what is needed, how the person can accomplish it, and always be there to help if the someone stumbles.

IBITDA—(*Income Before Interest, Taxes*, and *Depreciation Accounted for*) relates to the cash available from a performance period before interest, taxes, and depreciation are taken into account—a useful number for growing companies and stakeholders who need to support the cash needs for growth.

Innovation—used to be bandied around like motherhood, but as growth develops, markets and competitors get tougher, and "more of the same" is no longer good enough. One way to think of innovation is taking something successful in another world and bringing it to the world you are in.

Litigation—a dirty word if you are on the receiving end. *(See "Dealing with Mr. Big" or "Lawyer Isn't a Dirty Word").* It enters into a company's growth when the company becomes sizeable and is worth suing. Unfortunately, if you get sued, you already have lost even if you win the suit.

"One Of's" (inside)—important in growth and in planning the need for human assets—whereas senior staff may be capable of wearing several hats, further down in the organization the accounts payable clerk or the shipping and receiving clerk are just "one of," and if he or she gets sick or quits, it could cause havoc with the overall performance.

"One Of's" (outside)—as a company grows, the personal relationships with customers may not work if there is a hidden person, "One Of," who is part of the decision loop you never knew even existed.

171

Outside Help—in the form of outsourcing and off shoring; this has become more visible in recent years. One good philosophy is to outsource everything you can but never your core competency.

Plans—are born to be changed and quite often the preparation of a plan is more valuable than the plan itself.

Planning—should not be a boring exercise as many see it, but should be treated as a competitive exercise. Define it, make it, and track it along the way.

Priorities—are what drive a company, should be reviewed constantly, and reordered as necessary to provide the follow up path for making the plans a success.

Ratios—one use of the balance sheet depending on your view of the company. There are many useful ones. A quick ratio, which is cash and accounts receivable divided by accounts payable, is a condition of the near term cash viability. It better be greater than 1.0. A ratio of the total debt to the net worth can provide an overview of the company's health and the ability to borrow money.

Robust Growth—is synonymous with both compromises and changes, and requires the culture to live within this environment.

Scalability—the practicality of growing at rates with a balanced organization and affordability. Beware the spreadsheet wherein a nanosecond a new table can be created with little regard for human resources needed to support the financial numbers—it is easy to create tables showing the rate of revenue growth without the cost and resources tracking at the same rate, but it requires strategic thinking to have a balance between revenue and resource growth.

Strategic Goals and Strategy—are developed to meet the objective of the company and should not be mistaken for tactical goals, the tasks needed to get there.

"They"—is the invisible force that is needed to approve new and risky change, and it is interesting in that it takes a while for many managers in an autonomous situation to realize "they" is sitting there and they can change and approve whatever is needed.

Vision/Mission—Vision has many definitions, but I see it as the dream for the company, where as the mission is the basis for defining the vision as a business and providing the foundation for a business plan. Example: Vision—To be the best, most profitable manufacturer of bathroom fixtures and to be recognized in bathrooms around the world as the "King of the Crapper." Example: Mission—To provide premium innovative bathroom fixtures, utilizing a new technology for flushing, to the leading construction companies in the international market.

"What Ifs"—must be addressed if plans and agreements normally geared to success are blind to problems that might occur—the "What If's" anticipated are what to do if problems do occur.

Working Capital—by definition it is current assets (including A/R and inventory) minus current liabilities (includes debt to vendors and near term bank payments). It is obtained from the balance sheet, and there should be sufficient current assets on hand to cover the current liabilities, or there is a problem that needs to be addressed. A company's working capital may occasionally be undesirable, but if it is never above zero, the company will never reach its full potential.

Working Capital

There are some management terms, like ROI (return on investment) that many general managers and presidents do not totally understand. However, they would never admit this to their peers or bosses for fear of sounding dumb or inadequate, so they go along pretending they understand when they really don't.

Another such term is working capital and its derivatives, current ratio and liquidity. Everyone from banks to investors seems to be talking about working capital, because a healthy working capital can keep a company from going down the toilet. Unfortunately, if you don't understand what working capital is, it doesn't help you very much.

Usually working capital is discussed in negative terms, such as "Your working capital isn't high enough," "Your working capital should be above $1,500,000," "The loan is in default because the working capital covenant has been violated," or "The Company failed because they didn't have enough working capital." Don't these sound life-threatening?

Companies do run successfully and overcome the handicap of not understanding these terms by using common sense. However, once these ideas are made clear, the businessman has a much better appreciation of the company's situation, and he can better manage the company's working capital needs.

In effect, many companies are driven by working capital needs, even when they don't realize it, particularly if the company is managed from a cash perspective. Also, to successfully grow a business, you must maintain a healthy working capital.

Definitions

There are probably ten ratios associated with every line item on a balance sheet, but working capital is not a ratio, it is a real dollar figure. By definition, working capital is the current assets minus the current liabilities. It is a measure of how well the company is able to pay for the current liabilities using only the current assets. It is also a measure of the net amount of cash tied up in the invoices to customers (accounts receivable), the inventories in process, offset by the payments due to others.

After covering current liabilities, mostly made up of what is owed the trade, any current assets left over, after completion and converted to payments by the company's customers, are available to cover other operating expenses such as building maintenance, payroll, supplies, and capital equipment. If the working capital is marginal or low, then expenses other than those absolutely necessary must be delayed. These could include advertising and promotion, expanding sales overseas, new product development, regulatory qualification of products, and personnel expansion.

A company with low working capital operates hand-to-mouth, hoping that the current assets, especially inventory and accounts receivable, can be turned into cash quickly to cover accounts payable and other expenses. Lots of working capital alone isn't necessarily good if the inventory portion is overloaded and converts to revenue slowly. If so, planned expenditures have to be depressed, waiting for accounts receivable to be collected. Later you will see how to calculate the optimum working capital level for your sales level.

The ratio associated with working capital is called the current ratio, defined as total current assets divided by total current liabilities. Often managers and banks feel comfortable with a current ratio of two to one or more.

Since inventory cannot be transformed into cash immediately, there is a better measure of a company's liquidity, the quick ratio. This is defined as cash plus accounts receivable divided by current liabilities. Since many companies (particularly growth companies) operate with little cash, this ratio often boils down to accounts receivable divided by accounts payable.

Managers and banks will usually feel comfortable with a quick ratio of 1:1. However, a one to one ratio may be marginal, especially if accounts receivable take longer to collect than your suppliers will wait to be paid. The resulting cash flow problems can limit your business's growth. Also, ratios near 1.0 or lower can be devastating to your business, as the liquid cash will hardly pay the trade, let alone the other operating expenses.

In looking at a company's balance sheet, there are other factors that add into working capital, but inventory, accounts receivable, and accounts payable are the ones that dominate a growing company. The others have been left out for simplicity. For some companies, leaving debt and cash out of the working capital equations may be an oversimplification. Current liabilities do include near-term debt commitments, and a struggling company can have significant debt-service liabilities. Also, a company in good shape can have a significant amount of cash that should be added into the current assets.

Keep in mind that inventory, accounts receivable, and accounts payable get muddied up by the accountants with reserves and accruals, and a manager can go crazy trying to understand the liquidity condition of a company after the accountants get through with the figures.

A company that operates with little or no working capital can go on indefinitely, but it has no purpose other than perhaps to meet payroll. All a company's dreams and potential dissipate if it can't build up enough working capital to grow. Also, one of the most common reasons businesses fail is that they run out of cash. Planning and keeping a close watch on working capital levels can prevent overspending or premature spending on material, supplies, or payroll, and leave cash for other working capital items such as funding increased accounts receivable and building inventory. Without the capital to cover these increases, the company cannot grow.

Relating Working Capital to Sales Levels

Example 1:

In this example we are looking at a healthy manufacturing organization.

Assume that the GM (Gross Margin), defined as Price of Goods Sold less the cost of Goods Sold per month (COGS) is 50%, or 0.5 of the Price. The accounts receivable averages 60 days of sales, or 4 times the cost of goods sold. The inventory turns 4 times a year, or 3 times the COGS. Accounts payable totals 45 days of direct costs, or 1.5 times the monthly COGS. (There are certainly other things that are part of accounts payable, but the COGS is by far the majority.) Cash is equal to zero.

By definition, the working capital (WC) equals current assets minus current liabilities. Therefore, we have the following calculation:

WC = Current Assets – Current Liabilities

WC = (Accounts Receivable + Inventory) – Accounts Payable

WC = (4 COGS + 3 COGS) – 1.5 COGS

WC = 7 COGS – 1.5 COGS = 5.5 COGS

Sales is twice the COGS, so WC = 2.75 × the monthly sales dollars. The 2.75 is calculated as follows: 5.5 – ½(5.5).

Current Ratio = Current Assets / Current Liabilities

CR = 7 COGS / 1.5 COGS = 4.67

Example 2:

In this example we are looking at a company with a lower sales margin. If the GM is 20%, or 0.2, then the sales are 1.25 times the COGS. Therefore the A/R average of 60 days would only equal 2.5 times the COGS. The A/P and inventory figures would not change. Note how the results change.

WC = (A/R + Inventory) – A/P

WC = (2.5 COGS + 3 COGS) – 1.5 COGS

WC = 5.5 COGS – 1.5 COGS = 4 COGS

Sales is 1.25 times the COGS, so WC = 0.8 x the monthly sales dollars. The 0.8 is calculated as follows: 4 – (4/1.25).

Current Ratio = 5.5 COGS / 1.5 COGS = 3.66

Although the current ratio is still high at 3.66, the working capital drops to 0.8 which is less than 30% of its value in example 1, which says there is far less capital to work with than in example 1. This, in turn, means that there is less capital available to spend on needs other than trade payables.

In order to grow, a company needs enough working capital to support the increase in inventory and accounts receivable. The calculations below show the difference in the major elements of inventory, accounts receivable, and accounts payable when the company's sales grow 100% in one year. The growth in accounts receivable and inventory can be treated as cash investments. Increases in accounts payable amount to a loan from suppliers, and they will offset some of the cash needs for increases in inventory and accounts receivable.

Example 3:

Assume that at the end of year one, the sales are $1 million per month. Also assume that at the end of year two, the plan is to increase to $2 million per month.

The gross margin is 40% for both years. The profit is $300,000 in year one and would be $900,000 in year two, and will include an additional loan to cover the Account Receivables. The accounts receivable average 75 days, or 2.5 months of sales. Inventory turns are 3 per year, or 4 months of COGS. The accounts payable average 45 days of direct costs, or 1.5 months of COGS.

Relating all the accounts to sales yields the following:

COGS = 0.6 x sales

For sales of $1,000,000 per month, A/R = $2,500,000.

Inventory = 4 x COGS = 2.4 x sales = $2,400,000

Accounts Payable = 1.5 x COGS = 0.9 x sales = $900,000

For sales of $2,000,000 per month it is assumed A/R, inventory, and A/P will double.

Accounts Receivable = $5,000,000

Inventory = $4,800,000

Accounts Payable = $1,800,000

Putting the major elements of working capital in the balance sheet at year end will show the following:

Balance Sheet	Year One	Year Two
Accounts Receivable	$2,500,000	$5,000,000
Inventory	$2,400,000	$4,800,000
Accounts Payable	$900,000	$1,800,000
Working Capital	$4,000,000	$8,000,000

To fund the growth in accounts receivable and inventory would require an increase in working capital of $4,000,000. Some of this needed capital can be made up in profit ($900,000), but there would be a cash shortfall. This cash shortfall can be shortened if the bank will lend at the same conditions as they have for the A/R in year one. Assuming this to be $2,000,000 from the bank, the net cash shortfall will be $1,100,000. Therefore, in order to fund the growth, the company needs to obtain $1,100,000 in cash from investors, or sell off assets. If not possible, the company will not have the funds needed to cover the increase in working capital and cannot go ahead with planned growth. As a result, new investors must be brought into the company, so you will have to sacrifice equity to fund the growth. Of course spectacular profit (like 22% after tax, which seldom happens) could in theory fund the growth, but even then, the timing of orders, shipments, and collections would have to be perfect.

A company's management must focus on working capital both to make sure enough cash is available for growth and to make sure the company doesn't run out of cash. This important idea is one you need to understand clearly in order to manage your company well.

Section 3

Advisors/Consultants

From the first day of a startup, change occurs. With new changes in customers, sales, employees, and the environment (e.g., new regulations), the company is bigger on a daily basis.

Advisors come in many forms, including mentors, advisory boards, a board of directors and even paid consultants, the latter of which can be a necessary evil when cash is tight. However, if used correctly, they can also be a big addition to the company's growth and success.

The assistance from these advisors can include:

- Bringing new expertise to the various functions, including marketing and finance.
- Being a sounding-board for top management.
- Helping with new products and technology expertise.
- Filling temporary voids in the management team.
- Bringing new contacts in the marketplace.

The most difficult decision to make when employing a consultant is when top management believes they can do the necessary task(s) better. They may be right, but usually in high-growth situations, everyone is overstressed and no one really has the time to take on the task(s) at hand. *(See the chapter "Advisory Boards—The CEO's Secret Weapon.")*

Bank As Partners?

In preparation for a bank loan consider the following:

A bank *must* feel comfortable and confident that the borrowing party will have the wherewithal to pay back the loan. Included in the following are tips to help create that level of comfort.

<u>Assumptions in the Business Plan—Especially in the Cash Flow Section:</u>

The assumptions are the foundation of any plan including business, budget, cash flow, forecasts, and pricing. It's important to continually review these assumptions. If the results are not meeting expectations, inform the bank and take corrective action(s).

<u>Backlog Definition:</u> While a backlog is defined as the orders in-house from your customers, the best discipline is to define an order with a customer purchase order number, a delivery schedule, and the specifications or agreements for the product or services requires for/to delivery.

<u>Letter of Intent (LOI):</u> Some companies include a letter of intent (LOI) in the backlog, which can prove to be dangerous as the legal commitment for the customer's order may not be firm enough. I have seen companies produce material for an LOI that is promised to cover X number of months, only to have the customer back down on their promise. It helps the planning to provide a regular backlog report to include the margin and aging of the orders in the backlog.

<u>Bank Loan Checks:</u> I believe loan officers can too easily turn down a loan application for fear of it failing and having to report the failure regularly to their peers. For example, I have seen loan officers turn down loans because of such reasons as, "The guy in the downtown office turned this loan down." Truth be told, I doubt that there is a downtown office.

For example, I had two business friends who started a bank. I asked them to force a lost business report (i.e., loans rejected) on the loan officers. The result was a revelation for the numerous loan requests they turned down, including those that made sense. The bank then improved their hit ratio and business.

<u>Bank Hit List:</u> If you want to continue borrowing money from a bank, there's a very good reason to avoid getting on any bank's hit list,

including those customers who continually have late/missed payments and missing covenants. Besides agreeing to make payments against a loan, there are various performance ratios taken from a balance sheet as well as those meeting the forecasts for revenue and profit. These covenants include working capital and various other ratios (e.g., current assets divided by current liabilities).

Banks and Guarantees: Banks will require at least two (2) guarantees for payments concerning the ability to pay the loan, especially for a small company. In most cases, a majority owner will have to agree to a personal guarantee.

Banks in First Place: As a company grows and uses other avenues for capital, it can expect banking agreements to keep the bank in the #1 position for getting their money out first. In fact, many people in business believe that banks are only ready to lend money when you don't really need it. (Note: Keep in mind that banks are not investors and, therefore, they will only take a limited risk with their loans for start-ups and small businesses).

Important to consider in a start-up:

- Banks are not equity investors and risk takers therefore are tough on giving loans out to people just with a dream.

- Do not assume in future projections to automatically count on a bank loan because the numbers look good.

- There are other factors besides revenue and profit in qualifying for a loan like covenants, which are more related to items in a Balance Sheet.

Benchmarking

Benchmarking is a tool that gathers information in order to be able to compare the analytics of companies in the same market or industry. Applicable elements can include operating margin, revenue, pricing, and even employee compensation and efficiency.

Information gathered before and after establishing a start-up can provide vital information to help with the business, marketing, and operation plans.

One of the best benchmarking references for a start-up is a role model. One example for a role model occurred in a small engineering design company, which I was running at the request of its founder, an engineer, who wanted growth to $25 million. Through myriad information, we found a public company at the $100 million revenue level. We scaled it down by 4 to assume it was more like a $25 million company in our market. It wasn't perfect, but it was useful by helping us to plan our activities for manpower, facilities, and much-needed cash. Although the company didn't make it to $25 million, the founder ultimately sold it for $8 million.

In another case, an electronics manufacturing company had at least 10 competitors. One goal was to see what their gross margin was, and how it might be affected by R&D or marketing expenses. Tracking the competition this way was one element to factor into the strategic planning that helped h the success of the company. The company's revenue was growing by 30% annually and ultimately went public.

I have been aware of startup companies using role models like Victoria's Secret and Red Bull. These startups, besides using data from them in planning, it helped strengthened their vision in believing it could be done again.

When getting started, if you want to challenge existing companies in your market by niches or leadership, you can go either way. If it is a niche you seek, challenge the leaders' weaknesses; if leadership is your choice, then challenge the leaders' strengths.

It's easier for an ongoing company—versus a start-up—to obtain market information but there are many ways available to both. Information on public companies is readily available. There are company press releases, investment banking companies' reports and government regulations on public companies to provide information to the public.

As the chairman of a public company compensation committee, I hired a consulting firm to gather information on companies approximating our size in the marketplace. On another occasion, when I was with a company having good relationships with a supplier vendor, we were easily able to get competitor information on other companies who used this same vendor.

On more than one occasion in my career, we used advertising for jobs to gather information from sales personnel in areas in which competitors had personnel.

A good place to get useful information is from networking. I made it part of my senior staff's goals to network in marketing and finance organizations. Useful information can even be gathered from a customer after losing a bid.

Like all data, it depends on what you do with it. I have had salespeople who claimed they were the only ones to get the competitive pricing from a purchasing agent working for the customer. It made you wonder about the validity. Then there are salesmen who don't listen. In an experience with a large customer, for example, I was making my annual visit with our regional sales manager to get some inside information about our customer's future requirements. My salesman went on talking about 15 minutes (while providing answers to his own questions), and when he paused, Mr. Customer said, "You're doing okay; why don't you just continue?" In other words, the visit was a waste of our time.

In the real world, people are benchmarking all the time and may not even know it. On the other hand, I have friends who use consumer reports before buying anything personal—from a garbage disposal to an automobile.

Use whatever information you can get wisely. Simply put, for startups you don't know what you don't know, so seek all of the help and information you can from advisors who've been there.

As a start-up grows, the challenges it faces may change; however, if the elements being benchmarked (to create milestones) are cleverly selected, the data can be useful along the way. To build a company, significant changes are constantly occurring in manpower requirements. It is important to factor in changes in the culture and industry. As an example, at one time, when manufacturing was prevalent, it was possible to use $150,000 per employer when related to revenue. Today a company using the Internet to sell its services, when related to revenue, that figure could now be over five times that number per employee.

There are numerous other avenues for a company to acquire market and competitive information. See the list following below.

- their customers;
- their vendors/suppliers;
- job applicant interviews;
- focus groups;
- roundtable groups;
- trade shows;
- trade journals;
- news releases;
- networking;
- the company's accounting and law firms;
- investment bankers;
- consultants from the board of directors;
- advisors;
- Dun & Bradstreet;
- Google; and
- Facebook

Breakeven Alert

In a start-up company, careful usage of ash is essential. The majority of start-ups that failed were not related to a bad value proposition but, rather, because the company ran out of cash.

Breakeven is the level of revenue that covers all operating costs that can get a start-up company to the point of survival.

A breakeven in profit would be helpful and quite essential when searching for new investors—therefore, the cash breakeven point is essential for the company's existence. Eventually, Law 1 (referring to cash: the goesinnas must exceed the goesouttas!) in the <u>Laws of Management Physics</u> must occur for success to prevail. *(See the chapter entitled "Breakeven—The threshold for Success.")*

Cash Flow

One serious void when planning a start-up is a lack of forecasting cash flow. In fact, the term even seems to be new to the company's inexperienced founders. I seldom have seen a cash flow forecast in a 12-15 slide investor presentation.

The use of the funds that will raised may be shown in basic categories, such as marketing, engineering, or G&A. What is required to run the company is a timeframe on how long the cash is expected to last. The biggest failure for new start-ups is poor cash management, ranging anywhere from poor utilization of available cash or just basically running out of it. For instance, I have seen many technically-driven product companies run out of cash before the market explodes—and they are left out.

A report should be made that shows line by line places where cash will come in from and line by line the items that will be cash out. Cash in examples are cash collected from customers and cash from investors. Cash out examples are payments for purchase of equipment, auto expenses and salaries. It is very important to project the ins and out on when they might occur in time

Oftentimes, when a cash flow projection is provided, it is based on the profit and loss forecast, which doesn't include the working capital or hard assets (e.g., equipment) that will be required. It is not wise to do an accurate multiyear cash flow forecast without a balance sheet, and it always surprises me how many people seem to shy away from preparing one. Even in my consulting activities, helping small business presidents, some did not have a balance sheet. Granted, small companies can be successful without one; however, having one in place is vital to the success of the company, if the company plans robust growth. Although almost all of my clients said they wanted to grow, actually very few, "Busted $10 million," a symbolic revenue target that won't happen without major culture changes and an understanding of cash flow.

My advice to start-ups is that planning cash needs requires an extensive understanding of the elements related to a balance sheet (e.g., like accounts receivable [AR] and accounts payable [AP]).

Find out what kind of payment terms are normal in the market planned, especially as those terms relate to the time customers take to pay for the product or service involved. Think of AR as a loan to the customer, because your payments to suppliers may be required to be paid for their services before the customer pays you. The payment terms from your suppliers must be known. If you need a physical product to be manufactured, you may have to pay for it up front (with no credit rating) long before your sales dollars are actually collected.

It helps to develop a cash cycle. This would be the time it takes to get cash in from the customer related to the time it takes to pay all the cash out to produce the product. For instance the company may have to pay suppliers in 30 days, but the customer negotiates the company to pay in 60 days. It happens. During the early stages of a company—before sales and revenue occur—it is necessary to be very prudent with the disbursement of available cash. The accuracy of the first sales forecast (in dollars) and timing are also extremely important for the company to move forward. As mentioned earlier, too many great concepts and products die because the company ran out of cash.

Due Diligence

Following is a short list of what to expect in a due diligence exercise. It's a given that the experienced investor will perform such an exercise before writing a check.

There will be a review of all data presented, including presentation materials, business plans, product detail, and background on all team members. This requires being on guard from the very beginning to back up any information given along the way. It is to be expected that significant emphasis will be put into digging deeply into all available marketing information, which—starting with revenue—is the basis for forecasting.

Since long-term agreements may not have surfaced during initial meetings, data requiring careful review will include those agreements and/or contracts with company personnel, vendors, and customers. In essence, an investor will be looking for bad deals that can influence the performance going forward.

A big hurdle to overcome in order to move forward will be the individual (s) selling the potential of the company.

I have sat in on many presentations by entrepreneurs when a legal problem got mentioned and several investors got up and left the meeting.

Deal points (Term Sheet): Outside help might be required to get into all the details of the deal, ranging in anything from a letter of intent to any/all default clauses that might be applicable. This will be the document that defined what each party will received like the ownership if the deal made. In fact, an agreement cannot be finalized until all of the due diligence information is reviewed. The objective here is to be certain that all the information gathered will not provide any new risks going forward.

Verification of information: Key to an investor is IP protection; cash in, as adequate; all forecasts are realistic; getting to know the staff and members of the board of directors; and, most importantly, the probability for the investment return and potential for the exit plan. At various times in my career, I have been involved with all aspects of the financial projections, pricing of products, evaluation of the competition, and product development programs. It often appears that investors are looking for a reason not to do the deal. I also believe many investors are looking to verify the information to minimize their risks – to create a feeling of comfort.

Thorough due diligence will examine, in great depth, every aspect of the company and contain information that may enable an investor to walk away from the deal, if necessary.

Elevator Speech

The elevator speech—and the efforts beyond for raising money—are the most important personal sales activities an entrepreneur can experience.

The cash phase starts with image. The pitch should show passion and confidence but, for sure, not arrogance.

I don't know how the term "elevator speech" got started, but I learned early in my marriage—when I was in an elevator with my wife—that she could learn more about a person's life in a minute than I could learn in a lifetime. After running out of family and friend contributions, the pitch for money ultimately needs to go to strangers.

The first step in developing an elevator speech is to be sure to include three vital points:

1. there is a market need;

2. you have a match; and

3. you have a plan to develop a new market or penetrate an existing one.

It doesn't matter if the [elevator] speeches are 30-seconds, 90-seconds, or longer in length—just remember that the above three points are mandatory—and that the longer the pitch-time allowed, the more details can then be added.

The objective of the speech is to create an interest in the audience—whether it be one individual or a group—to ensure that the relationships to write a check continue to exist. (**Note**: *The best word I can think of for an investor to believe in is comfort. Do everything you possibly can to ensure that you make an investor comfortable so that their hand isn't shaking when they sign that ever-important big check.*)

Financing Follies

It's a cliché that there are millions of dollars out there searching for a place to be invested and make more dollars. Certainly there are many worthy companies and individuals who need cash. Why are there so few actual transactions? Why are so many winning ideas lost for lack of funds?

This is the number one issue among start-up and small enterprises: "How do I get the cash I need?" Unfortunately, these potential borrowers often start out very naively, believing that once they announce their business opportunity to the world the investors will be standing in line for a piece of the action. They soon become hardened after several false starts and rejections, but they still have trouble learning that the money is not yours until the check is cashed and the funds are in the bank.

This naiveté is illustrated over and over again in business plans I am asked to review. For instance they assume that an accounts receivable loan will miraculously appear as soon as it is needed. Of course, very few A/R loans actually occur as planned.

Why is it that some companies find private investors (angels) who are virtual strangers and others can successfully do public offerings, even with poor performance, low sales, and negative profit, while solid, on-going businesses with good financial performance can't even get a line of credit?

In my opinion, the key difference is the "storyteller", the person leading the company's fund-raising efforts. There are some people out there who can get lenders to commit just by announcing that they are thinking about starting a business. While some of it is trust earned by past successes, more often it is the storyteller's personality and charisma that creates the investor interest. Most of all, though, it is storyteller who knows who he's asking and how to handle them. I lost a client once because I suggested to the CEO that his Marketing Manager make the presentation to an investor group as a better choice.

In this chapter I present my perceptions of debtors and investors, which I hope will help you approach the task of raising capital more knowledgeably.

Investors – An Overview

To begin with, the famous complaint, "Banks will only lend you money when you **don't** need it," is often true. Its corollary is, "Plan ahead, and borrow money when you <u>don't</u> need it."

Another saying, "Investors want to own you," is also not far off the mark. There is a reason why venture capitalists are often called "vulture capitalists." If you accept this, and approach the fund-raising process with a healthy dose of cynicism, it will help you deal with the heavy hitters more effectively.

Before you commit yourself, you must know how lenders and investors think.

Friends and Relatives: The easiest place to borrow small amounts is from friends and relatives, but is it worth the aggravation? They will haunt you to death with questions like, "How is our money doing?" or "When can I plan to use the money for Joey's college tuition?" Many a friendship has ended over borrowed funds.

Angels: These are usually sophisticated investors willing to risk $50,000 to $250,000 on a stranger with a dream. Unfortunately, angels will most likely deal with the CEO/President as if they are dealing with a child.

Venture Capitalists: Venture capitalists are well-organized and have an organization that will sit on you. Their goal is to dominate a situation, and they will try to structure the deal so that they either have a majority ownership going in or will eventually get it.

Banks: Banks always want a sure thing, and they'd take your first born as collateral if you let them. They will structure the deal so that you've already defaulted on at least one part of the agreement before you even get out the door.

Senior Debt Lenders and Asset Lenders: They'll start by saying, "We're really not in the equity business," but somehow they manage to work stock warrants into the deal while you aren't looking. Be careful, because if you stumble, you will be amazed at how much ownership they end up with.

On the positive side, these investors are the people who write the checks. If you don't get them involved, your dream will evaporate and die. Table 1 lists many sources of funds. The trick is to match the source to your needs, and then, be a good storyteller.

Investors	Loans	Government
Relatives and Friends	Relatives and Friends	Small Business
"Angels"	Banks	Administration (SBA)
Venture Capitalists	Saving and Loans	Small Business
Foreign Investors Small	Small Business Admin-	Innovative Research
Business Investment	istration	Grants (SBIRs)
Corporations (SBICs)	Credit Cards	Government
Limited Partnerships	Mortgage Companies	Agency Development
SCOR (Private Place-	Assets	Contracts
ment)	Stocks and Bonds	State of California
Public Stock Sale	Life Insurance	Department of Commerce
Employee Stock Option	Equipment Leases	Guaranteed Letters of
Plans (ESOP)	Credit Unions	Credit for Exporters
Strategic Partners	Federal Housing	VA (Veteran's
Crowd Funding*	Administration	Administration)
Big Company Venture		California Industrial
Groups		Development Bonds
Kickstarter*		

Personal	Other
Cash	Customer Up-Front Money
Sell Bonds	Customer Progress Payments
Sell Stocks	Vendor Credit
Mortgaging on the House	
Selling life Insurance	

Notes:

1. SBIR grants are funds awarded by government agencies for special development projects. By law the agencies have to invest a portion of their budget in these programs. This can be a good source of funds for a developing company. One southern California company has been able to obtain twelve such awards.

2. Asset lenders require significant assets as collateral, making it difficult to get a loan for many service companies that will not qualify.

3. Crowd Funding—the government had changed the laws in allowing small companies in raising money including on the Internet.

4. Kickstarter is a company that provides a network of people willing to invest funds with no equity in return. The start-up may offer product in exchange when available of gifts. It resembles a

presale.

Preparing to Meet Borrowers

The first step in borrowing money is to firmly believe that you can deliver a good return on the investment and to be able to articulate both your need and your confidence that you can deliver. Investors have to be picky about who they write checks to, and they look far beyond the financial numbers in their evaluation of you and your company. Keep in mind that they are comparing you to all the many opportunities they have available, and you are competing against these invisible foes.

Investors will not make a commitment unless they are totally comfortable, and there are many things that can make investors nervous. However, many of these things can be prevented with correct preparation. The following is a list of the most common reasons why investors will turn down opportunities:

1. There is no business plan.
2. There is no vision.
3. The idea is a dream and not a realistic basis for a business.
4. There are no superstars on the management team.
5. The revenue projections are not supported by the market size.
6. They are not convinced the company can penetrate the market.
7. There are not proprietary advantages in the business as planned.
8. The plan is far too ambitious and therefore lacks credibility.
9. Their plans for borrowing from banks are naive.
10. There isn't an acceptable payout for the investor.
11. There is no exit plan for the investor.
12. The plan lacks common sense.
13. The management team doesn't have making money as a top priority.
14. And most important a lack of passion not displayed by the team.

Minority Investors

It generally starts with the entrepreneur, who says, "How about putting five or ten thousand into a new company I am forming?" This may fly with relatives and friends as a leap of faith.

Every investor expects to get a return, no matter how high the risk or the nature of the investment. When an investor chooses to put equity money into a privately-held company, he is willing to forego interest on his money, such as he could get from other types of investments available to him. Usually he hopes the company will succeed and go public, making the return on his investment 500% or more.

However, with little say in the direction of the company, the investor can only hope that something will happen to give him a pay-off on his investment. If the company doesn't go public, perhaps it will be bought by a public company, again giving him a value on his equity. Or, there is always the possibility of selling his stock, but it is very difficult to establish the value of privately held stock, and therefore very difficult to find a buyer.

There are two other methods by which the minority investor can realize a return. One, he might obtain a guaranteed buy-back from the company, but buy-back agreements are usually only offered to employees, not minority investors. Two, he may obtain an agreement that guarantees dividends issued periodically. Generally, though, the minority investor has little expectation of a dividend. Perhaps more favorable is a convertible note. This will be a loan that allows converting to stock at some agreed to price. The investors can collect interest on the note and later if the stock value climbs the investors can convert the loan to stock. It is normal as financing rounds are done the last one in will probably have investors expecting or demanding more in commitments.

Often, everything starts well, with the normal enthusiasm of a new company. Perhaps management hints that they'll go public as the company grows. Then time goes by, and the investor sees good things happening with revenue, profit growth, increased management salaries, bonuses, and profit sharing plans. Yet, despite all these encouraging signs, the minority shareholder is still stuck without a reasonable way to convert his investment into rewards. (*See the chapter on "Ownership in Section 3."*)

After watching this for several years, the investor's frustration grows, and sometimes, anger and resentment develop. After all, weren't these the "good guys," who believed in the company enough to make an investment without any guarantee of rewards?

You see, this is where the problem really began—at the beginning.

When more sophisticated investors make minority investments, they obtain agreements with pages of covenants that the company agrees to meet. And many times, later investors have all kinds of advantages over the original outside minority investors. The later investments may even be structured in the form of a loan with interest payments (or dividends) and the option to convert to equity. It is normal as financing rounds are done the last one in will probably have investors expecting or demanding more in commitments. One expectation is for the investors to get preferred stock rather than common stock. This will put them ahead of common shareholders when any payback is distributed.

Why, then, don't the earlier minority investors get similar treatment? The original investor has a higher risk than those going in later. First of all, the individual minority investors usually don't ask for definitions, commitments, or covenants on their investments. Secondly, the new start-ups don't yet understand what lies ahead in their dealings with sophisticated, professional investors. Meanwhile, the CEO is getting his salary, bonuses, medical, profit sharing, car allowance, etc. The sophisticated investors no doubt have a lot more experience than the first time investors and use that experience to get the most for their investments.

How can the individual minority shareholders be taken care of fairly? Assuming that the company believes that

    A. The risk is high, and taken in good faith, and

    B. Minority shareholders should see a pay-off

Then the following are some ways to see that the minority shareholder can be treated fairly. First off hire a lawyer who can cover the following:

1. Make sure from the start that the company's plans for paying out (for example, merger, going public, dividends, etc.) are clear.

2. Have a definition of management and employee rewards with caps that trigger dividends which must be paid before the caps may be exceeded.

3. Establish a dividend program when it would be appropriate.

4. Develop a stock buy-out plan to establish the value of a stock at a future time.

5. Treat the investment as a loan that pays interest while maintaining the investor's right to convert to stock.

It is important to recognize that whatever approach is used, it must be compatible with the company goals.

Ultimately, these goals MUST be well understood by both parties up front. In the final analysis, they need to ensure that there is a defined point in time, after the company has gotten established and seen some success, at which the minority shareholders will see a return on their investment.

Banks

The first thing you need to understand about dealing with banks is that they are not investors, and they want to deal in the short term not the long term. They recommend you use other sources such as insurance companies for long term loans. Too often borrowers get frustrated and disappointed when the bank is not caught up in their dream. The bank makes money on the loan money; they do not speculate on the future. Generally, they will not lend funds for the borrower to make acquisitions or develop product for futures. They want evidence that the borrower can make payments the day the loan is given. They will fund needs for working capital, including inventory and accounts receivables, and they want proof of collateral now.

In dealing with banks, approach them with the following in mind:

1. Banks will not usually tell you why you have been rejected. Today, they can hide behind "the regulators," using them as the bad guy, the excuse for turning down a loan. They will also use the lame excuse, "I tried hard for you, but the guy downtown shot the loan down." Someday I would like to meet that invisible guy downtown.

2. I believe loan officers would take a little more risk if bank management put more emphasis on their need not to lose business. It is too easy for a loan officer to reject a loan rather than stand up in front of his peers weekly to report on a loan that made him nervous going in. If rejected loans were analyzed more carefully, more risk might be taken, with greater rewards for all concerned.

3. It can help to look for banks that allow loan approval by an individual rather than by committee. With a committee you are relying on your loan officer to make the pitch to his committee, and this is scary. In that situation, it pays to make sure the loan officer (interface to the loan committee) is knowledgeable about your business and convinced you are successful. The more informed the bank is, the greater your chances of getting the loan.

4. It is worth the effort to present your business to the bank officials you are dealing with, and to try to get above the loan officer.

5. The financial cash flow projection must include a line specifically for payments to the bank. You should point out to them what actions and alternatives you plan if in fact the business doesn't go quite as you planned. An impressive report will show what can be adjusted, if necessary, in order to ensure that the bank gets theirs.

When you make the presentation asking for a loan, make sure you do the following:

1. Include a business analysis. Make sure your bank contact understands both your request and the nature of your business. Make sure they feel secure about what they know.

2. Make sure the bank feels comfortable with your management team. Get them to meet as many people as possible, and convince them that the company is strong enough to withstand the turmoil of key management staff leaving the company.

3. Make sure the bank feels sure that the company will survive a downturn. Show them a disaster plan under which the company could withstand a 20% drop in sales and still be able to make payments.

4. Make them believe that the company has liquidity, good performance, and adequate cash flow.

5. In any presentation to the bank, make sure there is always a line showing when and how the bank gets their money.

6. Always be prepared to offer collateral.

Remember, the bank will only lend you money if they believe you can pay back the loan on time.

Banks are trained to require two sources of repayment, cash flow from the business and collateral. The primary source, cash flow for short term loans and earnings for long term loans, needs to be supplemented by some form of collateral such as accounts receivable, inventory, or a mortgage. Banks are the happiest when receivables alone can cover the loan. Even when the loan is covered by receivables, the bank will also have first claim on all the assets. Then, if something goes wrong with the original plan, the banker will always have something to fall back on.

Now, here is where the banks become hypocritical for start-ups and small companies because after saying they will only need two sources repayment, cash flow and collateral, they say, "Oh, by the way, we would like a personal guarantee from the majority owner." This guarantee is almost universally required of small companies, so this talk about only needing two sources of repayment is bunk.

The banks say that the personal guarantee ensures that the borrower is committed psychologically to the business's success. Banks don't expect a great deal of security from the personal signature, and say that they may not even go after the individual. What they want is that individual's total support and dedication to making the business successful. The loan officers are reluctant to risk the bank's money if the borrower is reluctant to risk his or her own. In other words: no guarantee, no loan.

Keep in mind that the bank is always comparing the risks to the rewards. Since they work on a small return on assets (ROA), they have to be right 99% of the time. They need several good loans to make up for one bad one. Therefore, they also need to be convinced that you are in command of your business and will respond appropriately to any downturn. They also do not generally lend in high leverage situations, and might use 3 to 1 as the upper limit (the ratio of all liabilities to the tangible net worth). Anything above this ratio will probably scare them off. Banks are limited in the risks they can take from both a business and a regulatory viewpoint.

Since banks like NO surprises, keep them informed, especially when you are having trouble with the business or the loan. Banks can also give far more help than just credit. Use their services in other financial matters. For instance, if you plan to go to international markets, seek the advice of your banker.

It is important that you build a good relationship with your bank, and there are several ways to create and maintain this relationship:

1. Communicate with them in a timely manner, even when you have bad news.

2. Stay off the "bad" lists, like the overdrawn account list, the late payer list, and the personal exception report.

3. Keep the bank informed of trends in your industry and your goals for the company.

4. PAY THEM ON TIME!

Today, most banks will only lend money when (1) the company is profitable, (2) the debt to net worth ratio meets their criteria, and (3) the borrower is willing to guarantee the loan. It's true: Banks will only lend you money when you don't need it. Therefore, prepare ahead of time by developing a good relationship with your bank and demonstrating your commitment to repaying them.

Finance Companies

Finance companies are not the boogeymen that most borrowers think they are. They do generally ask for higher interest rates than banks, but they do not expect the borrower to guarantee the loans. Many companies that would buy a receivable from the company at a discount and then shoulder the responsibility of collection have now moved in to fill the void created by banks, and are offering asset lending and even bank lines.

Finance companies are interested in loaning money against the company's receivables, and they will even buy receivables from a company. The performance and stability of the company are important, but they are not nearly as important as with banks. The only collateral the finance company will require is the receivable, and normally, no one has to sign a personal guarantee. Finance companies like to loan money to a company if it will help that company's profitability.

Naturally, just as banks do, finance companies will evaluate the risk, considering the customer and the nature of the receivable. They will only accept quality receivables, and they may declare several types of receivables ineligible: international receivables, overly aged receivables, and receivables that include a high percentage of large customers.

The most important reason to consider finance companies is that they will be there when banks will not give you a loan. Their rates are higher, but with proper cash management and utilization of early cash availability, this impact can be minimized. In fact, the money is made available much sooner than even the best-paying customers that are given discounts (sometimes in a few days!). Companies that give customers a 2% discount for a 10-day return are paying at a much higher rate than they would with a finance company. And how many times does a customer unfairly take an early payment discount without paying in the agreed-upon time frame? I have heard small company presidents say, "I will never pay 2% per month a loan" only to never have the money to grow and meet their expectation without the money.

The most important thing in deciding between a bank and a finance company is to first truly understand your financing needs and to factor the cost of this financing into the price of the product. Cost of money should not be treated as a penalty for being in business; rather, it is a cost of doing business.

Sophisticated Investors
Raising Money the Hard Way

When it comes to investors, you must convince them that your vision is worth pursuing together. One may approach investors with arrogance and expect everyone to jump at the chance to buy in, but keep in mind that sophisticated investors are quite intelligent and knowledgeable. Most importantly, they have several similar experiences under their belts, and your plan will be compared to many others. You must grab the reader quickly, generate excitement over the opportunity, and clearly show potential investors how they are going to make money.

There are three things investors look for before exploring an opportunity: (1) a sensational idea, (2) a great team, and (3) a demonstrated market and the ability to penetrate it. If all three of these are present in a business plan, the investor is minimizing their risk and they will probably make the commitment. While more and more emphasis is being put on having the great team, the marketing plan must still meet some basic requirements. It must identify the market need, it must show that the product will meet that need, and it must define the plan and show the ability to penetrate the market. Unfortunately (or perhaps fortunately!) it isn't always possible to find all three ingredients, so investors must assess the risk of each opportunity before making a decision.

The Idea

The idea can take many forms, from a concept to a product ready to sell, but clearly it is the idea that hooks the investor, encouraging him to take the time to evaluate the complete plan.

Investors are always looking for that super product that has get-rich potential. The investor would also like to see a proprietary product or process to ensure that competitive edge. Of course, if the market is already developing and the company's product fits the need, it will attract even more attention. On the other hand, if you must educate the customer in order for them to buy the product, it is going to be low on the list. Also low on the priority list, are products that the customer can just as easily do without.

The investor loves to play in emerging markets that have a several hundred million dollar potential, because this will provide a much higher return on their investment. No matter how solid, plans that will not produce the expected return will be rejected. For example, let's say an investor is asked to put $1 million into a company for a 25% equity stake. The company valuation would have to be $20 million for the investors to get the 25% stake to be worth $5 million. If the revenue over 5 years is expected to reach $17 million, and the estimated company valuation will be $12 million in 5 years the investors will pass on this situation as the projection will hardly match the investors desire to get 5 times his investment in five years, especially with only 25% ownership.

Distributing plans cold to a group of investors seldom succeeds. Investors receive hundreds of plans to review, and they are far more likely to review the plans from the company that was referred by a credible source. Just like sending out resumes to look for a job, it makes sense to network, gaining access to the investors through others. Referrals can help a lot in getting an audience of investors or a business plan reviewed. I worked for a Venture Capital company and weekly, my task was to go through a stack of plans to see if worth passing to the next step. One rule was if the plan came with no cover letter or note from a friend or familiar contact recommending a review, I did not go past the cover. Also, even when the plan is looked at, the odds are small that it will be pursued. That is why the presentation must make such an immediate impact. The first paragraph of the executive letter must catch the fancy of the reader, or they will not even finish the executive letter. You must say everything in the first section, above all, how much money you're going to make for the investor.

If the plan catches the investor's interest, it will generally be turned over to an analyst for further review and analysis. When the process gets to a face-to-face meeting the storyteller must shine. Then, as before, your first priority will be to convince the investor that you know where you're going and that when you get there, everybody involved will make a killing.

The Team

Investors see many plans. If you realize that they have probably seen several for a product or market similar to yours, you will see why a team that believes in the vision becomes so important. If more people share the same vision, the investor will feel more comfortable placing funds at the team's disposal. Once the investor believes there is a market and that the product can penetrate that market, the team may become the deciding factor.

The make-up of the team is important. Venture capitalists like to go with proven winners. If the industry icon just mentioned that he is thinking of starting a venture, the investors will line up for him. Filling in the team with known people strengthens the team's fund-raising potential. The venture capitalists may even prefer a failed entrepreneur over a novice, because they will assume they will assume that the failed person will have learned from their experience. It is obvious investors will be more comfortable with a team working together in a garage with no income than a one man arrogant closed minded entrepreneur. It is important to have a committed set of advisors like an Advisory Board. This will give investors comfort if you have advisors who know the technology or market from the start of the company or growth project.

Top priority will be given to teams with strong knowledge of the market, as investors feel that other voids in the team's composition can be filled more easily. Therefore, the investor is more concerned with those who need to know how the product will be marketed and sold.

Technical entrepreneurs can let their egos get in the way, because they are convinced they understand the product, and because of this, they think it is a great idea for them to spearhead the market. This might be workable for initial sales, but with distribution channels becoming more complex, you MUST have a strong marketing team both to win the investor's trust and to succeed in the market.

Finally, many investors no longer accept that the person who conceived the idea and put the plan and team together will be president forever, insisting on change if the initial president doesn't cut it. Specialists alone will not make a company fly, and the team must have signs of superstars with broader skills among their number.

The Market

Investors want to feel comfortable, and one of the best ways you can help the investor feel comfortable is to clearly prove that not only does the market exist, but that the team you have assembled can penetrate that market. Saying that you can surely do 0.01% of a four billion dollar market is not good enough. What you must do is convince the investor that you can penetrate that market: numbers alone are not sufficient. The novice may not understand how important marketing is mostly perception so someone ready to talk about the market without talking face to face with potential customers will not impress most investors.

Obviously, the larger the market, the more likely you are to succeed, but large markets alone are only a start. For example, let's say your computer hardware market estimate starts at $3 billion. However, half the market is captive to major users, reducing the market size to $1.5 billion. Sixty percent of this is government users not serviced, reducing the market to $600 million. Half of this figure is users who will not be serviced by your company, reducing the market to $300 million. Finally, 50% of those left could find software that meets their needs, reducing the available hardware market to only $150 million. For the company to penetrate this market and grow to $75 million, they would have to capture 50% of the available market. Unfortunately, the competition is not likely to roll over and play dead, and the investors know this.

Breaking down the market in more detail and analyzing the product and sales channels will enhance your plan's credibility. Better yet, get a reputable marketing organization to provide input. After getting an estimate of market size, back it up with more information, such as the user's need for the product, the buying habits of the market, competition, and alternatives to the product, and service and maintenance patterns. Many plans fall short because they don't take the need to support and service the product into account. This is particularly true when the customer base includes users.

Probably most important is to have an organization and strategy to do the actual selling. Many times, great ideas fail because the company can't sell them. It's easier to develop products the market needs than to market the product after it has been developed or educate the market about its need. Today's computer and telecommunications markets are overwhelmed with sales channels. How simple it was when you only had two to worry about, the OEM and the user. Selecting the correct channel requires far more analysis and expertise than ever before. The Internet, web pages and social networks provide numerous channels to use like Facebook and blogs. It helps to have access to the talent to optimize the utilization of these channels.

It's difficult for an inexperienced manager to project just how long it will take to penetrate the market or to predict all of the hurdles that lie ahead. Teaming with an experienced investment group can help provide this insight. The normal tendency is to be overly optimistic about how fast the product will be accepted and about early sales levels. Unfortunately, a company will still fail if they get there too soon and can't hang on long enough. Many engineering companies with a great idea and product failed by running out of money and sadly were not their when the market exploded for the technology and similar products. I worked with a company involved with voice recognition 20 years before its market time.

Timing mistakes in sales can often be tolerated by the investor if you have clearly demonstrated that there is a market and the product match is evident. Continually adding direct input from customers (that the investor can verify) as well as top-down analysis is essential. Often, lists of customers who need your product and are buying have a lot more impact than the numbers alone. There is no better way to excite an investor about your potential market penetration than with letters from customers who say they need or are waiting for your product.

On the other hand, investors will shy away from products that have long gestation periods. There are several things that will increase the time required for market penetration: (1) a new market, (2) a product that requires educating the customer, (3) customer alternatives to your product (or even worse, alternatives to your product that require the customer to do nothing and that cost nothing). A turn off for investors is when the new start-up or growth project is dedicated to improving worldly problems. It goes like this, "If you aren't interested in making money, how can I make money?"

The timing of market acceptance is a vital part of the investor's decision and comfort level, so significant time, effort, and analysis should be put into this issue.

Tips

Start all plans from one month after the capital is received. Time has a way of slipping by, and if you put the plan on a calendar and then don't meet your own deadlines, investors will wonder why you can't perform up to your own expectations.

Investors do not always have to have majority ownership, and depending on how good the plan is, may put $1 million or more into a company for a minority position. How much ownership the investor demands will depend largely on the risk/reward ratio.

Entrepreneurs are often reluctant to yield ownership to the investor because they fear that they will lose control and doom the plan to failure. Not only is this usually incorrect, it is also self-defeating. Control can lie in the hands of the key players even if they only own a small percent of the company. It is far better to own a small percentage of a very successful, highly valued company than to own 100% of a failed company.

Investors want to make five times their investment in five years, and they won't go in unless the plan has a chance. However, keep in mind that if they get their return, a whole lot of employees will also be getting wealthy.

You have to believe in your own plan before you can expect strangers to believe in it and invest the money at their disposal. This belief can be developed by a well-conceived plan that clearly communicates the idea, the team, the market that needs the product, and how to penetrate that market in a timely fashion. Keep in mind everything will take longer than you think.

Among all the rejections, there are billions of new dollars being invested yearly, so keep trying!

Forecasting Need Not Be Rocket Science

The initial step in any business plan is forecasting, yet it is one of the toughest things to accomplish, especially in a start-up, because the start-up is faced with a new product, a new market, and a new experience—so where to start? Always start with the assumptions.

The more extensive the market research performed at the beginning to validate the product the better, along with customers' input can provide a higher probability for the forecast to actually take place. The assumptions can include the size of the market, the market potential, product availability, pricing, and the competition. The strategy goals should also be factored into the assumptions.

Once the market and revenue are forecasted, the other elements of the business plan—with emphasis on the operation plan—can then follow, thus providing a base for the financial projections.

The forecast is based on the knowledge of the market and the information available. A method for developing a multiyear forecast is to (1) assume the revenue goal and (2) define what the company will look like at that point—and then work backwards so as to fill in the gap to get there. For instance, if $2 million in revenue is a goal, define how many units (or customers) will be required, using the projected pricing. Then define the organization that will be required to achieve and support this projected level of revenue. This exercise can also provide a refresh on the business concept to build the company.

The forecast is based on the assumptions and "knowns/givens" at that point in time. In a dynamic situation, the assumptions should constantly be reviewed in order to determine what, if any, changes should be made to them. Refer to the business plan outline in Appendix A. Consider the outline like a diary adding to the sections as you go along. For example, as more information and experienced is gained, it may be necessary to make changes in the forecast, strategy, and/or plans.

The New Gross Margin

In the product world, it has been established that the gross margin equals the revenue minus the cost of manufacturing the product that includes the cost of material, direct labor to produce the product, and the overhead costs (including supervision, management facilities, insurance, and so on).

To be successful, the gross margin dollars must cover all the supporting costs including, administration, engineering, sales, marketing, and something left over for profit. The gross margin percentage equals the gross margin dollars divided by the revenue dollars. Margins of 40% can be healthy. Actually in the electronic manufacturing companies a margin of 6% might be acceptable.

In the move to software and internet product after the product was developed the gross margin can be above 90%. The costs to operate will include people to continue development and all the supporting costs to the products. But 90% for a one dollar disk or operating a website provides little dollars to cover all the other costs in a software company. Companies selling a service or application on the Internet or utilizing social networks need to be more creative with margins. The accounting needs to figure out how much of the total human element is to be charged to produce the product. Instead of gross margin consider the need to cover all the costs as added value. Therefore it becomes necessary to have enough revenue to cover the added value as well as the profit desired.

One approach is to pick revenue levels and decide how many customers and price are needed to reach that level.

A one person start-up that wants to cover cash for living expenses can calculate the number of sales. If the annual rate is $40 and the person wants to have an income of $4,000 per month, then 1,200 paying customers are needed. Of course to get to 1,200 customers other expenses are needed above the $4,000 per month—therefore 1,200 won't do it. This can start a cycle to get to the actual number.

If $2,000,000 is a level considered success with the founder, additional employees and covering investor's needs, 50,000 customers will be needed. The help in doing this kind of exercise will identify the impact of pricing needed to reach target goals. Now the need is to define the cost to support 50,000 customers—certainly more people are needed beyond the founder.

In the Internet and social network companies, sweat equity can go a long way in a startup with a small team as human capital is basically all that is needed to obtain and grow revenue. As noted above, pricing is very important in developing the needed added value (costs) not only in place but in attaining future goals.

A Guide for Success to Building a Company from Scratch—Up to Going for the Big Money

Once you decide to go ahead with your start-up company, there are three phases before you get to the big money. Phase 1, The Start – Building a Foundation, is the validation phase, Phase 2 is Going Forward – The Race, after the initial funding and validation and operating the company and Phase 3, is The Next Step for Big Capital.

Phase 1: The Start

- Building a Foundation—The Concrete.
- Vision—Make sure the team buys in.
- Mission—Provide the basics to build a plan.
- Business Plan—Be certain to put the emphasis on the assumptions.

The object of this phase is to validate your value proposition and customers who will buy into you product.

Alert: LOMP Law #12 – Do What You Do Best!

There are many definitions of a vision, but mine goes like this:

A vision must be a living thing, be it a dream or an idea that you believe in passionately—and you should eat and sleep it. It should also be inherent in making decisions in your daily life. It is the force that drives the company, creates team building, and provides all of your associates with the purpose for the company.

Alert: There will be a gap between the priority for entrepreneurs and investors in the money-raising activity that needs to be closed in order for investors to write a check.

The Vision is the dream and the Mission will play on the Vision and provide important elements that can be used to build the business plan. A business plan should include information on the subjects of the product/ service, the market and competition, financials and information for the investors like an exit plan.

(*See Appendix A for a more detailed outline for a Business Plan. During the time to construct a business plan, use the detailed outline as a diary filling in information as it is gathered.*)

The Team should include individuals who share the founder's vision. The employee team should have superstars who provide the operating—technical, marketing, and finance—disciplines. If this is not possible at the beginning, plan on adding advisors as necessary to fill the voids. Be extremely careful if/when distributing ownership, as a portion of ownership will be needed for future additions and equity transactions.

Alert: Equal Partnerships are doomed for trouble going forward. (Refer to the chapter entitled "Equal Partners Doomed for Failure.")

In building the team, it's advisable to look for people who have knowledge, curiosity, flexibility, a sense of responsibility, a continuous learning mindset—and, above all, passion.

In planning for the marketing strategy, avoid trying to be "everything for all people." Companies in early phase that try to do it all are one of the top three reasons for startups failing. At this stage, focus on the key that if you want to go after a niche in the market, go after the leaders' weaknesses. In other words, if you want to be a leader, go after their strength(s).

After the first half of my career in corporate America, I started working with small companies. No matter how big or strong the competition, we could always find a way to compete by selling the small company "positives."

For instance, during a competition for an engineering design contract against a super power, we were able to convince the customer to go with our small company. The reason we won: We promised the customer's engineers one hour per week with our small company's head of engineering, who was well known in the market for innovation.

Starting out with a niche can be a good strategy. I have seen start-ups become giants by doing so. I had the pleasure of being on the board for a company that changed their strategy when my friend and colleague took over early on, found a niche in the market and ultimately took the company public and becoming an $800 million revenue company and a leader in their market.

Alert: Trying to create the brand can cost millions of dollars of capital.

When evaluating getting into a market, I have seen a degree of difficulty grow, like in the following with a 1 being the easiest to accomplish.

Identify/Research a Market—Difficulty: 1

Define a Need in the Market—Difficulty: 5

Define a Competitive Match—Difficulty: 10

Penetrating the Market as Forecast—Difficulty: 100

Alert: Saying "getting .001% of a $4 billion market is a given" won't fly without demonstrating how.

The Business Plan Structure – The Basics

The company should develop a business plan to operate to, but the plan will be imperative when trying to raise money from outside investors. The plan should include at least the following.

Executive Summery – Paragraph 1 – The Story of the Business and goals of the company:

- The Business
- The Market and Competition
- The Management and Organization structure.
- The Financials
- The Payout and Exit Plan

Alert: If the first paragraph is not exciting and interesting, the reader will go no further.

Keep in mind that a Business Plan isn't only for an investor but it is also required when looking for bank loans as needed, and very important for setting goals and priorities for the team.

Alert: Entrepreneurs wanting investment cash should avoid being a savior of all the world's problems. Doing so would ensure that an investor would be thinking, "If your goal is not to make money, then how can I possibly hope to make money?"

Be careful in your early pitch and presentations to avoid breaking any of the "Guinness Book of World Records." You can avoid do this by researching industry norms, which will help you prevent: ridiculous growth rates (e.g., forecasting revenue in Year 2 to be $30 million; profit margins that are ridiculous. It is also dangerous to present unrealistic product development times, not practical, for getting your product or service out to the market.

Know that you can count on investors asking: "When will you reach a break-even cash point?" (See Appendix A for Investor Questions most likely to be asked in any presentation.)

Alert: LOMP Law #101 – Everything Takes Longer Than You Believe!

But when waiting for a return on investment it may take forever.

I have made "angel investments" that are over 10 years old. Although they are surviving, there has been no return in any form on my investments.

I once read in a Wall Street Journal article that in the venture capital world, 4 out of 5 investments fail. While several "survive," they also fail because for the investor none are getting a return on their investment.

It's important to make sure that any valuation you make for the company to use with investors is fair for both sides.

Never say to an investor group that your valuation is negotiable because that can be interpreted to mean that you don't believe it—which, thus, may be considered as a weakness by the audience you're trying to reach. If asked, a better answer would be: "If you're interested enough, do a due diligence and I believe you will see the valuation to be fair."

Alert: Anything times zero equals zero or $X0 = 0$. It's better to own a small percentage of a $100 million company than 99% of a company worth nothing.

Suggestion for entrepreneur: Review the chapter entitled "Would Be Entrepreneur before investing your time and money to starting a company for the first time.

Phase 2. Going Forward – The Race

In operating a company, it is wise to track and control.

- Cash flow
- Use of resources
- Burn rate
- Sales expectations
- Revenue and profit
- Milestones

Alert: LOMP Law #10: Reports are vital for a company

In any new startup company there may be voids in the operations as the early team may be lacking in experience. It's beneficial to plan for advisors to assist; therefore, look for counseling personnel with operating disciplines in the following aspects:

- Financial
- Technical
- Marketing

It's also a good idea to have a friend for spiritual guidance; additionally, look for people to serve on your fiduciary and advisory boards. It may be difficult to form a board of directors because of the risk involved to Directors with today's laws and regulations. Fortunately it is possible to delay forming a Board of Directors until legally required. To get people to serve on the board, you might need to provide directors and officers with (D&O) insurance.

It's normal for some start-ups to include friends and relatives on the board. They may lack experience in governance and government laws and regulations for today's businesses which could be dangerous.

One good solution is to build an advisory board. It might be easier to get these types of directors because there would be no fiduciary responsibility as the Board of Directors would have. I have often used "no hairs" and "white hairs" (i.e., former managers and executives) in the marketplace, willing to help, who can be very effective because they wouldn't need to worry about governance issues like members of the board would. *(See the Chapter on "Advisory Boards.")*

Alert: LOMP Law #100: Do not mistake advice for counseling. Counseling is advice that can be accomplished within the system.

Once funds are in and the company is started, it helps to have a roadmap—which can be the business plan expanded to an operating plan.

The most important report is one covering cash flow to project what cash will be required and from what source(s). The burn rate of cash; the amount of cash needs to be watch constantly especially before and during the time the revenue is zero or lean. Divide the total cash available by the amount of cash being used monthly. This will give you an idea of how long the company can go on. It is not unusual for a startup to run out of cash and must find a way to keep the team together. One way is to give the team equity in the company in place of the payroll.

As the company grows, plans need to be reviewed on a continuous basis. The foundation for any plan should be the assumptions which should be reviewed on a regular basis to determine if they need to be changed. A plan should not be cast in concrete – after working on it and filing it away for the end of a period, like each year, with no changes. For example, change will be necessary if the operating results like sales are not going as planned.

Alert: LOMP Law #10: Plans are born to be changed.

Since balance is important, it's necessary not to diverge from the plans too soon. The mindset to prevent this is to focus on the operating results. If misses can be corrected, male adjustments and do this before redirecting the company

Obviously, the sales forecast—and getting those first sales—is very important. Rather than "beating up" the individual who made the forecast, if sales are not occurring according to plan, analyze the reason(s) why to see if change(s) are required

Marketing Tips with Which to Live

Marketing is often based on perceptions rather than facts. At one time in my business career, I worked for a company that competed with IBM. Although there were areas in which our company could provide better field maintenance to our customers at a lower cost, many of our customers' purchasing agents thought it was safer to choose IBM, the multibillion, dominant leader in the marketplace. With that in mind, always remember…

- Rely heavily on Public Relations (PR).
- Customers like to deal with #1.
- Focus on your business plan.
- Avoid product "ego decisions" – sometimes you win by losing an order that would have been wrong and have harmed the company in some way.
- Put importance and energy into assumptions.
- Acknowledgement by a customer doesn't mean approval.
- An order equates to a privilege to serve the customer.
- If possible, create mystique, and differentiate your product from the competitors'.
- **Focus! Focus! Focus!**

Good marketing will be vital to growth; therefore, budget what is affordable to build an image and awareness for your customers.

To build an image and awareness, there are many elements to consider, including:

- Public Relations (PR)
  ◊ Free—not considered controlled copy
- Media
  ◊ Trade advertising—controlled copy
- Measurable
  ◊ Direct mail—controlled audience

- ◊ Radio/TV
- Trade Shows
  - ◊ Face-to-face contact
- Technical Articles
  - ◊ Image building
- Seminars
  - ◊ Highly controlled – limited audience
  - ◊ Internet and Webinars
- Newspapers
  - ◊ Undirected audience
- Internet and Web page
  - ◊ Uncontrolled – broad audience
- Social Networks
  - ◊ The "now" marketing

Selling tips:

- Sell to the highest level individual in the customer's company.
- Use titles for your salespeople (e.g., Vice President) to your advantage.
- Don't always ignore a salesperson's bad news input as it might be factual and not emotional
- Prevent too many layers of people between top management and sales personnel.
- Teach sales personnel to listen.
- Keep your customers' frustrations from your employees.
- As a company, avoid trying to be all things to all people.
- Support outside sales agents as your direct sales people.
- Use finder's fees from outside help to your advantage for both finding and closing sales.
- When negotiating, you have a choice between "Your Price, My Terms" or "Your Terms, My Price"—don't give away both Price and Terms.

Throughout the selling cycle, company personnel need to listen to the customers. It is best to really understand what the customer needs before presenting the product or a solution to a potential problem.

Sales managers usually live within a "funnel model," which relates to the potential for the opportunity along the way, and the fallout during various steps in order to end up with what are considered real opportunities. (So many to get so many out.)

As part of top management, I obviously always wanted to know the probabilities for an opportunity to turn into a sale. In the following list the stages of a sales can be given a priority for each stage 1adding 10% on a cumulative basis as the probability.

- Customer Awareness of our company
- A meeting with customer to find out their need
- The possibility of meeting the customer's need
- A meeting with the boss of the first customer contacted person
- Receiving a request for a proposal from the customer
- Being sure there was a budget for your product in the customer
- Meeting the person who had the authority to approve and sign an order
- A positive response from the customer regarding to the proposal
- Extended meetings with the customer to review details
- Probability for the order – 90%

Each step can have a higher probability until it reaches 90% or falls by the wayside. It is a fact that everything takes longer than you hope, but we did have a checkpoint. In the weekly proposal probability report, when an outstanding proposal reached 12 weeks, it would dropped in the following report, if not an order yet.

In a start-up company, it really helps to get that first sale in both Phases 1 and 2. It helps the relationship with company investors and is a great motivator for the existing team already in place. There is no better way to prove a value proposition than to get someone to pay for it

Alert: The Founder must expect to be the first sales person in the company to customers, suppliers, hiring employees and wooing investors.

Phase 3 – The Next Step for Big Capital

This phase assumes that the company is successful with growth, meeting its sales projections and the expectations in the business plan.

After operating the company for a period of time, when management wants to continue to grow robustly, it must recognize the need for the addition of capital above and beyond what the profit will provide. Usually, at this point, there could be a need for additional personnel, facilities, equipment, and definitely working capital.

Depending upon the amount of cash required, more sophisticated investors might prove to be more advantageous, rather than friends and relatives who initially made their investments.

Sophisticated investors are looking for sales and profit—a proven concept—and the ability to scale the company to higher revenue sales. Of course, the new investors' interest [to invest] will be more pronounced if the company has the newest technology in a growing market. But all of this is always needed to attract an investor.

To me, the best word to describe an investor's mood is comfort, which can come from credibility that builds trust. When credibility and trust peak, an investor will be more than willing to conduct a due diligence: and the more money involved, the deeper the due diligence exercise will be.

In building any projection for the investors, management should start with the first month in ant forecast because using dates is dangerous. It may take months to close an investor deal. If dates are used, a potential investor in the month of May, for example, might ask: "How did you do for the period of January through May?" Without the funding you are looking for, it is unlikely you will meet the forecast.

The forecast plan should begin at Month One as the date the money comes in. The initial investors should be asked if they are interested in investing again, because they may want to protect their ownership percentage. If they do not invest again the new capital in for equity will dilute the percentage ownership. Of course, additional investments can make the individual share value higher for the original investors. If the company is doing well, additional financing rounds will continue to build the value of the shares, even while diluting the ownership percentage of the existing investors. Whereas early investors may get common stock, later round investors can (and will) expect preferred stock, which gives the investor more rights.

The Team

Investors will look for credibility in the team. The more depth employees can add to their roles, the better. Individuals who "have been there" (especially in a successful start-up), coupled with a board that has experience and advisors with specific experience related to the company's requirements, is very important to investors. Additionally, it is very important that the CEO and other members of top management have open minds and be good listeners.

Alert: In any discussion with investors, company management must be very careful not to be defensive or "put the listener down."

There are tips on dealing with an investor, a number of which follow:

- Always present the market need first
  - ◊ To get the investor's attention
- Investors will ask if any personal cash is put in by the founder
  - ◊ It helps if some in indicates believing in the potential
- Make investors comfortable
  - ◊ Extends the financial projections to show when an ROI occurs
  - ◊ Credibility breeds trust, trust breeds comfort, and comfort brings investments
- In any forecasts, it is wise to avoid plans that would put the "Guinness" growth records to shame
- How to use funds:
  - ◊ If asked "What would you do with $500,000?" be quick to answer if the request is for far less money
  - ◊ Be fast on your feet with a credible answer
- The company's motives must be financial
  - ◊ Investors won't relate, otherwise
  - ◊ Logic from investors, "If you don't want to make money, how can I make money?"
- Get enough money the first time
  - ◊ Obtaining further capital will cause the company to pay dearly, if it falls short going forward
- Use the best "storyteller" in the company for investor presentations
  - ◊ It doesn't have to be the Founder/CEO
- Make investors believe
  - ◊ They want to – that's why they're listening
- Make a plan for growth

◊ That's the only way to get a return on investment(s)

There are reasons why an investor won't buy the business plan:

- No passion
  - ◊ "If you don't believe first, how can I believe?"
- It's an opportunity and not really a business potential
  - ◊ Many ideas aren't supportive of a vision
- No plan and/or exit plan exists
  - ◊ Which makes it difficult to get anyone's attention
- Market penetration is not convincing
  - ◊ Not a big enough market to have enough sales for an investment return
- No proprietary advantages
  - ◊ Makes you one of the "bunch"
- Valuation of the company is not credible
- The piece of the company for the investor is too small
- Too ambitious plan (i.e., $12 million plus revenue in the first year)
  - ◊ Kills credibility
- Scheduled bank borrowing is naïve – too soon in the plan
  - ◊ Credibility problem again
- Market growth potential insufficient bad marketing plan
  - ◊ Can't support a business
- Payoff for investor is not good enough
  - ◊ All investors have some criteria
- Team is weak
  - ◊ People required to make it work

The Investor

There are various feelings in an investor's gut and they look for it. . Following are three:

- Market! Market! Market!

- Team! Team! Team!
- Comfort! Comfort! Comfort!

Investors are seeing positive trends for entrepreneurs in presentation. For instance:

- Willing to give up CEO position (at some point)
- Acceptance of outside help
- Willing to give up fair amount of equity
- Better understanding of managing a business

In summary, for the steps for an entrepreneur along the way:

- The first question to ask and answer is: "Is it a business opportunity?" Companies can easily be formed but a business is when founders and investors are getting a return on their investment
- Then…believe in your dream.
- Convert the vision to build a plan to build a business worth investing in.
- Make "them" believe.

Alert: Are you ready to work 70 hours per week for several years to reach the payoff?

(Refer to Section 3 for more assistance in preparing for an investor. See chapters on the "Elevator Speech" and "The Presentation" in Appendix A for an a presentation example, called Nuco.)

Hiring—Interviews

At any level, the interview process should include the potential supervisor of the applicant, and there should be at least one other person (beyond human resources personnel) conducting the interview.

One caution, however, is to beware of the supervisor who fears hiring someone that might be better than themselves. In a growth situation, all hires should have growth potential.

I once had a supervisor in our test department who had an insecurity mentality. It became a concern because he turned down so many applicants for any job opening in his department because he was afraid of hiring someone—anyone—better than himself. Unfortunately, it took us a couple of months and several interviews to realize this.

I have seen companies grow to $2 million or $4 million in revenue when the #1 person was able to perform several functions to get to that point.

There comes a time in a start-up or small-growing company when senior-level people need to be hired. It may take a while, but the top person eventually recognizes that to grow, experienced personnel additions are necessary. Oftentimes, an experienced marketing person is required (especially if the founder is an engineer).

Referrals from friends and associates are the first level of contact. While this concept is basically a good one, the lack of experience can be harmful. Many times the first senior hired-person fails. The first case; because the candidate looks good and sounds good, but primarily only because s/he's spitting out impressive buzz words that make them sound qualified, but fails as the performance doesn't match the image. The second reason is the person never had a chance as the owner really wasn't ready to give up any control or trust. The problem is the cultural difference that can be present, which includes the question: Is the #1 person really ready to turn over responsibilities that involve trusting a [new] "stranger." Frankly, 50% of the time, failure is assured when a hired employee is the first experienced senior person brought in to be in the #2 position of the company.

The way to prevent this potential failure is to get help from experienced people during the interview process, and by conducting an extensive background check that includes verification of a candidate's previous jobs.

To be considered as well is that a new person coming from a larger company may not be ready to make the transition to a smaller one. For example, I once interviewed an individual from a billion-dollar company who said he was ready because he had a 12-person group and understood the culture of a small company, which prompted me to ask one question that shot him down: "Did you ever have to meet a payroll with no bank balance?"

Early in my business career, especially with a small company doubling its earnings annually, I/we had to learn: "Don't hire anybody that worked for IBM or GE, unless they had two other jobs since leaving them."

When it comes to hiring key people (or what I call superstars), there are several reasons for shooting down the applicants and saving valuable time.

Following is a synopsis from my book, The Laws of Management Physics, called *"Hiring Smarts."* I have often told my clients that if they truly consider themselves to be the best game in town and want to find a superstar, they should buy into the following hiring practices:

1. *Don't hire* someone who is currently unemployed. While this won't sit well with the millions of unemployed, remember: You're looking for a superstar; therefore, that person has to be in demand. If laid off due to unfortunate circumstances, the individual in demand will have no trouble walking into another position.

2. *Don't hire* someone who has jumped from job to job too quickly. Instability is a drawback in any position.

3. *Don't hire* someone who has followed their boss from job to job. You will seldom find a leader among those who have followed all their careers—and the superstar is a leader, not a follower.

4. *Don't hire* someone who isn't focused. This person is generally responsive to any job and doesn't make it clear what they are interested in—in other words, they don't really know where they're going or what they want to do.

5. *Don't hire* someone who made more money in their two previous jobs; and don't hire someone who will take a significant cut in pay. There may be some sound reason the candidate wants to join the company, but if you are paying less than s/he got paid in their two previous jobs, the mindset of your candidate is way off. Someone who isn't ambitious on their own behalf will probably not be ambitious on your behalf, either. In other words, this is obviously not a good fit.

6. *Don't hire* anyone who hasn't done research on the company prior to the interview. Why hire someone who is not interested enough in the company to find out something about it?

7. *Don't hire* someone who has not been a winner. Once a person has had a taste of being on the winning team, nothing else will do – they must get there again.

8. *Don't hire* someone who doesn't seem basically intelligent or someone who has no common sense. It's amazing how good a person sounds when they know all about the specific job(s) they've done. However, you need to make sure that they can "walk across the street without jeopardizing traffic."

9. *Don't hire* someone who has failed to achieve success in their previous (and/or current) company. Do you really want to hire a CFO from a company that's going bankrupt? Or an engineering manager who hasn't released a newly-designed product for several years?

10. *Don't hire* someone who will accept any job available (e.g., barber to brain surgeon). This just demonstrates how dangerous this type of person can be.

11. *Don't hire* someone who was "fading" while with their previous company. In the reference check, find someone to decode all the fancy titles.

12. *Don't hire* someone who has worked in the industry for several years, consistently earning far below the norm. This strongly indicates that the person has a problem you'd be crazy to voluntarily inherit.

Based on my experience, another suggestion that might help when planning the element of time is that when you're hiring a senior person you have yet to meet, from the first meeting it could take in excess of three months for that individual to actually come onboard.

There is one criteria and the top of my list for hiring and that is look for passion.

Investors and comfort

Comfort—a key word for locking up investors.

In any presentation to an investor they must get a feeling of comfort to continue their interest. Comfort can come from credibility that builds trust that builds comfort. Presentations with numbers and statements that defy Guinness records credibility turn investors off. Arguing with investors also can turn them off. And when asked, "what is the valuation of your company?' and getting a response, "It's negotiable," can be death to toward any comfort. Investors want you to believe so they can believe in what you say. Stand by your ground. An answer like, "It is X and I believe if you are interested in doing a due diligence I believe we will convince you."

An investor must be comfortable enough so their hand isn't shaking to prevent them from signing the big check.

The Lawyer as a Partner

For a start-up, it is necessary and important to get **legal help early** in the process to get the legal information to protect your idea, minimize your personal and investors risks, optimize the organization costs, cover how to treat partners and employees, and form **an affordable partnership with the lawyers.**

Following is a list of questions topics and questions to review with a lawyer to help build the foundation for a successful company, and a partnership.

Keep in mind there are **people out there with suing on the mind** and they will wait until the company is worth something in the future before doing so.

Legal Structure

- When is it necessary to form a legal entity?
- What is the best legal structure for a startup going forward?
- What is the best state to form a corporation?
- Are there any tax advantages I can gain by the form and state regulators?
- When is it necessary to move up from an S-Corp?
- When is it a legal necessity to form a Board of Directors?
- What is the difference between a Board of Directors and an Advisory Board?
- What lies ahead to consider to change the corporation structure?
- What is D&O insurance—is it legally required?

IP Protection

- How do I protect my idea/product?
- What is the difference between copyright, a patent and a trademark?
- What is patentable and how long is a patent effective

- Are there disadvantages to filing a patent?
- What is a typical cost for a trademark or patent?
- What is the probability a patent will hold up and what are typical costs to fight attacks?
- What is the definition of copyrights and is it meaningful
- What is an NDA and is it useful?
- Should I use an NDA for hiring employees or offering investors?
- What do I have to do protect my domain name
- When should I consider legal protection globally? Is it effective?
- Tell me about the so called trawls
- Do I have ownership of the effort by the people working on developing my product
- Are there places I can go to get information at the very beginning to see if my ideas for names, domains, patents, trademarks are available?

OWNERSHIP

- Why are many equal partnerships doomed for failure?
- What are good methods of compensation to use for additional employees?
- Are there alternatives to providing equity to give directors, advisors, key employees?
- Contracts/Agreements
- What should I look for and is usually lacking in a contract or agreement?
- Will a handshake hold up in court?
- Is it true no written agreement can be the worst kind?
- Is it necessary to have Product liability insurance?
- When is a business license needed?

Are there recent laws affecting startups—from local and state?

- Or Regulations?

What is the Lawyer's role in a startup?

CAN A STARTUP AFFORD A LAWYER?

Marketing and the Web

It's a given that the Internet, along with the myriad social media networks, have created channels for marketing products. However, until the product actually gets out there and potential customers try it, it's like selling an invisible unknown. Since many services may be as low as $5 per month, to "make a business" the company will be required to generate thousands of paying users of these cyberspace sources. Because of the wall between suppliers and customers, various methods must be tried to get the latters' feedback.

When the Internet first became popular within the investment world, many businesses depended upon it for their sales. Of course, the obvious question was, "How will you get customers to go to your site and look at every page?" Well, with the help of Google and Facebook, etc., the Web has developed even more quickly, thus providing a direct path from customer to supplier versus the actual physical product that a customer could see, touch, feel, try, and then, if interested, buy it—a very different approach to selling an application or service.

The Internet, on the other hand, provides a most effective strategy by offering customers limited usage of the product, at no charge; therefore, the startup costs to get initial customers can be greatly reduced because facility and inventory costs are significantly lower. The product must be pitched on all levels of social media available today, and will need some sort of gimmick to attract the customer's attention (e.g., the free offer is the best). The value/price factor can be used when the customer likes the product and wants to keep it.

If a customer needs and sees a physical product, they'll buy it. With an Internet product, however, although a customer may "like the sound" of a specific product, they may not commit until the network or chat room has a significant number of users who discuss and recommend it. After gathering cost information to market a physical product it might be reasonably possible to scale the forecast as the sales channels are more visible and direct customer contact may be possible. But with the Internet product because of relatively low revenue per customer it might require reaching thousands of unknown potential customers to justify the cost of development.

A plan to reach the thousands of unseen customers requires whatever amount of experience and expertise an entrepreneur can obtain from advisors who have already been there.

Outsourcing

The manufacture of the computer and telecommunications industries exploded over the last half of the 20th century, with the manufacturing part starting in the 1960s with the transistor radio and hand-held calculators.

I had the opportunity to start an operation in Asia for a parent company in Southern California. The company was a manufacturer of ferrite core memories for computers (before semiconductor memories were even born). It required lots of labor in the assembly operation in Southern California. We only had 50 direct laborers assembling these items The work was tedious and, frankly, as we grew, we would not have been able to hire the number of people required in the U.S.

Early in the 21st century, I served on the board of directors for a Southern California company assembling flexible circuits for cellphones. I don't believe that we could have hired the 20,000 people in Southern California that we had in China. At first, we started utilizing the labor in Asia by providing the material and detailed manufacturing procedures. Over time, however, our Asian partners were able to perform all of the manufacturing steps and then, eventually, the engineering and even the marketing requirements.

In manufacturing, the advantages were clear and beyond just the mass numbers of labor available. By maintaining in Asia the overhead requirements and lower costs for manufacturing engineers, purchasing, testing, and operating personnel, we were able to give purchase orders for the finished product to our other facilities/partners. The advantages included: fewer employees (by being more efficient), less infrastructure, a greater control of inventory, a reduced number of skills required in-house, and far better cash flow requirements. But most importantly, to produce our products, the need and cost for equipment was greatly reduced.

I have said it often that I believe there would be no computer and telecommunications market as to size and availability of products as we know them today if it weren't for outsourcing to Asia.

Of course, there could be disadvantages if outsourcing is not done properly, including less control of the process, IP, and other unique processes, as well as disclosing and exposing the company's customer base, but it is a good option that should be considered for growth.

The Virtual Company

In recent years, starting at the very start of inception, it's not unusual to find a company technically outsourcing all of its operating functions, including marketing, engineering, finance, and manufacturing. I have made an investment in a virtual company where everyone except the president is an outsourced function, making it possible to get the most talented and experienced people and resources in place almost immediately when the company is formed. Long-term employee commitments can be limited to just paying for the service; they are not required for the long-term.

The Start-Up

Based on my experience as an angel investor, coach, and mentor of start-ups, from day one I review the situation to see if the company is better served by outsourcing a function (e.g., sales distribution). There is, of course, the entrepreneur mentality to give up any/all control. In fact, the ultimate in outsourcing is to find an experienced partner to take the "idea" for a product or service and help make it a success. In my experience, however, most ideas are just that, ideas—not a foundation for building a successful company.

An angel organization I belonged to at one time supported 100 entrepreneur presentations per year and (on average) funded one per month. There were many that never even reached the presentation stage. With a partner from day one, the founder's idea can: (1) cost less as far as their personal investment is concerned, (2) get there quicker, and (3) create less stress. The probability of success can be increased and weighed against losing a degree of control and perhaps even less of a reward. To succeed, the alternative of going it alone is a future of 80-hour weeks for a seemingly countless number of years.

Ownership and How to Lose a Friend

An engineering friend of mine owned his own engineering design company. He called to talk with me about a great new product opportunity. Not unlike many engineering design companies, over the years he became increasingly frustrated providing designs and products that made big money for his customers [based on his designs].

He had been contacted by an individual—successful in the marketplace in which he worked—who came to him with a great idea. This individual had numerous contacts and even some customers that verified the value of the product and were willing to pay for it when it became available. After much discussion, my friend suggested in forming a company to exploit the idea.

My friend asked me how the ownership in the new company should be divided. Based on what little information I was given, my answer was: "While you will do the design and provide the level of technical support going forward, your potential partner has the idea, knows the market, can form the sales channels, has the contacts, has identified the customers, and is willing to leave a high-paying job; therefore, I believe this marketing guy should own the majority—right?" With this answer, needless to say, I wasn't surprised when my engineering friend got up and left, sticking me with the check.

For the record, even though I started out as an engineer, I have had many engineering friends and clients who do not understand that…**"It's all about MARKETING."**

Ownership, Founders, and Minority Stock

Ownership is a valuable asset; therefore, its distribution should be considered very thoroughly and carefully.

Founders

I have seen two extremes: First, the founder is reluctant to and against giving any ownership to anyone else (which most often results in a failure to grow or attract key individuals and investors to purchase equity in the company). Second, if the founder is permissive during the distribution process and feels good about it, they will often times give out too much stock up front, which results in regrets in the future when it comes time to attract key personnel and raise equity funding.

An even worse case scenario is the sadness and frustration that occurs when the new owners stop performing or, even worse, leave the company with only partial ownership. Before any distribution is made, the various laws and regulations that relate to minority owners should be explored and discussed with an attorney. To see what fits, future ownership in the form of stock options is also worth discussing. On the other side of the recipient, getting stock in a private company may end up in a dead end if the founder owner never plans to go public or sell the company.

For example, there are methods such as Stock Appreciation Rights (SARs) that can result in an employee having value in the stock (or cash) when leaving the company. The latest approach I used for giving stock or stock options out for new employees was to structure a plan that gave them ownership over a specific period of time. After 90 days, the employee was given stock or options that vested on a periodic basis. While the target vesting time was established, if for some reason the employee was terminated, the stock/option schedule stopped (or was terminated) as well.

Who should get stock? Well, that all depends upon the value of the company. Five percent (5%) for the initial designer may seem to be too low; however, to be considered is that after the design has been completed, the value of the employee may decrease. As an alternative to "too much" ownership, a plan providing a smaller percentage ownership and royalty dollars in the product if it sells can be utilized.

It's always best to carefully consider who and how much may be required for stock distribution, especially if the company continues to grow.

As to outside investors buying into the ownership, when possible it's a good idea to try to maintain control with the majority ownership as long as practical, which means owning over 50.1% of the stock. For instance, two steps (i.e., selling an ownership at 20% and another at 35%) still allows the 50.1% or more percentage ownership for the founder. Or, selling 20% leaves the founder and team with 80%; then selling 30%, still leaves the founder with 56%. Granted, the prior example is an oversimplification, but it illustrates what can happen. Simply put, the more money raised, the greater the dilution in the percentage of ownership that will occur for the company's current owner(s). New investors will always have a say about what ownership they will get for their investment in the terms and condition in a term sheet for their money investment round.   In that case, if is best to keep in mind that although the present percentage of ownership will be diluted; with each investment dollar, the value of the company should go up; and since the number of shares is still owned by earlier investors and owners their value will grow.

Ownership – Minority

I once read that "Minority ownership in a self-style business; a company that never gets to the point of equity transactions, can be worse than kissing your brother or sister."

With my drawer full of company stock certificates (that have no value), the many failed promises of going public, or the owner's failed promise to find someone to or buy the company or make a major equity investment, I wholeheartedly agree with that statement.

The minority owner should ensure that there is an agreement up-front that defines how the stock will be valued if at some point in time it is necessary to leave the company. I was able to help employees get stock by convincing a 100% owner to define the value of the company through the use of a specific formula. Then, if someone left the company, we would apply that formula to determine the employee's value so we could buy them out.

In the formula noted above, we used the net worth as the foundation of the formula, which allowed the owner to take out a predefined, fixed compensation value equal to $500,000 a year (total) - no matter how well the company performed. This money could be in any form he wanted like having his children on the payroll. In the formula we had that control needed for calculating profit and the additions to that went to retain earnings and the net worth. If the company succeeded the net worth would increase and when some left the piece they owned would have an increased value – allowing them to leave with some value for the time they put in and the contribution.

Many founders never learn anything—times zero equals zero. Better to own a small piece of a successful company than 100% of a company with no outside valuation.

The Presentation

When soliciting investors to buy in, the presentation is a must. Following are the most important points to include to prove what the investors' opportunities are:

1. Prove that the market has a need – Investors like to ask, "Is there a 'pain' that needs relieving?"

2. Prove the company has a match for the market need with a product or service.

3. Prove the company has a plan to develop a new market or penetrate an existing market.

In many cases today, there is no active physical product or service for the startup as yet; therefore, the more information detailed in the presentation, the better chance to "reel in" the investor's interest. There are investors who will not even consider listening unless the founder has validated the value proposition and potential customers. Since customers who indicate they like the value proposition may not be enough, it's necessary to convince the investors that customers will pay for the product or service—and there is no better way to convince anyone that the concept is proven than to have an order in place and a customer ready to pay for it.

From an investor's viewpoint, the four considerations necessary for them to make an investment are:

- What capital (cash) is required?

- What are (1) the company dollar valuation and (2) the investor's share?

- What is the exit requirement?

- What multiple will the investor get for their ROI, and when?

The total presentation should include:

- The market need

- The match – solution to the product

- The market strategy and plan

- The product

- The competition
- The management team
- The financial summary
- The company validation and funds requested
- The use of the funds provided
- The exit plan

(See Appendix A for an example of a presentation.)

As mentioned earlier, if an investor shows an interest it helps to have a business plan; and if an investor doesn't say no or go away, by all means follow-up. On the other hand, if an investor continues to procrastinate or even goes so far as to actually say no, push to find out what the hurdle is that's preventing them from investing. To this question, I have heard, on occasion: "My wife doesn't think we should." So…ask to meet the wife.

Entrepreneurs should not get defensive because of any questions asked or fight a new idea. Tough questions from investors are good. Perhaps they want a response to knock down a hurdle that's been keeping them from moving forward.

Alert/Caution: Make sure everything you say in a presentation or business plan can be backed up.

As touched on several times throughout this book, the final step before an interested investor signs on is for them to do a due diligence, which enables them to verify everything you have told them. *(See Appendix A for a sample of the topics covered in a due diligence investigation.)*

It is expected that investors or investing organizations will want a representative to serve on the board of directors. At some point in time, investors will also want to see marketing and operating plans. *(See Appendix A for suggested outlines for these plans.)*

The basis for the final agreement will be a term sheet, which will define what each side is contributing to the deal, and what each gets for doing so. In other words, a term sheet covers the terms and conditions (T&Cs) for the final contract, which will include: the funds put in, the ownership mix, and any rights the investors want to reduce potential risk. It's imperative to engage legal help at this stage of the relationship to help close and finalize the ultimate agreement.

Entrepreneurs and investors will start out with a large interest gap about doing a deal together. To the entrepreneur the vision is a living experience that is part of their daily life, but to the investor it might be one in a hundred potential opportunities. You can expect if a "turndown" professional investors will not drag things on and on any longer than necessary.

Risk Management—Risk Taking

Before risk management comes risk taking comes first. Arguably there is no other business risk higher than starting a company from scratch.

Going the route of a start-up puts at risk; personal time, personal funds, personal assets, personal image and extreme pressure.

I have seen start-up companies exist for years before crumbling into ashes. There are ways to reduce that risk including:

- The more advisors from the start, the better he chance for success. *(See Chapter on "Benchmarking" for helpful insight.)*

- The more information up front the better the chance for success.

- The greater the market need and the validation of the Value Proposition match.

- The better the business plan the better the chance for success.

- The better the management team, the better chance for success.

- The higher the cash raised the better the chance for success.

- An investor needs an emotional feeling to make a decision and minimize the risk and that is comfort in the entire program. The list above will help the feeling of comfort.

Alert: The highest risk for an entrepreneur is the risk of not starting the start-up.

Scaling Alert

While defining the business and operating plans required defining the future of the company and achieving success, it's normal initially for a start-up to concentrate on validating its customers and potential value.

But it is particularly important to explore the pricing by doing an exercise starting with a targeted revenue goal that is a success point to continue growing organically or providing an ROI to investors and to the founder. For example, if $2 million in revenue is a target for success and the product will be priced at $200 per year for the company's customers, logically speaking, 10,000 customers will be required to provide this revenue. The result should give the team planning to start thinking about how to get there. However, while this estimate may create concern, the numbers alone aren't all that's required. To attain the credibility, planning in depth is needed to achieve the numbers.

The point about picking a target can help define the effort to get to it. An exercise should be made to define what the company will look like at the target point. Since the start-up is close to zero, this exercise will demonstrate what needs to be done to get there. I have seen a number of entrepreneurs pivot their value proposition after doing this simple task. Sadly, I have also seen a couple of would-be entrepreneurs give up when they saw the reality of what might lay ahead. (*See the chapter entitled "Scaling Resources Up to Grow."*)

Based on my experience with high-tech product companies, I have seen entrepreneurs shot down in an investor presentation because, when challenged about their growth numbers, they respond with, "What? You don't think I can get .001% of a two billion market?" (this, of course, raised the question of "How?").

Nowadays, with the increase in Internet and social media involvement, the primary response is being changed to: "What? You don't think I can get hundreds of thousands of customers out of over six billion people in the world?"

In most investor presentations, someone in the audience is invariably bound to ask, "Is the product scalable?" Software products became popular because scaling the product (e.g., like a disk) was easily producible – but the "how" questions were still there, and the emphasis is on the scaling of human capital to support the product became very important. However, scaling is still focused on marketing the product and the ability to build a customer base.

Scaling the product isn't the only a need concern. It helps to build marketing and operations plans to detail what is needed for the organization led by people and the activities that needs be added to define what is necessary to operate at various levels to get to the target goal. *(See an Operations Plan Outline and a Marketing Plan Outline in Appendix A.)*

Strategic Partners

Strategic partners form an alliance to increase the probability of meeting strategic goals. It is possible that each partner can maintain their legal independence; however, the closer the working relationship(s), the higher the probability of success. Obviously, each partner believes there is a better chance of success with the partnership, because it can take many forms, including marketing, sales, and/or product development.

For start-ups, I believe it's wise to consider a strategic partnership from the beginning. I can say that in all my years of experience, the majority of start-ups have gained from partnerships rather than going it alone, even though this is not the normal attitude or mindset for the entrepreneur with a dream and a vision. As mentioned before, I'm pretty certain that I've lost several friends who had passionate ideas until I told them that what they really had was an opportunity rather than a business, in which case their usual response was, "I'll find someone who will tell me what I want to hear."

Anyone can form and build a company, but it's not a business until the founder and investors start to get their investment back.

As part of an angel investment group, it's not unusual that several investments have passed the 10-year mark. Some are still going, with the original founder in charge, but there is no ROI for any of the outside investors.

In a recent article in a financial newspaper, it stated that 4 out of 5 investments fail, meaning that the investors never got a return on their investment. All do not collapse; they just manage to survive.

So, with a new contact asking for my advice, my first question is whether their product or service is just an opportunity or if it's capable of building a potential business that will attract investors. The potential of the strategic partnership is that it can grow faster with lower financial risk, put less strain on the founder and his family, and offer a chance for faster financial rewards. It's important to consider that a marketing partner, with numerous contacts and a sales channel already in place, can start the customer validation process sooner and with much greater activity.

Established partners are seeking increased sales revenue and a wider selection of products. The established partner may be capable of adding technical and management potential as part of the start-up team. And with the ever-increasing regulations and litigation culture, by having a big brother the start-up can provide experience that would otherwise need to be built up from scratch. A partnership is an alternative to an entrepreneur's plan for growth. Marketing/sales are not the only potential partner(s). A start-up with a product can also find a manufacturing company as a partner.

In recent years, the virtual company has come into its own. I am aware of companies now where most of the requirements— from product development to marketing and accounting—are outsourced. I know of two companies—one that basically just has the CEO and founder as an employee of the company, while the second has the CEO and the head of marketing as its only employees.

As a director, I have watched a company grow, from start-up (with outside strategic partners) and then, over time, taking over those services themselves as the company grew.

The key to finding a successful partner is to be sure that: the strategic goals are similar, the cultures are compatible, the staffs complement each other, and the agreement includes all of the necessary basic assumptions before being turning over to the attorneys for further fine-tuning.

The investment community and large companies are looking for new products and innovation—and the technology that goes with it.

There are several forms of alliances with big companies, including providing the design, manufacturing rights, or even a royalty agreement. I have seen several companies in the health care industry develop their product with government grants and then, at just the right moment, sell the rights to that product to a big medical company.

Starting with a strategic partner may help an entrepreneur to be successful faster—with less financial risk and stress—but the entrepreneur partner in sharing may also sacrifice the potential of higher rewards but at a later point in time. However, with the experience and success the entrepreneur may want to do it again.

The Changing Product Development Cycle and Marketing Assumptions

In the early stages of the computer industry, it was common for the development of products (e.g., computers and peripherals) to take well over one year, even with hundreds of people in engineering diligently working to get the products to market. In the airplane industry, for example, it took Boeing over three years to get the 787 Dreamliner developed.

In today's world, with more and more products shifting to services on the Internet or applications for the myriad electronic gadgets (lead by the iPhone, of course!), it incredibly takes a lot less time. Some of these software products or applications can be developed by one person, and depending on the energy of that individual, it can be accomplished by merely sitting at a computer for X number of weeks.

In my recent experience as an "angel investor" and my activity with start-up "incubators," I see numerous false assumptions that are hurting start-up companies.

In the past, with emphasis on manufactured products, many business plans started out with assumptions based on hearsay or naivetés. For instance, almost every business I have encountered had cash flow projections, including assumptions about when the business would start to do "okay"; meanwhile, of course, a bank loan was inevitable. In my early angel investments, most were with start-ups led by engineers, many of whom believed that because they had a great product, investors would line up in droves at the door.

In the Internet world, over and over again I see start-ups believing in several dangerous assumptions because they believe their Web page are sensational; therefore, they believe that they have the answers to all questions that may be raised in this regard. In an investor group, after such a presentation making such claims, someone in the audience will invariably ask: "How do you plan to get people to your Web page?"—a question for which not all have good answers.

Another potential devastating assumption can be depending on advertising on the Web page or in a chat room to carry the growth in revenue and the positive cash flow required to build a successful business. There are other bad assumptions (particularly relating to scaling the number of users or believing that $40 a year per customer can build a business), but those mentioned earlier should not be treated as "givens" before validating." But, because if they're not and planned anyway, many companies seeking investors while using the optimistic "givens"— companies that are not prepared to present a good case—will most assuredly stumble and most likely fail.

Certainly, it's always important to focus on proving the concept and validating the customers—but also important is validation of the assumptions. Validation can be accepted by having creatable backup.

The Way It Was vs. The Way It Is Now

Long before most new, would-be entrepreneurs were born; published information or data accumulated over time were the only resources start-ups had to rely on for their business planning activities.

Strategic planning exercises, business plans, proposals to customers, and marketing research could take days or weeks to put together. Competitive information could be very difficult to find in the open market. All of these activities could also require a team of people to accumulate and accomplish the work required. Putting a business plan together could be very tedious. Spreadsheet data software for PCs did not exist.

The $100 million company for which I was president was very guarded about allowing any information to leak anywhere outside the company. As a result, whenever we hired someone from a competitor, the new person was amazed at the size and level of business we were doing.

Sales channels were limited to original equipment manufacturers (OEMs), end users, or distributors. Except for selling directly to the end user, manufacturers were buffered from the ultimate customer.

Then companies spend a multitude of money to cover the expenses required for physical travel to/from their customers. Big companies were known to spend millions of dollars on sales meetings to "get the word out." There was Santa Claus and Peter Rabbit, but there was no Internet, email, PCs, iPads, iPhones, Social Networks, Facebook, Skype, and the like.

I once sat on a panel discussing the greatest technical products or events in the second half of the 20th century. Most of the panel touched on the technology: Internet, PCs, mobile phones, tapes, and disk drives. When it came to me, I offered "a break-up of the Bell Telephone Company." Why? Because, with their monopoly and "snail's pace" operating culture used at that time, there would still be no Internet today. I also touted that without the move of manufacturing to Asia (with their tremendous manufacturing volume capability); there would be no computer or telecommunications industries as we know them today.

Microsoft was smart and created a big outside market that complimented their software. Innovative application people, with all kinds of creative software, helped accelerate the path to handling and manipulating data to fractions of a second, thus overcoming the "back in the day" slow way.

Now, one click of a mouse can change years of business projections in less than one second; whereas, it would take hours or days for a similar operation in the early, dark age of computers.

Software programs were developed to handle massive amounts of data and then be able to find information in less than a fraction of a second. Inexpensive software programs can now be found for most company operations in developing a strategy and running a business. Large companies (e.g., Google and Facebook) are capable of handling data for thousands upon thousands of people at the same moment. Hardware provided the technology advances to help expand bandwidth, which was required to develop the software for applications expansion.

A laptop PC now has more power and capability than the mainframe computer of the past, which helped IBM become a monolith giant in the computer industry.

And, as an example of what I have seen in my lifetime: As an engineer, I designed the flip-flop, the core of a computer. Its 19" by 4" size was a box – with only one flip-flop. Today, Intel can put billions of flip-flops on one tiny chip.

The result of all these technological advancements is that, within hours, a start-up can send out myriad emails to gather all the data required to define and structure a company, as well as get the word out to the world by utilizing the Internet, their website, blog, Google, Facebook, Apple, Twitter, and so forth.

Imagine that when hardware was king in the U.S. computer industry, it would take at least five people (e.g., the president, a salesperson, the manufacturing manager, someone from purchasing, and a direct labor person) to get a product in and out the door. With the "tools" now available, a product can be developed for sale by one person sitting at their PC. The tools now available have aided participants in the mobile phone market to create hundreds of thousands of applications for their product.

Imagine, from three sales channels then, there are numerous channels available now to get a product out and into the marketplace. We can expect the Y generation students—those coming out of engineering and business schools—to be the driving force required to accelerate the continual development of products for the marketplace.

Trust comes from comfort, comfort comes from credibility.

Validating the Value Proposition and the Customer

There are very intelligent and creative people who, in just one meeting, can come up with several great ideas—BUT, can these ideas be turned into a business? Based on my experience as an angel investor and consultant to start-ups, the answer is, "Rarely."

At one time, I belonged to an angel investment group that had 96 entrepreneur presentations per year; on average, 84 didn't get funded. The 96 to face the group were selected by a review committee from at least five times that number.

For the record, I am of the opinion that anyone can form a company today, even online. However, many get funded but go nowhere. Very few develop into a business, which is defined by me as when a company has reached a point of stability, with positive cash flow, and there's a chance for the founder and investors to eventually get a return on their investment.

Besides my angel experiences, I have mentored company presidents of small businesses; and, I also have experience with start-up "incubators," which help entrepreneurs with a dream to get developed to the point of seeking investors. I have seen start-up founders invest dollars and numerous hours of time before validating their dream, idea/concept, and product. I recommend against doing this.

The Internet and Google can provide reams of information, numbers, and other relevant data. The marketing data alone helps to encourage entrepreneurs to go further. I have witnessed numerous presentations of great ideas, as well as countless other presentations by entrepreneurs that lack direct face to face customer contact information. Much of marketing skill is dealing with the perception of customers and I have yet to see the customer perception derived from numbers. Unfortunately an internet product may be difficult to contact customers directly face to face; therefore in becomes necessary to get as much contact information as can be. Then there are others who have talked with family and friends, getting a big "go" from them. Even with customer contact information, the entrepreneur can be misled. For instance, I have seen customer interview information with comments relating to an idea as follows: "like to have," "need to have," and/or "got to have." These comments may have validated the concept or product, but this type of input lacks the validation of a customer when asked, "Will you pay for it?"

In essence, ideas are merely vapor until all of the necessary validation steps are accomplished.

For example, I can tell many friends, "I have come across a process that will turn dirt into gold; are you interested?" The answers would be: "Great!", "Yea!", "Let me in!", and, "Hell yes!". I then point out the minimum investment will be $50,000 and get, "I'll get back to you." "Let me think about it.", or, "I've got to go because I'm late for another meeting."

Most start-ups I have come across are new to the experience of validating the customer. The entrepreneur—driven by the passion of their dream—can't see all of the roadblocks that lie ahead. The answer is to start with an open mind and seek as many experienced advisors as possible to help along the way.

My recommendation to entrepreneurs is to validate the value proposition and the customer before spending too much money and time on the dream.

Would-Be Entrepreneur

If you are going to develop a business plan or look for investors for the one you have completed, beware. There are dozens of plan outlines and texts on making a business plan, but your passion and commitment must also come across. You need to get the investors' attention. Keep in mind that your plan must convince a stranger to share in your dream and then leave them comfortable enough to write a large check giving you cash.

Some people will tell you that the most important things an investor looks for in an investment are market, market, and market, while others will tell you they are team, team, and team. I believe those three things are comfort, comfort, and comfort.

Start with common sense and ask yourself, "Why would I invest in this venture? Is there a market need? Does the product meet that need? Can the team penetrate the market and make money at this?"

The First Encounter

Most of the investors you encounter will be strangers, so you have to work that much harder to convert your dream into a business plan. You must get into that investor's comfort zone, and to do so, you must do the research and select the investors that are comfortable with your market and the product you are presenting.

Find the latest buzzwords that are of interest in the investment community, such as biomedical, nanotechnology, software as a service; Internet 3. Even more importantly, avoid those that are dying, because you might not even get anyone to read the plan. Be aware that scalability and customer service, no matter what the product, are always "in." For example, hardware products are slipping unless the company is service-minded and the product is part of a larger solution.

Keep in mind that investment companies receive hundreds of business plans a year and can't possibly give all the attention you would like to your plan. The chances of them accepting or returning a cold phone call are slim to none, and the chances of getting a response to a plan sent in cold are just as low. To increase your chances of getting a response from an investor, look to a referral to give you credibility.

To help the investor reach a minimum comfort level, you will need to include the following items in your plan:

- Market Definition
- Products
- Market Penetration
- Costs
- Alternatives
- Management
- Financial Performance
- Revenue
- Return on Investment
- Profit
- Capital Needed
- Competition
- Valuation
- Exit Plans
- Marketing Differentiation
- Product Differentiation
- Marketing Barriers
- Product Barriers

The plan must have an exciting summary up front, sometimes referred to as the executive letter. This letter should cover the following points:

- Here is where I'm going.
- Here is how I will get there.
- Here is why you, Mr. Investor, should come along.
- Here is what the rewards will be.

Your plan must also have credibility in order to earn the investor's confidence. Avoid the Guinness Record Syndrome, which will sink your plan before you even get it off the ground: Don't show a plan that projects one of the following:

- Spectacular growth while competitors stand still.

- Higher sales per employee than what the industry has ever experienced.

- Profit margins never before experienced in the free world.

- Costs so low they are lost in the noise.

- Penetration into an existing market to grow by over 30% before the competitors respond.

- "Hockey stick" growth where 90% of revenue growth occurs in the last 10% of the plan period.

- A product for which the best alternative is for the customer to have no alternative as an alternative.

- To solve all the world's problems, but doesn't make money.

Don't try to dazzle the investor. Stay on firm ground. Make sure you're entering an emerging market and not a mature or fading one. Avoid market statements that can't be verified. Understand that the sophisticated investors usually know much more about the market in question than you might, and they probably have more resources they can rely on for verification as well. Make sure your dream has enough depth to develop into a business and isn't just an opportunity that would be better off with a strategic partner from the beginning.

Comfort! Comfort! Comfort!

There are three aspects of your presentation that will be particularly important in developing the investor's comfort level: how well you will deal with the market, how strong is your team, and how carefully and realistically you've planned.

The Market

Getting your investor comfortable with the marketing plans requires that you do four things:

1. Prove that the market and the need exist.

2. Prove that your product meets that need.

3. Prove that you can penetrate the market with your product.

4. Prove that no one else is already meeting the need.

If you can prove these four things, the investor will be able to have confidence in your marketing plan.

The Team

It helps to have a team that has worked together for a while and shares the same vision and enthusiasm as the leader. You must have someone who believes in your dream as strongly as you do. The investor is looking for a team that is willing to commit to working 100 hours per week and hock their houses and put their families into debt to make this dream become reality. Also important, have proven winners on the team, people who have done it before, especially if they are known in the marketplace. The venture capitalists may even prefer a failed entrepreneur in the management team before they will fund the company over a novice because they will assume he or she has learned from his experiences.

The Plan

Don't assume the reader knows as much as you do about the subject. Make sure the first paragraph captures all the most important information: the dream, the need, the solution, the reward, and the role of the investor. You have to capture the investor's interest so he or she will read beyond the first paragraph and maintain that interest throughout the executive letter so the investor will pass this plan along to his or her analyst.

Investors expect the arithmetic in the financial section to be correct, but they will discount it to some extent, mentally cutting the revenue in half, delaying the growth, or changing the growth rate. They want to make sure it will work under adverse conditions as well as ideal ones.

Extend the plan for a long enough period to show that the return on investment occurs on time. Provide a running line in the plan that shows the investor's return on investment. Finally, make sure there is an exit plan for the investor (and for yourself!), or any valuation of the company up front is useless.

Be Fast on your Feet and Other Tips

- Keep in mind that you are asking for a lot of money, so be prepared to explain in detail how you plan to spend it.
- Put on your salesman's hat, as this is a selling experience
- Always be ready to state your personal investment to date.

- Be ready to articulate your cash needs and explain how that cash will be used.

- Convince the investor that you, too, are in it to make money, or he or she won't believe that you will make money.

- Be a good story teller, or have someone on your team who is.

- Once an investor is willing to give you the time, he or she really want to believe in your dream. He or she is asking you to be convincing and overcome any hurdles in confidence.

- Investors get excited about investing in product development, marketing, and needed inventory, but he or she doesn't like to have their investment just cover rent and payroll.

- An investor may stay in a situation forever so long as he or she doesn't have to put more money in.

- Make sure your financial performance goals are high enough to make the investor comfortable.

- Usually, you only get one shot at an investor. Make sure you ask for enough cash up front, and if further rounds of investment will be needed, where they might come from.

- Have an idea of an exit plan, and if it might be to sell to a strategic partner, provide a few names of potential buyers.

- Remember, the investor is looking for COMFORT! COMFORT! COMFORT!

- Make the investor so comfortable that his or her hand isn't shaking when signing a check.

- Comfort breeds trust, trust brings investment.

Summary

Start by understanding that your priorities and the investor's priorities are very different. This business opportunity is very high on your priority list: it is your dream, and quite possibly your livelihood. On the other hand, to the investor, you are just one of hundreds of similar stories about the "perfect" investment. Keep trying to find the hurdles between you and the investor and knock them down. Close the priority gap.

When all is said and done, it will not be the written plan that will close the deal. It will be you and your team with your excellent story and your conviction that will make the investor comfortable enough to sign on the dotted line.

One important personal note to add. I will not invest in a start-up when the entrepreneur has majority control of the company, because I will be unable to change the management team if the company is not performing according to the plan.

The Laws of Management Physics

Law #1

The Goesinnas Must Exceed the Goesouttas.

To run a business successfully, the cash deposited into a company over a time must exceed the cash out.

Law #2

Profit Is The Muscle of a Corporation; Cash Is the Blood.

Companies can run for a long time with negative profits, but without cash they will die.

Law #3

A Staff that Stays Together Cannot Grow Together... at the Same Rate.

A staff that stays together can only grow from experience, and with different education, personalities, motivations, and reactions to change, the rate of growth will vary for each member.

Law #4

For Every Delegation, There Must Be a Control.

Whenever a responsibility is delegated, a control should be established to ensure that the task is done correctly.

Law #5

Customers Will Ultimately Forget Poor Delivery or High Prices, But They Will Remember Poor Quality Forever.

Customers will be reminded every day of poor quality. They will be aggravated if the product isn't working or performing to specifications. Never aggravate a customer this way.

Law #6

Many Times Nothing Can Be Better than Something.

Allowing a bad situation with an employee to continue can be more devastating than having no one in that position.

Law #7

Good Collections Start with a Well-Defined Purchase Order.

Most likely a customer will pay only for what he purchased, so the documentation must reflect in detail what the customer is buying.

Law #8

When Telling Someone Something They Do not Want to Hear, You Must Tell Them Five Times Before It Finally Gets Through.

It is important to be sensitive to what may be "bad news" to a subordinate. When it requires action, you must tell them over and over.

Law #9

When the CEO Starts Every Sentence With "I," You Are in Trouble.

This is particularly true regarding legal matters. Haven't you heard, "I will go to the Supreme Court if necessary"—with no regard for what is good for the company.

Law #10

Plans Are Born to Be Changed.

The process of planning can be more useful than the plan itself.

Law #11

You Cannot Be All Things to All People… Effectively.

Trying to be all things to all people (which is really an inability to focus) and poor cash management are the two things most likely to kill a company.

Law #12

Do What You Do Best.

Doing what you do best is so obvious, yet this law is often violated because of the desire for new experiences and ego satisfaction.

Law #13

The Second Question Is the Most Important.

Unfortunately, many times the first question is asked in hope that there will be no need for the second question.

Law #14

Anything Times Zero Equals Zero.

I have often marveled that a high-tech entrepreneur who's had ten years of math never learned that anything times zero equals zero. Hence, he is reluctant to give up any ownership when raising money, passing up an opportunity to own five percent of what could be a $100 million company to keep 100 percent of their zero-value company.

Law #15

Do not Put Costs in Place Anticipating Growth in Sales.

The key word is anticipating, as growth seldom develops as fast as expected.

Law #16

There Are Many Times You Can Win by Losing.

Avoiding a bad deal can be a winning solution.

Law #17

Success Is Relative.

Success cannot be judged by results alone' it must be judged against goals and objectives.

Law #18

The Best Way to Motivate Competent Senior Employees Is to Remove the DeMotivators.

Senior, key employees can be motivated more by knocking down hurdles that hinder spirit and performance than by motivation efforts.

Law #19

Do It Right the First Time.

This should be the most obvious of all good management laws, as it saves time, energy, costs, and management focus to do it right the first time.

Law #20

One Path to Success Is to Continually Search and Hire People Better than Yourself.

A good manager must be secure enough to do this. A real plus is that better people will push the hiring manager to do better.

Law #21

Most Often, Creativity Is Better than Imagination.

In my dictionary, imagination is the ability to come up with ideas having no limitation, whereas creativity requires innovation to solve a problem within the limits of the system.

Law #22

The Longer Something Takes to Happen, the Less Chance It Has of Actually Happening.

Confucius may have been the first person to say it, but it is still hard for some people to understand this principle. It manifests itself in many ways.

Law #23

Your Price, My Terms; Your Terms, My Price.

An effective approach in a negotiation is to make it clear that the other side cannot have both favorable price and favorable terms.

Law #24

At Some Point, the Monthly Revenue Level Has to Change to Match the Bookings (New Orders) Level.

It is dangerous to hold on to people and expense levels to match past revenue levels when new bookings are decreasing.

Law #25

Issuing a Third Top Priority Kicks out the First One on the List.

Everything cannot be labeled top priority, although people have a tendency to try. In some organizations, like manufacturing, when a third priority is given, it kicks out the first one.

Law #26

You Cannot Test Quality into a Product; You Must Design and Build It In.

The best way to achieve good quality is with a good design. All the testing in the world will not improve the basic quality of the design.

Law #27

No Contract Is the Worst Kind.

Verbal agreements and implied understanding will play havoc with a relationship when it starts to come apart.

Law #28

Making People above You in the Organization Comfortable Is Extremely Important.

The boss, owner, or director can only make judgments based on your inputs and the perceptions they determine to convey their confidence.

Law #29

The Easiest Product for Your Sales People to Sell Is the One You Don't Have.

Salespeople get bored easily and like excitement, therefore they have a natural tendency to sell features and future products that you do not have yet. They love to keep the customer's interest up and pitch "new" all the time.

Law #30

High Growth Is Synonymous with Compromise.

Growth requires stretching the system beyond its capabilities and old procedures. Existing methods become cumbersome, therefore the new dynamics demand compromises. If you can't accommodate compromise with your management style, stay away from high growth.

Law #31

Upper Management Has the Right to Talk to Anyone, but they Should not Chew Anyone out or Give Priorities.

Owners, directors, and bosses have the right to communicate with anyone in the company in search of information about company matters, but they must be sensitive to the impact of that conversation on those they speak.

Law #32

People Tend to Fight Giving Price Increases.

Managers can find all kinds of reasons for delaying a price increase because it is unpopular with the customers, and therefore uncomfortable for the manager to have to tell the salespeople. Salespeople have an even tougher time, because they want to be loved by the customer. Price increase risks deterioration in that relationship.

Law #33

Defining the Market Is not Enough; You Have to Prove You Can Penetrate It.

Some of the worst management fumbles happen when you are talking to upper management or investors. Along these lines is the manager who says, "If the market is X billion dollars, don't you believe I can get 0.001 percent of it?" The answer should be no!

Law #34

Going around the System to Expedite Creates More Problems than It's Worth.

It is far more efficient and effective to expedite within the system. More often, it is better to put energy into improving the system than in looking for ways around it or even in violation of it.

Law #35

Management Must Make Timely Decisions with the Information and Resources Available.

Given enough time, just about anybody can solve the problem; win the situation, or do the job right the first time. However, we don't always have the luxury of time.

Law #36

It Is Easier to Find New Products for the Market You're in than to Take Your Product to a New Market.

Being established in a market allows you to find other needs within that market. You can then take advantage of relationships you have already established to increase sales.

Law #37

The Quality of a Product as Perceived by the Customer Goes down as the Customer's Need for the Product Goes down.

When the customer's need for the product goes down, their quality requirements go up, to find a way out.

Law #38

The Answer to a Question often Depends on Who's Doing the Asking.

The answer an employee gives to a question will depend on whether it's his peers, his supervisor, the department head, or the "big cheese" doing the asking. People have a tendency to tell the asker what they think the asker want to hear, particularly in sticky situations or when they fear that an honest answer will get them into trouble.

Law #39

It Is Difficult for a Single Manager to Manage Companies through the Entire Life Cycle of a Company.

Managers have difficulty working in all the vastly different environments of start-ups, growing companies, stable companies, and companies in downturn cycles.

Law #40

When an Engineer Tells You not to Worry, It's Time to Start Worrying.

Engineers are generally eternal optimists, and they often find it difficult to recognize failure.

Law #41

In Negotiations, Before You Drop a Price, Ask for and Get Something in Return.

If you drop a price with no recourse, the potential customer will jump on this and continue to come back for more.

Law #42

Multiple Disciplines Can Be Performed Well by Good Managers, but only Special Personalities Can Do Sales Well.

Sales personnel, by nature, have to have a large degree of insecurity, a high tolerance for indignity, a strong competitive nature, and a well-disguised mean streak to outdo the customer.

Law #43

The More a Company Lacks Goals and Objectives, the More Time It Takes to Make Good Decisions.

When managers are making hundreds of decisions every hour, most of them have to be based on a good feel for the situation in order to be made quickly.

Law #44

It's Okay to be Bold with a Good Backlog, but Arrogance Can Lead to Oblivion.

Be careful when things are going well. Arrogance leads to complacency and indifference to competitive factors in the environment, customer needs, and customer sensitivities.

Law #45

Never Tell the Sales Staff Your Lowest Possible Price if You Want to Get More.

The sale staff wants to win and with a bit of natural impatience, giving them the lowest threshold price is handing them a torch burning at both ends.

Law #46

Never Let an Engineer Discuss Prices or Estimates with a Customer.

Engineers like to deal in absolutes, and apparently have banned the word contingencies from all their technical books.

Law #47

Be Wary of Promises that End up in Negotiations after You've Lost Your Leverage.

By nature, there are no negotiations after you have lost your leverage. It is best to define and make the best deal up front while you still have bargaining power.

Law #48

Backlog that Extends beyond the Competitive Lead Times for Delivery Can Be Harmful.

Competitive delivery dates must be met, and if you are overbooked, it is better to pass on an opportunity. But it is also dangerous, because customers can be very fickle, and once they are forced to find an alternative source, they may never come back.

Law #49

Good Marketing Depends More on Customer Perceptions than It Does on the Product.

Having the customer perceive you as the first or the best can overshadow shortcomings in your product or service. It's the customer's perception of you that matters. No matter how good you are, it doesn't matter if the customer has a negative opinion of you or a positive image or your competition.

Law #50

Underestimating Performance Can Be as Bad as Overestimating It.

There is no doubt that missed forecasts resulting from overestimating performance can hurt a company; however underestimating what the company is capable of can result in unused potential and lost opportunities.

Law #51

When Managers Get overly Excited about New Things, They Tend to Let the "Bread And Butter" Business Suffer from Neglect.

New opportunities may create excitement and challenges, but management must not lose sight of what is paying the bills.

Law #52

Having too Many People in Place Can Reduce Efficiency, Increase Costs above Budget, Make More Scrap, and Lead to Inventory Write-offs.

Therefore the need to balance the organization in a downturn should be done as soon as the need is identified.

Law #53

The Most Effective Way to Approach a Disagreement Is to Assume You Are Wrong and Work Hard to Prove It, But When You Can't, then You Know You Are Right.

This is a good policy for a quality organization when confronted with a customer problem. Be wary of your people who always start out with the "customer is wrong" attitude.

Law #54

Plans Tend to Show Greater Optimism Downstream and often Falsely Justify Near-Term Actions or Inactions.

Most growth plans have a hockey stick effect, but seldom does the upturn occur when planned.

Law #55

We Tend to Overkill a Situation with People rather than Spending More Energy on Analyzing The Problem.

Beware of increasing middle management, program managers, and coordinators to solve problems caused by weaknesses in the system.

Law #56

We Tend to Overload People and then Be Forced to Compromise on Accepting the Results.

It's hard to criticize or try to get more from people who are already overwhelmed. This is especially true for personnel who are underpaid.

Law #57

Often Emphasis to Reduce Costs by Concentrating on the Payroll Overshadows the Real Potential of Significantly Reducing Material Costs in Costs of Goods Sold.

Labor in manufacturing has become a small percentage of costs and inventory, therefore it's better to go after material costs as a way to increase margins. In today's manufacturing culture, reducing overall material costs, even by a modest amount, may result in savings that are more than the entire direct labor cost.

Law #58

Authority and Responsibility Are not the Same: However, They Should Be Consistent When Delegating One or the Other.

In many growth situations, the responsibility given to individuals is far out in front of authority, because authority requires trust, and trust can be slow to occur.

Law #59

Training Seems to Be a Lost Art in American Business.

Sadly many budgets do not even include a cost account labeled "training."

Law #60

Reports Are the Vital Signs of a Company.

The best way to monitor the progress of a company is to schedule its reports with defined metrics. The discipline of a scheduled report requires the provider to check and define the company's progress to be able to provide the correct information.

Law #61

Unrealistic Goals Can Be a De-motivator.

Goals, to be effective, must be motivational and measurable. Setting unattainable goals to achieve what is required is a de-motivator. It will lose focus and endanger achieving the real goals.

Law #62

Inexperience Tends to Distort Decisions Based on Principles alone Versus "Real" World Experience.

Personnel who are growing tend to look for the perfect world and therefore must be guided until they recognize the reality of the situation.

Law #63

Lateral Communications Can Be a Key to the Success of a Company Operating Efficiently at the Senior Staff Level.

Managers who compartmentalize their staff by having communications bounce back and forth are dangerous and will not gain the most from the staff members.

Law #64

Success Comes When You First Say What You Can Do, and Then Do What You Say.

This is what a boss expects from you. Respect comes from credibility; trust comes from respect.

Law #65

One of the Most Difficult Weaknesses to Detect in an Experienced Person Is a Lack of Basic Intelligence.

People successfully performing the same function for years, (e.g. production control) can seem intelligent and must be tested from time to time before being placed in a new situation or position.

Law #66

Don't Make Long Hours Worked and a Good Attitude the only Criteria for Being an Effective Worker.

One superefficient person can accomplish more than ten mediocre people.

Law #67

If You Plan to Operate with Integrity in Your Professional Life, You Have to Be Prepared at Times that Some Will Do a "Number" on You.

The "Black Hats" will always be looking for ways to beat a system, and don't let a bad experience change fine ethics or values.

Law #68

In a High Growth Situation, Little Time May Be Spent on Improving the Efficiency of the Present or Planning the Future.

This is dangerous, and new methods must be found for new situations. To do so, don't hesitate to look to outside help. Try to assign someone to look to the future, or as time goes by you will be discussing the same problem over and over.

Law #69

Business Plans with Losses or Market Deterioration Usually Aren't Approved by Superiors, but Rather Acknowledged.

It's unlikely that those above you will approve an undesirable plan, so don't expect an "okay" to mean approval. "Okay," in a response to many situations in our culture does not mean, "yes" or approval, it means "I heard you." Then look for constant pressure to improve.

Law #70

Undercapitalization Breeds Inefficiency in Management and Can Dilute the Real Mission and Purpose of a Company.

The lack of capital can deter a great team from ever attaining their potential. Do not expect great things from an undercapitalized company. Lack of working capital limits a business to "just getting by."

Law #71

The More Successful You Are and the Higher the Growth Rate, the More Cash Is Needed.

Do not mistake profit for cash, as the rate of cash needed for additional working capital can far exceed profit.

Law #72

Even the Most Senior Managers Can Act Like Children if It Appears that a Competitive Situation Exists among the Staff.

Try to avoid managers having their own agendas. Even effective individuals can seem to have conflicting ideas and often must be reminded they must have the same objectives to make the company successful.

Law #73

Financial Controls Do not Limit Management Freedom, but force You to Think before You Act.

Managers can't be allowed to run free with their spending. Good management establishes an approval and authorization process for its managers.

Law #74

Growth of a Company Requires Having People Who Can Continue to Make Necessary Changes in Their Style and Objectives.

The president's role is to set priorities, constantly reassess the priorities, and change priorities as needed. Growth brings new challenges and the need for change on a daily basis.

Law #75

The Tendency of a Manager in Trouble Is to Blank out the Problems by Talking about only the Pluses.

This is one sign that a manager is in over his or her head.

Law #76

You Can Know too Much About a Customer, Adversely Affecting Your Performance. By Taking Things for Granted, You Can Hurt Yourself by Abandoning Your Normal Good Mode of Doing Business.

Be wary of affiliates with inside information on a customer, as it might be out of context and be misleading, or worse!

Law #77

When Changing a Responsibility or Authority, Always Tell the Person from Whom You Are Taking It Before You Tell the Person to Whom You Are Giving It.

Often you may decide to change an employee's authority or responsibility after speaking with that person. If you have already spoken to the person to whom you'll be giving the authority or responsibility, it will confuse everyone and weaken the top manager's image.

Law #78

Without Meeting Revenue as Planned, All Plans Are Doomed for Failure. Revenue Is King.

Cash is blood, profit is muscle, but revenue is bigger. Many managers do great in meeting the expense budget, but fail on meeting revenue goals thus creating great losses.

Law #79

A Senior Staff Is Paid to Tell how to Do Things and not Give All the Reasons Why Things Won't Work. Leave It to the Leader TO Decide if the Cost, Time, or Risk Are not Appropriate.

Ding the staff member who immediately gives reasons for failure whenever a new idea is brought up. The reaction is often generated by fear of additional workload.

Law #80

Many Decisions Are Made More Difficult by not Having the Economic Understanding.

A mature company makes decisions based on marketing and economic skills. It is important for all your key personnel to understand the financial operations and subsequent results, in a company.

Law #81

Breakeven Points not Understood Limit Controlled Reaction to Downturns.

Understanding the breakeven point is part of the foundation for running a successful company. Part of this is the need to know the revenue level for covering expenses on as short a time period as a pay period.

Law #82

The First Time One Is Asked to Do a Budget Forecast, It Seems to Take Forever, but then They Become Easier and More Accurate after That.

Management should be tolerant of managers doing budgets for the first time and offer patience. This is particularly true if no background or history of date is provided.

Law #83

An Engineering Fix to a Problem Can Create other Problems, but an Engineering Design Change Solves the Problem.

"Band-Aids" ultimately can cause problems. This is particularly true in software designs.

Law #84

A **Centralized Organization in a High-Growth Rate Company Can Be a Hindrance to Success! But, a Decentralized Organization Structure Can Breed Redundancy in Many Functions.**

Organizations are born to be changed and should be continually reviewed to optimize cost and effectiveness.

Law #85

Forecast of Sales for Acceptance of a New Product Will always Take Longer than Planned.

Good products will, however, eventually exceed forecasts and last longer than originally thought. Be wary of the early successes. Usually a dip occurs before the product really takes off.

Law #86

Don't Fix It if It Isn't Broken, Unless You Are Planning a Change in Strategy.

Today, a new strategy is needed with global competition, customization, and an increased need for customer service forcing it to happen. Change becomes the norm to enable growth.

Law #87

I Have never Met a Good Controller that I Liked Personally.

Controllers have to be pragmatic but tough. "No" becomes the most important word in their vocabulary to be able to control expenditures in their company.

Law #88

A "Good" Boss Is a Person Who Lets You Operate the Way You Like.

There are numerous definitions of a good boss, but in the final analysis, the one who lets you operate and accommodates your style will help you grow.

Law #89

Successful Management Has the Correct Mind-Set, Which Is a Proper Combination of Perception, Perspective, and Priorities. This Leads to Planning and People.

Most tasks and programs have a higher chance of success if the proper mind-set is present at the start.

Law #90

Numbers and Their Relationships Serve as a Great Motivator for a Group.

Employees want to see how their contribution helps an organization. Metrics can help this more so than goals that can't be measured.

Law #91

The First Thing Investors Look for in Evaluating an Opportunity Is the Team.

In a growing market, many teams will submit plans to investors. In most cases, they will look alike. So the selection hinges on the people. The more people who believe in the plan, the better chance for success.

Law #92

We Often Wait too Long for People to Develop into a Role Rather than Take a "Firmer" Directing Hand.

It is demoralizing for employees to recognize a person problem long before management does. Then when someone finally decides to make a change, it is already too late.

Law #93

Do not Assume that Your Staff Knows Your Priorities unless You Tell Them.

Companies get off track for lack of direction, and staff personnel tend to guess at what the boss wants.

Law #94

Most People Like to Be Told how They Are Doing even if there Are Some Negatives.

A weakness of many managers is the reluctance to confront subordinates regarding their negative performance. Accordingly, avoiding discussion of negative attitudes or behaviors becomes a part of the management style.

Law #95

Innovation Is the Ability to Take Ideas and Success from a Past Life and Apply It to New Situations.

This is why it is so important to eventually bring personnel with new and creative ideas into the company to accelerate growth and success.

Law #96

Recognition of a Job Well Done Is High on the List of Motivating Employees, and at Times Can Go Farther than Money.

Bonuses are short-term motivations and may provide no motivation at all when they are expected. Recognition of employees, particularly to their peers, is high on the motivational chart.

Law #97

Listening to Employees Is only Part of the Equation and Must Be Followed by Using the Ideas Solicited, Giving Feedback, and Praised When Used.

Good communication includes a two-way process of sending and receiving.

Law #98

It Should Be Understood and Obvious that in a Loss Situation, All the Ratios % to Sales Such as Overhead and G & A Are Bound to Be out of Line.

Presidents should try to explain what can be expected regarding overhead and General and Administrative cost ratios, as well as understanding the present bad numbers.

Law #99

Big Companies Are Loaded with Budget Managers, whereas Businessmen Run Companies.

Budget managers manage to the numbers planned. Businessmen manage to the results needed. It is far easier to meet an expense budget than a revenue number and cash planned.

Law #100

Do not Mistake Advice for Counseling.

Superiors and directors may tend to give "advice" without understanding the situation. Advice can be stating the obvious. More welcome is counseling. This is advice that can be taken within the system and resources.

Appendix A

Business Plan Outline
Treat as a Diary in Developing

Executive Summary

Market Need (pain)

Company Match

How to Penetrate Market

Outside Help and Reward

Product/Service/Process

Driven by the Value Proposition

Market—to include credible back-up

Market Position—goal—to be Perceived by Customer

Marketing Plan

Competition—table if possible

Concept—Company Status

Potential Growth

Management Team

Operating Plan

Money Needed

Company Valuation

Use of Money—if to be Raised

Exit Plan—needed Personally as well as for Investors

Financial Projection Summary—sales/cost/profit

EBITA—Schedule could Help

Appendix—following can be helpful

- Customer List
- Articles
- Testimonials

- Strategic Partners

Financial Schedule Details

- P&L
- Balance Sheet
- Cash Flow Projection

Note: No need for a business plan before you validate your Value Proposition and customers.

Questions Often Asked By Investors

1. How much ash are you asking for to get to success?

2. What can you do with the present request?

3. How much money has been raised so far?

4. How much have you put in?

5. What will be the sales channel?

6. Is your market strategy based on market studies?

7. What is the valuation and how did you get there?

8. Why did you pick this market?

9. What is your value equation?

10. What is your secret sauce?

11. Do you have any IP?

12. How much money are you asking for and what will you do with it?

13. What is your exit plan?

14. What might the return on the investment be?

15. How long will it take you to break-even cash wise?

16. What is your marketing strategy?

17. How long has the team been together?

18. Who will be the direct competition?

Alert: A sophisticated investor will do a due diligence before making an investment that will include validating any claim you make.

Marketing Plan Outline

Reference "Canvas" for basic information

Basic Elements for a Marketing Plan

The Vision and Mission

The Product/Services

- Validation of the Value Proposition

Market Research and the Competition

- Differentiation

Market Strategy, Definition, Size and Availability

- Sales Channel

Marketing and Sales Collateral

- Promotion Strategy

Organization and Budgets

Forecasts—By product, Segment and regions

- Sales Revenue
- Profit Margins

Useful before developing a business plan.

NUCCO, Inc.

NUCO, INC.

President : Name
949-XXX-XXXX
Name@aol.com

What Business Problem Do We Solve?

❖ NUCO is in the stereographic low cost 3D video presentation industry.

❖ NUCO 3D provides, surgeons, radiologists, schools-of-medicine instructors, and other healthcare professionals, for the first time, with a variety of powerful, yet very low cost, 3D-color graphical, anatomic-manipulation systems for MRI and CT Scan images. Thereby: Shortening the time and enhancing the learning process of medical surgery students

❖ The company has developed four computer system products to satisfy several major industry markets starting with the MRI segment of the medical care market.

❖ NUCO can take raw data from an MRI disc discuss and process to a 3D TV or monitor output device to provide more useful information to aid analysis

2

NUCO's Health Care Markets
Being Pursued

MRI/CT SCANS & ANATOMY VISUALIZATIONS		
Marketing Segments	Southern California Facilities	U.S.A. Facilities
Medical Technology Schools	220	4400
Medical Therapy Centers	120	2400
Teaching Hospitals	8	160
Secondary Schools	50	1200
Hospitals	30	1800
Private Scan Centers	110	2200
Surgical Medical Groups	75	1500
Totals	613	11260

4

Competition

FEATURES	NUCO	ComX	ComY	ComZ
MRI/CT 3D Scan	Yes	No	No	Yes
Large Screen Projection	Yes	No	No	Yes
Flat Screen 3D TV Display	Yes	No	No	No
Trocar Surgery Assistance	Yes	No	No	No
Color Coded Tissue	Yes	Yes (manual only)	Yes	No
Tissue-Type Filtering	Yes	No	No	No
Ease-of-use & Intuitive	Yes	No	Yes	No
Complete plug & play, turn-key solution	Yes	No	No	No

5

NUCO'S Management Team

❖ President and CEO, xxxxx

- xxxxxxxxxxxxxxxxxxxxxxxxxxxxxxxxxxxxxxxxxxxxxxxxxxxxxxxxxxxxxxxxx
xxxxxxxxxxxxxxxxxxxxxxxxxxxxxxxxxxxxxxxxxxxxxxxxxxxxxxxxxxxxxxxxx
xxxxxxxxxxxxxxxxxxx

- Marketing Manager, xxxxxx

- xxxxxxxxxxxxxxxxxxxxxxxxxxxxxxxxxxxxxxxxxxxxxxxxxx
- xxxxxxxxxxxxxxxxxxxxxxxxxxxxxxxxxxxxxxxxxxxxxxxxxx

❖ VP Operations xxxxxx

- xxxxxxxxxxxxxxxxxxxxxxxxxxxxxxxxxxxxxxxxxxxxxxxxxx
- xxxxxxxxxxxxxxxxxxxxxxxxxxxxxxxxxxxxxxxxxxxxxxxxxx

Chief Technical Officer xxxx

❖ xxxxxxxxxxxxxxxxxxxxxxxxxxxxxxxxxxx
❖ xxxxxxxxxxxxxxxxxxxxxxxxxxxxxxxxxxx

6

NUCO Is Seeking $350,000

- **Use of Funds**
  Expanding marketing and sales program
  Hire full time engineer for future development
  Add necessary people infrastructure
  Provide working capital
  Achieve profitability

- **Year One**
  Marketing/Sales $100,000
  Engineering $100,000
  Support Team $100,000
  Breakeven by the end of year 1
  Sales in Month 4 after capital in
  Total Cash in ALREADY
  Founders $190,000
  Outside investors $140,000

7

NUCO Profit and Loss

	YEAR 1 (AFTER FINANCING)	YEAR 2	YEAR 3
TOTAL SALES	$543,750	3,250,000	7,355,000
COST OF SALES	326,250	1,787,500	4,045,250
GROSS PROFIT DOLLARS	$217,500	1,462,500	3,309,750
% MARGIN	39	45	45
OPERATING EXPENSES			
TOTAL EXPENSES	$243,550	$915,000	$2,200,000
PRE TAX PROFIT (LOSS)	($26,050)	$547,500	$1,109,000

Resources Needed Beyond Capital

* **Absolute**
  - Sales Channel
  - Sales person from the Medical Market
  - Full Time Engineer
* **Desire**
  - Strategic Partner to Help Marketing
* **Potential Partners- also to buy the company**
  - XXX, LLC
  - XXX, Inc.

The Deal to The Investor

- Investment Required -$300,000
- Present Valuation $660,000
- Strategic Partners or Sale by end of Year 3
- ROI 2.5 to 5X

10

Operation Plan Outline

The Need for an Operations Plan is to turn the Company Goal and Strategy into Tactical Tasks and an organization to make goals happen.

Start from:

- Where do you want to be?
- Where are you?
- How do you get there!

First Needs

- The Product
- A Forecast
- Pricing Goal

Build a Plan to include:

- Manufacturing of Product/Service
- Resources needed and planned to include:
  * Personnel
  * Facilities
  * Equipment
  * Outside sources
  * Customer support
  * Timing and milestones
  * COST (BUDGET)
  * Getting further along – policies, procedures, logistics and quality plans will be needed

Useful in any scaling exercise.

Appendix B

The Changing Environment

- Products faster time to market
- Rapidly changing technology
- Customer is king or queen
- Quality has risen as a requirement
- Customization of products
- Customer service quality is expected
- Open architect for electronic gadgets
- The increasing importance of the Internet
- Globalization
- Outsourcing
- Better, Faster, Cheaper
- Social Networks utilized for marketing

Truism—Values

- Do it right the first time
- Put customer satisfaction high on the list
- Everyone is a customer service person
- There are customers inside as well as outside
- The customer is right until proven wrong
- Quality is everyone's business
- Honesty is the norm
- Fair pay for a fair day's work
- Provide a challenging environment for people "growth"

Mindset—The Key to Success

- Mindset—the proper combination of:
  - ◊ Perception
  - ◊ Perspective
  - ◊ Priority

◊   Planning

Management Law
- If you can't track or measure it, it isn't a good goal! (this from Peter Drucker)

Finance—Myths
- I'll never pay a finance company 30% interest for a loan!
- My pricing formula will guarantee a 20% profit margin.
- I'll be able to get an accounts receivable loan whenever I need it.
- I'll be able to finance the growth from my profit.

Truism
- Losers do their best!
- Winners outdo their best!

Communication

Do we really speak English? All though my career I heard these expressions that may have been understood only by the person spitting them out. In my International experience they really were a detriment. For instance, in a negotiating deal with a Chinese man in our head of sales used the term "Slam Dunk" several years long before Yau Ming, an BA star become a household word in China. In another experience while at a meeting in Yugoslavia, my ego was crushed when the person heading the other side said, "Would you please let Mr. A (an Italian on my staff), speak as I understand his English is much better." Now with the Internet and social networks are creating a new language.

Here are several expressions that can confuse a discussion:

- Man you are in deep yogurt and you are up the creek without a paddle
- Do I need an instant replay to get the message across?
- Last month you went 0 for 4 and if you don't start hitting, I'll be all over your back when I return
- You better get a point guard out on the lne, and go to a full court press
- We need an all-out blitz
- You may luck out this week as it is a slam dunk
- We may still be n trouble for the month even though te fat lady hasn't sung yet
- We may all be I the same boat, but I am not going down with your Titanic
- In fact, I have an ace in the hole because I got in the lottery round
- You better hit the bomb, so go for the hail Mary as we are passed the two minute warning, but don't think you can see the forest for the trees
- My heart bleeds for you, but we are not going back to square one
- You have me climbing the walls and I will be in a bind if you don't cut the Mustard

- So this is the acid test and you better come up with a hat trick and go deep or I will be all over you back

Management Philosophy—One Liners

Businessmen manage a business, Budget managers manage the numbers.

Sometimes it is easier to sell a bad product with good support than a good product with poor support.

Remember when they used to say, "You can't be fired going with IBM? Now your boss will be upset if you don't look for alternatives to IBM.

When a company is struggling it's easy to make a quick impact by identifying the obvious: inventory is too big and unbalanced, collection estimates are too optimistic, market estimates are too ambitious, etc. but the difficulty is correcting the problems.

A company drifting down is like a marriage in trouble: if it took 3 years to reach a low point, it will take three years to get back and usually the people involved don't want to work at it.

In the early stages of a company's growth, an owner's mentality "drives" the company culture, but maturity occurs when leaders find they no longer can carry the company on their shoulders.

When trying to raise money from investors, keep in mind you eat, sleep, live your vision, but the investors have many opportunities—so you must first find ways to reduce the gap between priorities.

When you ship a product or provide a service that doesn't fit or work in their product or system even though it meets the agreed to specifications your attitude should be "we have a problem so let's fix it together."

For every action, there is an equal and opposite reaction, Isaac Newton: so for every delegation there should be a control.

A customer's perception often can be more important than facts in selecting a product or service.

Companies can suffer more from a lack of good management decisions than from bad managers.

You can expect everything to take longer than you think

Death and taxes are inevitable, but I guarantee time will also pass by, so plan your precious time intelligently.

Mindset—The Key to Success

Mindset—the proper combination of:

- Perception
- Perspective
- Priority
- And planning

Time Management—Time Killers

- Procrastination
- Reactive management
- Interruptions
- Lack of delegation
- Long phone calls
- Bad meetings
- Duplication responsibility
- Poor instructions
- Never ending tasks
- Too much grunt work
- Not able to say "No"
- Committee decision mentality
- Easy distractions
- Small talk too long
- Do it wrong the first time
- No plan

TRUISMS and Myths

Decision Marking Truism

Accept what is needed to be done:

In the time allowed, with the resources available and the information available

By understanding the consequences

Finding ideas on how to do, not how not to do

And the final decision maker will decide on the risk, cost, use of resources and priorities

Avoid starting without all the reasons it can't be done

Organization Truism

- In management theory, it teaches you to structure the organization and find the people to fill the positions
- In real life and growth, you build the organization based on the manpower skills available and how fast you can bring the outside personnel to fill voids

Truism—Values

- Do it right the first time
- Put customer satisfaction high on the list
- Everyone is a customer service person
- There are customers inside as well as outside
- The customer is right until proven wrong
- Quality is everyone's business
- Honesty is the norm
- Fair pay for a fair day's work
- There will no "not invented here" (NIH) factor

Book List

Dick Dadamo Presents:

Busting $10 Million series

A collection of books dedicated to enhancing managers understanding of all operating disciplines, including finance, marketing, engineering, and manufacturing particularly related to growth.

The Laws of Management Physics – A Handbook for Hands On Managers

A bible for indicating the cultural changes ahead for growing companies. The 51 Laws and the chapter on Management Lies – A View from the Top provides an insight not often understood by the inexperienced managers.

The Laws of Management Physics – A Guide

The LOMP Guide presents in basic form 100 laws that can help managers make the changes in the culture that are needed for successful growth. The LOMP Guide presents basic hands-on experience for a growing or changing manager.

Will the Real Inventory Stand Up and Be Counted—Unscrambling the Methods and Madness of Manufacturing Inventories

This book is dedicated to the many manufacturing managers who are constantly beat up for having oversized inventories when upper management doesn't understand how much of the inventory they have no control over.

Marketeer or Pied Piper, Salesman or Con Artist? Managing Growth through Marketing

Dadamo professes that much of marketing is common sense and tries to break-down the barriers that Marketing and Sales people establish because they have access to the customer.

Finance: It's Not Just For Bean Counters Any More!

All you ever wanted to know about Finance without Having to Bridge the GAAP!

A true epistle for non-financial managers, but also a perspective that may be different for financial personnel.

Planning As Exciting As It Gets Or Plans Were Born To Be Changed

This book is a guide to help emphasize the importance of planning for all aspects of business.

The Anatomy of a Growing Company

This book is to give growing company managers an idea of what lies ahead to support their new experiences to limit the slowing down of the growth by speeding up the learning curve.

For more information and special deals, contact Dick Dadamo at dickd@cox.net

Notes

Notes

Notes

www.ingramcontent.com/pod-product-compliance
Lightning Source LLC
Chambersburg PA
CBHW051626170526
45167CB00001B/81